Ilija Trojanow

D1823517

CONTEMPORARY GERMAN WRITERS AND FILMMAKERS

Edited by

Julian Preece (Swansea University)
Frank Finlay (University of Leeds)

Editorial Board

Professor Stephen Brockmann (Carnegie Mellon University)
Professor Friederike Eigler (Georgetown University)
Dr Michael Minden (University of Cambridge)
Professor Moritz Baßler (Westfälische Wilhelms-Universität Münster)
Professor Sabine Hake (University of Texas at Austin)

Volume 2

PETER LANG

Oxford • Bern • Berlin • Bruxelles • Frankfurt am Main • New York • Wien

Ilija Trojanow

Edited by Julian Preece

PETER LANG

Oxford • Bern • Berlin • Bruxelles • Frankfurt am Main • New York • Wien

Bibliographic information published by Die Deutsche Nationalbibliothek.
Die Deutsche Nationalbibliothek lists this publication in the Deutsche National-
bibliografie; detailed bibliographic data is available on the Internet at
http://dnb.d-nb.de.

A catalogue record for this book is available from the British Library.

Library of Congress Cataloging-in-Publication Data:

Preece, Julian.
 Ilija Trojanow / Julian Preece.
   p. cm. -- (Contemporary German writers & filmmakers ; 2)
 Includes bibliographical references and index.
 ISBN 978-3-0343-0894-6 (alk. paper)
 1. Trojanow, Ilija--Criticism and interpretation. I. Title.
 PT2682.R56Z83 2012
 833'.92--dc23

                    2012039080

Cover image © Peter-Andreas Hassiepen, 2011

ISSN 1664-6916
ISBN 978-3-0343-0894-6

© Peter Lang AG, International Academic Publishers, Bern 2013
Hochfeldstrasse 32, CH-3012 Bern, Switzerland
info@peterlang.com, www.peterlang.com, www.peterlang.net

Printed in Germany

Contents

vi

A Note on Citation and Translation

In order to make this book, which is the first in either German or English on Ilija Trojanow's growing literary oeuvre, readily comprehensible to non-German speakers we have translated all German quotations into English and only give the original German in the case of Trojanow's own writings, which are the object of our study. Readers without German will become familiar with the original titles of his major books, for which reason we do not translate titles such as *Der Weltensammler* as *The Collector of Worlds* each time that they are mentioned. English titles of untranslated works are not italicised, thus *EisTau*/Melting Ice. The publication details of the editions consulted by each contributor are given in footnotes at the beginning of his or her chapter. Most of the translations are our own, but when Trojanow's books have been published in English (as three thus far have been), some contributors have opted to cite the published translations instead. Again, this is made clear each time in the chapters concerned.

Biographical/Bibliographical Chronology: Ilija Trojanow

1965:	born in Sofia, Bulgaria, which was from 1945 to 1990 part of the Soviet bloc, and ruled from 1954 to the collapse of communist eastern Europe by President Todor Zhivkov, General Secretary of the Bulgarian Communist Party
1971:	the Trojanow family flee communism and settle in Kenya after passing through Yugoslavia, Italy, and the Federal Republic of Germany. Trojanow first attends the English-speaking Kenton College, then the Deutsche Schule in Nairobi
1977–1981:	in Germany
1981–1984:	in Kenya
1984–1989:	student of Law and Ethnology in Munich
1989:	founds Marino publishing house, specialising in African literature
Early 1990s:	returns to Africa, living mainly in Cape Town in post-Apartheid South Africa, and spends time travelling
1993:	begins to publish. *In Afrika. Mythos und Alltag*/In Africa. Myths and Realities (Munich: Marino). Republished by Deutscher Taschenbuch Verlag (Munich: 1996) and Frederking & Thaler (Munich: 2001)
1994:	*Naturwunder Ostafrikas*/Natural Wonders of East Africa (Munich: Frederking & Thaler)
1996:	publishes first novel, based on his family's experiences of fleeing Bulgaria, *Die Welt ist groß und Rettung lauert überall*/The World Is Large and Salvation Lurks Around Every Corner (Munich/Vienna: Hanser); and (with Chenjerai Hove) *Hüter der Sonne. Begegnung mit Simbabwes Ältesten/*

Guardians of the Sun. Encounter with Zimbabwe's Elders (Munich: Frederking & Thaler)

1997:   his second novel (with Rudolf Spindler) *Autopol* (Munich: Deutscher Taschenbuch Verlag) first published as an experimental 'work in progress' on the internet; *Afrikanissimo. Ein heiter-sinnliches Lesebuch*/Afrikanissimo. A Serene and Sensual Anthology (Munich: Piper)

1998:   moves to Bombay/Mumbai in India

1999:   *Hundezeiten. Heimkehr in ein fremdes Land*/Dog Times. Coming Home to a Foreign Country (Munich/Vienna: Hanser), republished as *Die fingierte Revolution. Bulgarien, eine exemplarische Geschichte*/The Simulated Revolution: Bulgaria, an Exemplary History (Munich: Deutscher Taschenbuch Verlag, 2006); and *Zimbabwe* (Munich: Polyglott)

2001:   *Der Sadhu an der Teufelswand: Reportagen aus einem anderen Indien*/The Sadhu on the Devil's Wall. Dispatches from a Different India (Munich: Frederking & Thaler)

2003:   *An den Inneren Ufern Indiens. Eine Reise entlang des Ganges* (Munich/Vienna: Hanser). Translated by the author with Ranjit Hoskoté as *Along the Ganges* (London: Haus, 2005)

2004:   *Zu den heiligen Quellen des Islam. Als Pilger nach Mekka und Medina* (Munich: Malik). Translated by Rebecca Morrison as *From Mumbai to Mecca* (London: Haus, 2007)

2006:   *Der Weltensammler* (Munich/Vienna: Hanser). Translated by William Hobson as *The Collector of Worlds* (London: Faber and Faber, 2008)

2007:   moves to Vienna. Begins to write occasional column entitled 'Schlagloch' ('pothole') for the Berlin left-wing daily, *die tageszeitung; Nomade auf vier Kontinenten. Auf den Spuren von Sir Francis Burton*/Nomad on Four Continents. On the Trail of Sir Richard Francis Burton (Munich: Deutscher Taschenbuch Verlag); and (with Ranjit Hoskoté),

Kampfabsage: Kulturen bekämpfen sich nicht – Sie fließen zusammen/Calling Off the Fight: Cultures Do Not Fight Each Other – They Flow Together (Munich: Blessing)

2008: *Der entfesselte Globus. Reportagen*/The Unchained Globe. Dispatches (Munich/Vienna: Hanser); *Kumbh Mela. Indien feiert das größte Fest der Welt*/Kumbh Mela. India Celebrates the Greatest Festival on Earth (Munich: Frederking & Thaler). Film of *The World Is Large and Salvation Lurks Around Every Corner* (dir. Stefan Komanderev: Bulgaria/Germany/Hungary/Slovenia)

2009: (with Juli Zeh), *Angriff auf die Freiheit. Sicherheitswahn, Überwachungstaat und der Abbau bürgerlicher Rechte*/Attack on Freedom. Security Mania, the Surveillance State and the Demolition of Civil Rights (Munich/Vienna: Hanser)

2010: (with Susann Urban) *Oberammergau. Richard F. Burton zu Besuch bei den Passionsspielen/Oberammergau. Richard F. Burton. A Glance at the Passion-Play*. Zweisprachige Ausgabe/bilingual edition (Zurich: Arche); (with Susann Urban) *Fühlend sehe ich die Welt. Die Aufzeichnungen des blinden Weltreisenden James Holman*/I See the World by Feel. The Memoirs of the Blind Globetrotter James Holman (Munich: Malik, 2010)

2011: *EisTau*/Melting Ice (Munich/Vienna: Hanser); *Hinter der roten Sonne. Die schönsten Abenteuergeschichten*, edited by Ilija Trojanow and Susann Urban/Behind the Red Sun. The Most Beautiful Adventure Stories (Berlin: Aufbau, 2011)

2012: (with Anja Bonhof) *Stadt der Bücher*/City of Books (Munich: LangenMüller)

JULIAN PREECE

Preface

Ilija Trojanow shot to attention in the literary world with the publication of what to date is his central work, *Der Weltensammler/ The Collector of Worlds*, a biographical adventure novel about the British soldier and explorer, Sir Richard Francis Burton (1821–1890). The novel was praised by critics and sold in high numbers. Among the reasons for its success we must count the sensuality of its narrative and Trojanow's ability to retell a classic story of derring-do from the age of European colonialism for our own multicultural and – as he would say – neo-imperialist times. *Der Weltensammler* was too a novel that the German-speaking countries perhaps needed to read in 2006: as a contribution from the realm of the imagination to discussions about identity in the wake of the American-led 'war on terror' and to the ongoing German debates about immigration and the value of culturally heterogeneous societies. Trojanow was also part of a growing phenomenon of non-German born authors opting to express themselves in the German language. In his fiction he is concerned with travel and migration: a family's flight across borders to a new life in a new land (*Die Welt ist groß und Rettung lauert überall*/The World Is Large and Salvation Lurks Around Every Corner); the social nightmare of prison convoys on a dystopian motorway network (*Autopol*); three of Richard Burton's celebrated expeditions to India, Arabia, or East Africa (*Der Weltensammler*); or a cruise voyage to the imperilled Antarctic ice cap (*EisTau*/Melting Ice). For all these reasons he embodies a certain vision of Germany and Austria as places of international cultural communication at the beginning of the twenty-first century. His readiness to make his views known, to make a stand with a provocatively placed article or interview, or even with full-length books on subjects such as the surveillance state or relations between the West and the Muslim East (his answer to Samuel Huntington's 'clash of civilisations'), have raised his profile as a public intellectual further.

As Ilija Trojanow argues with the world, in this volume of essays we have tried to honour his engagement by arguing back with him when appropriate. *Der Weltensammler* is a focus of attention in four of these essays (those by Caitríona Ní Dhúill, Ernest Schonfield, Ben Morgan, and Eva M. Knopp) and a point of reference in most of the others. His three other shorter novels are subjected to critical scrutiny, in some cases for the first time in a scholarly format. After literary fiction, Trojanow's genre is undoubtedly the travel book. Ernest Schonfield compares his two accounts of a pilgrimage to Mecca, one a retelling of Burton's journey in the 1850s, the other a report on his own hajj one hundred and fifty years later, with Burton's own best-selling Victorian travelogue. Christina Kraenzle assesses Trojanow's re-negotiation of the traditional genre boundaries in his travel writing, in particular the book ostensibly about *Der Weltensammler*, in which he reflects critically on his own novel and his research into it: *Ein Nomade auf vier Kontinenten* / A Nomad on Four Continents. In the concluding chapter, I attempt to characterise some of his other travel writing with reference to the practice of 'reportage'.

What we hope will emerge is a critical portrait of a many-sided contemporary writer, whose best works are deceptively rich, perhaps straightforward to read but not easy to apprehend in full.

Most of these essays were first presented as papers at a symposium entitled 'Blurring the Lines: Ilija Trojanow as Traveller, Essayist, Novelist' held at Swansea University on 7 May 2010. I am grateful to the Austrian Cultural Forum and the Swansea Centre for Contemporary German Culture for their support, as well as to the contributors for their participation.

JULIAN PREECE
Swansea, October 2012

Interview

Vienna, 6 September 2011

JULIAN PREECE: Good afternoon, Ilja Trojanow.

ILIJA TROJANOW: Ilija.

JP: Ilija Trojanow.

IT: How you pronounce Trojanow does not matter but Ilija is important because the additional syllable makes it into a completely different name.

JP: The other German-speaking author from Bulgaria that I know is of course Elias Canetti. It is remarkable that you should have what was originally the same name.

IT: It is remarkable because it is not the just the same name and the place we come from. We both left Bulgaria at the age of six and another strange thing is that we both first spent time in an English-speaking country and learnt English before we learnt German. That makes English our second language. And we both ended up at one time or another in Vienna and we are both interested in power. Thus, there are several things that we have in common, although obviously he is a completely different author in other respects.

JP: On the subject of language: what has always interested me is this decision in favour of German instead of English when you came to write or in the case of *EisTau*/Melting Ice, your most recent book, even Austrian, as there are some Austrian expressions in it. Why don't you write in English seeing as you first went to an English-speaking school? I find it marvellous that you chose German, but it does not seem an obvious thing to have done.

IT: I know that two hearts beat in your breast as well and I don't know how you will react (some are horrified, others delighted) when I say that I do believe that German offers a prose writer more variety. If I were a poet I would have stayed with English. When I do write poems, which is seldom enough, I write them in English. But German offers me far more possibilities when I write prose. It is like an instrument which can produce every sound, including sounds that have not yet been heard. German is, as is well known, very exact. It has an immense bureaucratic tradition, that means it can be pedantic, it can be exaggerated to the point of parody, it has a tendency to over-exactitude, it can be extremely rigid, stiff, or abstract, it has an immense facility for abstraction, for abstract concepts, but on the other hand, it can be very sensual. I think that one problem that the Germans have with their own language – this began if I am not mistaken in the age of Romanticism – is the prejudice that the Romance languages are more musical. This Romantic prejudice then assumed a new guise as the German language was contaminated during the Nazi period. Many post-war writers had a problematic, antagonistic relationship with their own language. Many did not acknowledge that their language also has a gentle, erotic side. As an outsider my perspective is different. If you read Celan out loud, or Trakl, the sensuality of the language is enticing. Then there is also the opportunity to beat your own path through the forest of words. One of German's most striking features is compound nouns and adjectives. A very good example is 'Weltensammler'. Every now and again, at least once a month or so, there is a reference in the German newspapers to someone being a 'Weltensammler', a word that did not exist before my novel was published. That shows you that you cannot only create words but also enrich the language. For an immigrant that is important. There is a saying by Chinua Achebe, which has stuck in my mind since I read it when I was young because it reflects my situation, that he wanted to carry on writing in the foreign language until he had left his mark on it. That is precisely my point too because as a migrant you have the urge to be visible. As you take your first steps you are not only invisible but also unwanted. It is a combination of not being seen and not being wanted. In order to overcome that, you have to work very hard. In my childhood and adolescence I was told 'you have to be better than the others because you have so much catching up to do'. As refugees we had no connections, no money in the bank, we arrived with just one suitcase.

JP: And you did that first of all in Kenya and after that in Munich.

IT: Yes, that's right. And you know that you can never let up. I can still remember how Mr Sainsbury in Kenton College after I had been there for a year looked around the class after he had handed out the yearly reports and said: 'Shame on you boys, how can you let a damn foreigner beat you!' He didn't say 'damn', I added that, but he said 'how can you let a foreigner beat you'.

JP: They were all British at this school?

IT: There were Africans, that is Kenyans and Kenyan Indians, but of course it was very British, it was as if the Colonial era was still going on. There were all these references to England. It was a little bit of England exported to Kenya. There is another aspect that is especially relevant for Germany (far more so than in England or in France), where migrant authors were suspected of not knowing German properly. No doubt there used to be one or two who did not know it properly but by the time my generation came along, all those that I know, those that you have invited to Swansea for example, they have full command of the language. That means that if we diverge from standard linguistic usage we know exactly what we are doing and do it on purpose. In my case at the beginning there were mutterings and insinuations that you could tell I was not a native speaker. That is true, but in a different way: we have a different approach to the language and perhaps a different determination to leave our linguistic footprint.

JP: As someone who has also done his best over lots of years to master German I know how much work and practice you have to put in. You have to know all the rules and so forth. You began at ten or twelve.

IT: Twelve.

JP: The same as me.

IT: You are absolutely right. It is also a question of how much you read. Between the ages of around fourteen and nineteen I kept a record of all the books that I read. When I looked back recently, in the best year I counted something like 300 books. I nearly read a book a day.

JP: And most of those in German.

IT: Yes.

JP: Coming to the question of literary tradition and role models, whether from the present or the past, can you say which authors have influenced you? Was it more authors who wrote in German that you looked up to? I have picked up from your essays and comments that you tend to mention international names or authors who write in English rather than German ones. You mention Canetti and Grass but that is about it.

IT: You are right and that is interesting. The thing is that I came to literature before I came to the German language. In Kenton College we had a library and it was fairly well stocked, I did a lot of reading there, and I suspect there were mainly books by English-language authors, so I read them. Also, I spent three pivotal years between the age of sixteen and nineteen in Kenya and gradually came to realise what kind of a ghetto we whites were living in. I wanted to free myself from this ghetto and did two things. The first was to take a rucksack and go off to do all those things which were forbidden, by travelling into the bush and staying in the dingiest hostels or sleeping out under the stars. The second was to read African literature and that is another unusual influence which makes me stand out from other German-language authors. I must be just about the only one who was marked at such a young age by African literature.

JP: Who wrote in English.

IT: Because I was in Kenya, of course, yes they wrote mainly in English. Authors like Chinua Achebe, Ngugi wa Thiong'o. Later on and still to this today Nuruddin Farah was very important to me. But also many others, it is a long list. There are other connections in the background which link up things which I did not even realise could be linked. Questions such as: what kind of attitude does one have towards story-telling, to narration itself? You either have an attitude which is characterised by scepticism and ambivalence, dominant in Germany in the decades before I became active in the field of literature, with all those meta-levels, the whole idea of the postmodern, of being artful, the great distrust of story-telling itself, but in my case Bulgarian fairy tales were my very first literary influence, and later African literature that has an affinity with the oral tradition. I did not go in search of this. Looking back I can claim it as part of my poetics but I got there more by chance than anything else. Because of the constellation of the Balkans and East Africa I was closer to orality. To this day I prefer books which really give you the feeling that a narrator is speaking to you. I can admire someone who shows me how his narration is constructed, displays his *scaffolding*, so to speak, but it does not really get me excited. By all that I do not mean to say that I am a naive narrator. You can combine the two traditions.

JP: I would like to come to the questions of literary fame and writing for the market, now that you have some renown as the author of *Der Weltensammler*. Is there not a contradiction in your books between serving the market and serving literature? I see a distinction between books such as *Gebrauchsanweisung für Indien*/India: A User's Manual and lots of the travel books and the literary works that you have published.

IT: You are quite right about the difference. But there is no contradiction. You get to the point where you will do anything to survive. Earlier on I had absolutely no money. I took the hardest of all routes by giving up my degree to found a publishing company. We published African

literature which of course did not make any money. At the same time
I did some journalism. All these things were necessary for me to earn
my living, to survive. In literary history this is not something which is
out of the ordinary. Lots of well-known authors have done the same
thing. I was recently in Lisbon and I was very amused to discover that
the first ever book to be published by the great Portuguese writer
with the great number of pseudonyms, Fernando Pessoa, was written
in English, *A Travel Guide to Lisbon*.[1] I began to dip into it, and it is
unbelievably bad.

JP: Really bad?

IT: Yes, but then I thought, poor Fernando must have needed money and
so he quickly banged out a travel guide. He had to do it in English
because in those days the tourists were all English. With respect to
Gebrauchsanweisung I think I have to contradict you slightly because
in my view it is an educational book. It is part of a series which sells
in great numbers and it is intended to introduce readers to India in a
very different way to the one that they are used to or may be expecting. It offers a new perspective, a new way of looking at the subject. If
I tried to do the same thing in a respectable book of essays published
by Hanser I would get wonderful reviews but the book would be read
by 3,000 people. *Gebrauchsanweisung* has so far sold around 80,000
copies and I have the satisfaction of knowing that a great number
of German travellers to India have gone there with my book, which
subverts all the clichés about India that are trotted out every day in
the media and in most of the other travel guides to India. I see that
as part of my task, I do not write for posterity or to be admitted into
the pantheon, but in order to touch my fellow citizens in some way
or to raise doubts in their mind. If I do that by being popular or by
producing a book for a series like that, then that is not a problem as
far as I am concerned.

---

1   Fernando Pessoa, *Lisboa: o que turista deve ver/What the Tourist Must See*, bilingual
     edition (Lisbon: Livros Horizonte, 1992).

JP: And you did that with the Mecca book as well.

IT: But in my view the Mecca book has literary qualities. I don't think that it is flat or popularising. That's why lots of Germans have problems with it.

JP: But you wrote and published it at a time when the west was saying lots of nasty things about Muslims and Arabia because of Iraq and all that and you came along and said, no, it is all very different. You even confessed affiliation to the religion itself, didn't you?

IT: No, that is the problem, people can only think in black and white. I have explained roughly 7,000 times that I do not believe that if you are a spiritual person that you have to belong to a religion. On the contrary, I would even suspect that this restriction by a dogma or an ideology is contradicts my understanding of spirituality. I cannot convert to Islam or confess allegiance to it. I find the question wrong. I have explained that often but people still don't understand. You can say it hundreds of times but they still come back and ask: are you a Muslim or aren't you? People are stuck in this binary thinking. They use it to try to discredit me in the newspapers, even when I am talking about climate change or something else. Some say: he is an Islamic agent who just wants to distract our attention from the real problems.

JP: You get reactions like that?

IT: Yes. Let me give you one example. I think I sent you the lecture that I gave in Groningen about how I set about writing a novel on climate change. Once a year someone is asked to give a talk in the main city church on a major contemporary topic. It is very prestigious because the talk is printed in full in Holland's leading newspaper. There is also a long interview. When it appeared, a newspaper, a weekly newspaper of the extreme right, what's the man called, Lubbers?

JP: Geert Wilders?

IT: Yes, that's right. Lubbers was someone else.

JP: I don't think he was so bad.

IT: Yes, I got them mixed up. Geert Wilders said this is a clear case of a Trojan horse who for a while now has been telling us rubbish in order to distract our attention from the real and true danger, which is the Muslim takeover of Europe. In Germany on websites such as 'Politically Incorrect' or 'The Axis of Good' you get similar things. Sooner or later there comes the point when you develop a thick skin and you think that it can't be my problem how people misunderstand me on purpose. I think that my whole oeuvre shows that I am as radically removed from a religiously aligned position as one can be. It is quite impossible to categorise me as either a believer or an atheist, which is supposed to be a clear distinction. Some people refuse to accept such a life in the in-between, in these liminal spaces. That is why Richard Burton was such an obvious topic for me because he had the same problem throughout his life. The multifarious complexity, which as far as I am concerned goes hand in hand with freedom, has to be defended all the time against labels and prejudices.

JP: I would like to move on to Richard Burton and the *Weltensammler*. It struck me when I re-read the novel recently that Burton by the end of his life is in some way a failure.

IT: Yes, I agree completely. It is a novel about failing.

JP: Really? I am glad to hear that you agree. I thought I was the first to come up with this idea. In the third part ...

IT: The third part is very sad. I think that lots of readers did not notice that because it is narrated in such a colourful way. There is action and adventure.

JP: Especially in the first part, with the love story and so on.

IT: No, I mean the third part, there is such a lot happening and Sidi Mubarak Bombay is such a charismatic character that lots of readers have overlooked the profound sadness. Burton gets to a point where he betrays himself, not just his material aim of finding the source of the Nile, but his own standpoint. He falls back into colonial ways of thinking and behaving.

JP: He is an imperialist himself at the end.

IT: Exactly, he falls back into all those colonial positions which he had rejected when he was in India. I wrote the end of the chapter with a great sense of mourning.

JP: Another thing which has struck me reading your prose fiction is that each time you have a new narrative approach. *Autopol* is entirely different from *Die Welt ist groß* which is different from the *Weltensammler* and now *EisTau* is narrated in a different tone. I have been reading the latest novel by Martin Walser[2] over the summer because the *Times Literary Supplement* asked me to review it and there all you can say when it comes to the style is that it is the same old Walser sound that you either like or you don't like. He does what he does terribly well but you can tell that it is him.

IT: You are quite right. I have heard at least ten people react like that to this novel over the summer. Either they say, great, a new novel by Walser or they say, it's rubbish, useless, full of the usual pathos.

JP: And this time with *EisTau* you have got inside the head of this glaciologist.

IT: I have to butt in because this is central to my understanding of the way that I write. I want each work of fiction, each literary work that I write to be a new departure. There is nothing that I fear more than repeating what I have tried out already. I have little interest in churning out something time and again that one has already tried and maybe even mastered. For me it contradicts a fundamental principle. I believe that in all my books I try to demonstrate hidden complexities and to explore new ways of seeing and expressing myself. I cannot do that by using the same structures or the same style, the same literary form. My poetic ambition requires me to find a new approach for each new theme.

---

2   Martin Walser, *Muttersohn* (Frankfurt am Main: Suhrkamp, 2011).

JP: On the other hand, there are lots parallels, for instance between Zeno
      Hintermeyer in *EisTau* and Richard Burton. Hintermeyer is a failure
      too, is he not at the end of his life?

IT: Yes, but ...

JP: And your view of women, the way you portray female characters, you
      get accused from time to time, whether in your presence or not I don't
      know, of having a very traditional, chauvinist view of women, in the
      relationship between Burton and Kundalini, for instance. I once gave a
      talk on *Der Weltensammler* and someone in the audience complained
      that the first thing that Burton did when he got to Bombay was go to
      a brothel (and I had not even noticed that it was a brothel).

IT: In Basel there was a seminar organised by Germanists on the sub-
      ject of German literature and voyages of discovery. A woman from
      Vienna gave a talk about me. She criticised me for the fact that the
      shimmering ambivalence evident in every other respect of my writing
      was absent when it came to the female characters. On the one hand,
      I take this criticism seriously, on the other, it is ahistorical. Why does
      Richard Burton go to a brothel straightaway? First, because that is
      what he did in reality. Second, because in those times most men did
      the same. Third, to this day, men still do the same. It is a sign of our
      hypocrisy that we do not accept how widespread prostitution is in our
      society. The numbers are sensational. Every third German man goes
      to a brothel at some point. There are 300,000 registered prostitutes in
      Germany. It is a mass phenomenon. In those days, in 1842, there were
      hardly any European women in India. Where else was he supposed
      to go? The relationship with Kundalini is by the standards of that
      time to a certain degree fanciful. Such relationships were themselves
      a mass phenomenon, often based on contracts between master and
      female servant. What the feminist reading seemed to overlook is that
      Kundalini has her own voice, and she tells her own story, she tells it in
      such a way that she confronts Richard Burton. She has her own voice
      and her own dignity.

JP: She deceives him and she never stays the whole night with him.

IT: Such were the social restrictions. In the Arabian chapter there cannot be any women, that is obvious, it would be absurdly unrealistic if there were.

JP: There is one, when Burton goes into a harem to treat the wife who cannot conceive.

IT: Where it was possible, I included women, but once he gets to Mecca and Medina then there cannot be any women. The only thing that I regret is that I did not make more of the character of Sidi Mubarak Bombay's wife. There are lots of female readers who have remarked that she is a wonderful character. I could have developed her into a more influential character. The reason that I did not had nothing to do with my view of women but that I was focussed on a different topic. You notice sometimes when you look back at what you have written that you were concentrating on certain aspects, thus overlooking others. With the new novel I am not sure – one woman has criticised me again for my treatment of the female characters, but I have also heard from several female readers that Paulina is my best female character to date. At last there is an interesting female character, even if she is not the central character. I think the jury is still out. My wife says that I just pick themes which tend to exclude women. She may be right. Why I do that I don't know.

JP: We don't have time to analyse that now. Ilija Trojanow, I thank you very much for this conversation.

TRANSLATED BY JP.

ILIJA TROJANOW

Weltbürgertum heute: Rede zu einer kosmopolitischen Kultur / What Being a Citizen of the World Means Today: On Cosmopolitan Culture (translated by Seiriol Dafydd)

This lecture was delivered on 25 January 2010 at the Thalia Theatre in Hamburg to open the first Lessing Festival (Lessingtage – Um alles in der Welt/Lessing Festival – About Everything in the World) which has since become an annual event.

1977 kam der Film *Amar Akbar Anthony* in die indischen Kinos. Darin flüchtet ein ehemaliger Häftling vor einem Mafiaboß und überläßt seine Frau sowie die drei gemeinsamen Söhne ihrem Schicksal. Die Mutter erblindet, die Brüder werden ausgesetzt und von Fremden adoptiert, der erste von einem Hindu-Polizisten, der zweite von einem muslimischen Schneider und der dritte von einem katholischen Priester. Sie tragen die Namen der jeweiligen Tradition, ohne sich ihrer Herkunft bewußt zu sein. Der älteste Bruder namens Amar wird Polizist, der mittlere namens Akbar Sänger und der jüngste namens Anthony, gespielt von der Ikone des indischen Kinos, Amitabh Bachchan, ein Taugenichts, der gelegentlich das Gesetz reizt. Sie ahnen es schon: auf verschlungenen Pfaden kreuzen sich die Lebenslinien der Brüder, sie helfen einander, sie singen zusammen ein Lied, sie besiegen den bösen Mafiaboß, sie erkennen sich als Brüder, sie finden zur Mutter zurück, der erneut Augenlicht und Söhne geschenkt werden. Die Familie ist wiedervereint, doch mit keiner Geste wird angedeutet, daß die Brüder ihr adoptiertes kulturelles und religiöses Selbstverständnis ablegen könnten, in keiner Szene führt ihre Differenz zu Konflikten. Die Handlung ist an hanebüchenen Zufällen kaum zu überbieten, und doch ist *Amar Akbar Anthony* ein moderner Filmklassiker, der regelmäßig auf einem der 101 Fernsehkanäle Indiens wiederholt wird. Auch wenn die Handlung unwahrscheinlich ist, so sind seine Ideale und Emotionen glaubhaft und bewegend.

21 Jahre später erzählt ein ähnlich angelegter Film ein ganz anders gelagertes Drama. In Mahesh Bhatts *Zakhm* lebt eine Witwe in Bombay mit ihren zwei Söhnen, Ajay, einem Sänger, und Anand, Aktivist einer rechtsextremen hinduistischen Organisation. Doch entgegen dem Anschein, die Familie sei hinduistischen Glaubens, sucht die Witwe von Zeit zu Zeit klammheimlich eine Moschee zum Gebet auf – sie ist von Haus aus Muslima, hat aber jahrelang in wilder Ehe mit einem Hindu gelebt und ihm versprochen, die Kinder nicht als Moslems aufzuziehen. Als im ganzen Land wegen der Zerstörung der Babri-Moschee durch Hindu-Fanatiker Unruhen ausbrechen, wird die Witwe, die ihren wahren Glauben so lange verheimlicht hat, Opfer ihrer wahren Religionszugehörigkeit. Fanatiker greifen sie auf der Straße an und zünden sie bei lebendigem Leib an. Mit 80-prozentigen Verbrennungen wird sie moribund ins Krankenhaus eingeliefert.

In 1977 the film *Amar Akbar Anthony* was released in Indian cinemas. The film tells the story of a former prisoner who is on the run from a mafia boss, leaving his wife and their three sons to their fate. The mother becomes blind and the sons are abandoned and adopted by strangers, the first by a Hindu policeman, the second by a Muslim tailor, and the third by a Catholic priest. Each son takes his name from these respective traditions without having knowledge of his ancestry. The eldest brother, Amar, becomes a policeman, the middle brother, Akbar, becomes a singer, and the young-est, Anthony (played in the film by the star of Indian cinema, Amitabh Bachchan) becomes a good-for-nothing who occasionally has brushes with the law. The reader will have already guessed how the story works out: the brothers' lives intersect in intricate ways, they help each other, they sing a song together, they defeat the mafia boss, they recognise each other as brothers, and they find their way back to their mother, who regains her eyesight at the same moment that she finds her sons. The family is reunited but no gesture suggests that the brothers can cast off their adopted cultural and religious identies; and in no scene do their differences lead to conflict. The plot can hardly be beaten for outrageous coincidences and yet *Amar Akbar Anthony* is a modern film classic that is regularly repeated on one or the other of India's 101 television channels. Even if its plot is implausible, its ideals and emotions are credible and moving.

Twenty-one years later a similarly structured film tells the story of a very different drama. In Mahesh Bhatt's *Zakhm* a widow lives in Bombay with her two sons, Ajay, a singer, and Anand, an activist in a right-wing extremist Hindu organisation. Yet contrary to all appearances that the family follows the Hindu faith, from time to time the widow makes clandestine visits to a mosque in order to pray – she is actually a Muslim but was cohabiting for many years with a Hindu, whom she promised not to raise the children according to the strictures of her own religion. When unrest breaks out across the country due to the destruc-tion of the Babri mosque at the hands of Hindu fanatics, the widow, who has concealed her beliefs for so long, becomes a victim of her true co-religionists. Fanatics attack her on the street and burn her alive. She is taken to hospital, at death's door, suffering eighty percent burns.

Der ältere Sohn Ajay muß nun um ihr Andenken und gegen die Rach-
sucht seines Bruders kämpfen, der die Realität als Negativ wahrnimmt,
überzeugt davon, seine Hindu-Mutter sei von Moslems ermordet worden.
Der Leichnam einer Frau, die ein religiöses Doppelleben führte, wird zum
prototypischen Zankapfel. Die Fanatiker verlangen die Verbrennung des
Leichnams, da die Frau als Hindu gelebt habe, der älteste Sohn will ihren
letzten Wunsch erfüllen und sie begraben lassen. Die einstigen Ideale von
Amar Akbar Anthony sind in *Zakhm* (was auf Hindi 'Wunde' bedeutet)
zerbrochen, der Freiheit der individuellen Wandlung sind Handschellen
angelegt worden. In den zwei Jahrzehnten dazwischen haben die Dogma-
tiker auf allen Seiten zu den Waffen gegriffen. Tribale Identitäten werden
nunmehr auf Kosten eines feindlichen Anderen konstruiert und aggressiv
verteidigt. Nicht nur in Indien, oder im Nahen Osten, sondern zunehmend auch bei uns. Und auf einmal erweist sich der angeblich altbackene
Gottfried Ephraim Lessing als Denker von prägnanter Aktualität. Wenn
wie in diesen Tagen in diskursiven Ritterspielen die Lanzen für und gegen
Aufklärung oder Glaube, Toleranz oder Selbstbehauptung, Freiheit oder
Krieg gebrochen werden, ist es an der Zeit, sich des ersten kosmopolitischen
Autors deutscher Sprache zu besinnen, der nicht nur ein Freund Moses
Mendelssohns sondern auch am Islam interessiert war (er übersetzte u.a.
Voltaires Essays 'Von dem Korane' und 'Geschichte der Kreuzzüge'), und
der eine bedenkenswerte Parabel bei uns popularisierte.

Der Staub jahrhundertealter Binsenwahrheit liegt auf der Ringparabel. Sie ist übertüncht von dem Anstrich des Geläufigen, Allzugeläufigen.
Auf den ersten Blick bietet sie nicht mehr als den kleinsten gemeinsamen Nenner einer vermeintlich toleranten, säkularen Gesellschaft.
Aber galt das nicht auch für das Prinzip von Habeas corpus, das wir als
gegeben und geschenkt erachteten, bis es ohne Not ausgehebelt wurde?

Ajay, the eldest son, must now battle to honour her memory and resist the temptation, to which his brother succumbs, to exact revenge. Perceiving reality in a negative light, his brother is convinced that his Hindu mother has been murdered by Muslims. The corpse of a woman who led a religious double-life becomes an object of contention in a way which we can see as prototypical. The fanatics demand that the corpse be cremated because the woman lived as a Hindu. The eldest son wishes to comply with her last wish and have her buried, as a Muslim. The ideals of *Amar Akbar Anthony* are shattered in *Zakhm* (which means 'wound' in Hindi); the freedom for individual transformation is now repressed. During the two decades between the two films dogmatists on both sides have reached for their weapons. Tribal identities are henceforth constructed at the cost of the hostile 'Other' and are defended aggressively, not only in India or the Middle East but also increasingly here. All of a sudden the allegedly old-fashioned Gotthold Ephraim Lessing proves himself to be a thinker whose relevance could not be more contemporary. If, as today, we are debating the pros and cons of the Enlightenment versus Faith, tolerance versus self-assertion, or peace versus war, it is high time to recall the first cosmopolitan author of the German language, who was not only a friend of Moses Mendelssohn, but was also interested in Islam (he translated, among other things Voltaire's essays 'On the Koran' and 'History of the Crusades'), and who popularised a parable worthy of our consideration here.

I must begin by blowing away centuries' worth of dust which encoats Lessing's ring parable from his play *Nathan the Wise*. It all seems familiar, all-too-familiar to us, but this appearance is deceptive. At first glance the parable recommends no more than the lowest common denominator for a supposedly tolerant, secular society. But was that not also true of the principle of *Habeas corpus*, which we took for granted until it was annulled without due cause?[1]

---

1   According to the principle of *Habeas corpus*, arrested suspects must be charged with an offence within a short period (usually twenty-four hours) or released. In the wake of the 'war on terror' following the 9/11 attacks, the period was extended in the United Kingdom in cases of suspected terrorism.

Und wird nicht eine Bischöfin, die an die Friedensethik als Teil einer Tradition gemahnt, die von allen Rednern alltäglich im Mund geführt wird
wie ein rachenputzendes Lutschbonbon, öffentlich gekreuzigt, als habe sie
zum Kannibalismus aufgerufen? Auch das gute alte Lied muß halt immer
wieder mit frischen Stimmen gesungen, die zentralen Fundamente einer
zivilisierten Gesellschaft in jeder Generation zu neuer Selbstverständlich-
keit gebracht werden. Genauer betrachtet offenbart die Ringparabel, wie
auch *Nathan der Weise* als Ganzes, eine profundere Haltung zu Vielfalt
und Vermischung als unsere Erinnerung diesem Klassiker zugesteht. Nicht
zuletzt wegen der Herkunft und Metamorphose einer Parabel, deren Gene-
sis an vergessene kosmopolitische Realitäten erinnert und deren verschie-
dene Varianten den Mißbrauch jener kultureller und religiöser Differenz
repräsentieren, die der Machtpolitik seit je als liebstes Werkzeug dient.

   Welchen Ursprung hat nun also die Ringparabel? Lessing selbst gibt
als Quelle Boccaccios *Decamerone* an und zwar die dritte Erzählung des
ersten Buches. Allerdings hat Boccaccio diese wie auch viele andere seiner
Geschichten nicht selbst erfunden, sondern sich aus einem überaus reichen
Reservoir an Fabeln, Parabeln und Allegorien bedient, das sich als narratives Grundwasser unter den Religionen und Kulturen ausstreckt, etwa die
Geschichten aus Tausendundeiner Nacht, die auf den altindischen Sammlungen *Vetala-pancavimsati* (*Die fünfundzwanzig Geschichten vom Vampir*),
Kathasarit-sogar (*Ozean der Flüsse von Geschichten*) und *Panchatantra*
basieren. So stammt die zweite Geschichte des zweiten Tages, in der Rinaldo
seinen Besitz verliert und wiedererlangt, aus dem Fabelbuch *Panchatantra*,
ebenso die zweite Geschichte des dritten Tages, in der König Agilulf takt-
voll versucht, es mit dem Stallburschen aufzunehmen, der seine königliche
Ehefrau verführt hat, eine charmante Erzählung, die heute noch in ganz
Indien beliebt ist. Die fünfte Geschichte des dritten Tages über Zima,
der die Liebe einer verheirateten Frau mit List und einem schönen Pferd
gewinnt, stammt aus dem *Hitopadesha* (*Anweisung für das Wohlbefinden*).

And what of the bishop whose vilification amounting to a public crucifixion could not have been more intense if she had called upon the population to embrace cannibalism? Her offence? To celebrate the ethic of peace as part of a tradition which itself is invoked daily by orators as if it were a mouth-cleansing hard-boiled sweet.[2] The old favourites must always be sung anew by fresh voices. The central foundations of a civilised society must be re-scrutinsed by each generation as a matter of course. On closer inspection, Lessing's ring parable, like the whole play in which it appears, reveals a more profound attitude towards diversity and intermixing than we may remember. The parable's profundity is not least a consequence of its origin and the narrative metamorphoses it underwent before it reached Lessing. Its variations remind us of forgotten cosmopolitan realities; the abuse of cultural and religious difference, which the powerful have marshalled to their advantage for as long as anyone can remember, is stamped on it too. What, then, are the origins of the ring parable? Lessing himself cites Boccaccio's *Decameron* as the source; the third story of the second book. However, Boccaccio, as with a number of his stories, did not make it up, but rather helped himself from a very deep well of fables, parables, and allegories, drawing from a kind of narrative aquifer which lies beneath the surface of our religions and our cultural traditions. If we drill down deep enough, we reach, for example, the *Tales from the Thousand and One Nights*, some of which are based in turn on the old Indian collections *Vetala-pancavimasti* (*The Twenty-five Stories of a Vampire*), *Katha-saritsagara* (*Ocean of the River of Stories*), and the book of fables, *Panchatantra*. The second story of the second day in the *Decameron*, in which a certain Rinaldo loses and recovers his property, comes from *Panchatantra*, as does the second story of the third day, in which King Agilulf tactfully attempts to be a match for the stable-lad who has seduced his queen. This delightful story is popular across India to this day. The fifth story of the third day, dealing with Zima, who wins the love of a married woman by means of deceit and a beautiful horse, comes from the *Hitopadesha* (*Instructions for Wellbeing*).

---

2   This is probably a reference to Margot Käßmann, a bishop who came under intense criticism for her public opposition to the presence of German troops in Afghanistan.

Von dort ging sie ein in eine Sammlung mit dem Titel *Die Geschichten von Sindbad dem Seefahrer*, die zu Zeiten Boccaccios in einer lateinischen Version weit verbreitet war. Die neunte Geschichte des dritten Tages über verworrene Liebe zwischen Gillette und Bertrand beruht auf einem der bedeutendsten Dramen des Sanskrit, Kalidasas *Shakuntala* (das übrigens Goethes Wohlwollen fand), damals in einer französischen Version aus dem 11. Jahrhundert in Umlauf.

Boccaccios Verfahren war keineswegs einmalig. Im Mittelalter gedieh der Import von Mythen und Legenden. Auch jüdische Autoren beteiligten sich an der Verbreitung orientalischer Geschichten, etwa indem sie arabische Sammlungen ins Hebräische und daraus weiter ins Lateinische übersetzten. So floß das *Panchatantra* durchs Arabische und Hebräische, bevor es im 12. Jahrhundert Johannes von Capuas *Directorium vitae humanae* (*Anleitung für das menschliche Leben*) nährte, eine berühmte Anthologie moralischer Geschichten. Die Verbreitung der Ringparabel nahm einen ähnlichen Weg; sie taucht als jüdische Erzählung in al-Andalus auf, wird ins Lateinische übertragen und gewinnt einige Jahrhunderte später nach dem Ende der Reconquista an Bedeutung, als das vereinte christliche Spanien nichts Dringlicheres zu vollbringen hatte als die Vertreibung aller Juden. Salomo ben Jehuda Ibn Verga, sephardischer Flüchtling und Chronist der Verfolgungen, führt das Gleichnis als Argument gegenüber einem christlichen König an, die jüdische Minderheit nicht zu verfolgen.

Die Parabel war nicht nur in das *Decamerone*, sondern auch in die *Gesta romanorum* gewandert, jene Exempelsammlung des 14. Jahrhunderts, die so gänzlich falsch benannt ist, denn es finden sich darin keineswegs nur die ‚Taten der Römer', sondern Geschichten aus allen Herren Ländern. Es ist die erste weltläufige Anthologie, ein Füllhorn an Themen und Geschichten, antike Stoffe stehen neben alttestamentarischen, christlichen Legenden neben Volksschwänken. Ein Fundus, der ganze Heerscharen europäischer Autoren inspirierte und Handlungselemente für die Dramen Shakespeares und Marlowes lieferte. Der Großteil der *Gesta romanorum* basiert auf der Sammelarbeit eines Mannes, der zu den dramatis personae von *Nathan der Weise* gehören könnte, einem zum christlichen Glauben konvertierten Juden namens Petrus Alfonsi. 1066 in al-Andalus geboren, zog er nach seiner Konversion in den Norden, zuerst in die Normandie und dann nach England.

This story enters a collection entitled *The Stories of Sindbad the Sailor*, a Latin version of which was widely available in Boccaccio's time. The ninth story of the third day regarding the entangled love affair between Gillette and Bertrand is based on one of the most important Sanskrit plays, Kalidasa's *The Recognition of Sakuntala* (which was, incidentally, favourably received by Goethe). In Boccaccio's day it was available in an eleventh-century French version.

Boccaccio's method was by no means exceptional. The importing of myths and legends was a flourishing trade in the Middle Ages. Jewish authors, for instance, aided the circulation of oriental stories by translating Arabic collections into Hebrew and then into Latin. In this way the *Panchatantra* progressed through Arabic and Hebrew before feeding into Johannes von Capua's *Directorium vitae humanae* (*Instructions for Human Life*), which was a well-known anthology of morality tales in the twelfth century. The ring parable was launched in a similar fashion; it appears as a Jewish story in al-Andalus, gets translated into Latin and becomes more significant a few centuries later after the *Reconquista*, when united Christian Spain had nothing more urgent to accomplish than to drive out the Jews. Salomo ben Jehuda Ibn Verga, a Sephardic refugee and chronicler of the persecutions, cites the parable as an argument designed to persuade a Christian king not to persecute the Jewish minority.

The parable had by then not only found its way into the *Decameron* but also into the *Gesta romanorum*, a fourteenth-century collection of anecdotes and tales which is totally misnamed, since it is not only the 'deeds of the Romans' that it chronicles but stories from all over the world. It is the first cosmopolitan anthology, a cornucopia of themes and stories, with material from classical antiquity and the Old Testament placed side by side with Christian stories and comic folk tales, a treasure trove which has inspired hosts of European authors and playwrights, among them Shakespeare and Marlowe. The majority of the *Gesta romanorum* is based on the collecting done by one man, who could himself belong to the dramatis personae of Lessing's *Nathan the Wise*. He was a converted Jew named Petrus Alfonsi. Born in 1066 in al-Andalus, after his conversion he headed north, first to Normandy and then to England.

Als Leibarzt von Heinrich I. und dessen wichtigster Gelehrter bei Hof, erlangte er durch Publikationen zu einer Vielzahl von Themen literarischen Ruhm. Nur eines seiner Bücher ist uns noch bekannt, das einzige, das nicht der Belehrung, sondern der Unterhaltung diente. Die *Disciplina Clericalis* (*Unterweisung für Kleriker*), 1115 fertiggestellt, ist eine Sammlung von 34 Geschichten, die er aus dem Arabischen ins Lateinische übersetzt hatte: eine kleine, repräsentative Auswahl aus der Erzähltradition von al-Andalus, so beeindruckend, daß sie Generationen von Lesern und Zuhörern im christlichen Europa begeisterte. Die *Disciplina* ist die erste Sammlung von Erzählungen in der lateinischen Literatur des Mittelalters. Die kosmopolitische Pointe dieser Anthologie besteht darin, daß der Konvertit diejenigen, die ihn bekehrt hatten, für die Kultur, der er absichtlich den Rücken gekehrt hatte, begeistern konnte.

Aber die Ringparabel hat nicht nur viele Väter, sie entstammt zudem einem Ring an Geschichten, einem Reigen an Parabeln, denn die erwähnten Geschichtensammlungen funktionierten nach ein- und demselben dramaturgischen Prinzip: eine Rahmenhandlung umklammert die disparaten Teile. Auf diese Weise ordneten nun auch die ersten westeuropäischen Prosaisten ihr phantasievolles Material, Boccaccio sein *Decamerone* und Chaucer die *Canterbury Tales*, die beiden einflußreichsten Erzählwerke der Renaissance. Wenn also Lessing dieses Verfahren ebenfalls verwendet, wenn sich bei dem Konflikt zwischen Saladin und Nathan eine Falltür zu einer anderen Geschichte öffnet, bedient er sich einer gemeinsamen Erzähltradition, und es stellt sich nicht nur die Frage, wer im Besitz der Wahrheit ist, also des einzig wahren Ringes, sondern auch, wer eigentlich erzählt: Lessing oder Boccaccio, Nathan der Weise oder die schöne Filomene aus der florentinischen Jeunesse dorée, Vishnu Sharman oder Scheherazade, ein höfischer Sanskritdichter oder ein jüdischer Gelehrter aus Córdoba. Und wenn sie alle miteinander die Parabel geschaffen haben, von der wir heute noch zehren, wenn sie über Jahrhunderte jenseits aller Grenzen unsere narrative Grundversorgung organisiert haben, wie ist es dann um die Deutungshoheit und das Wahrheitsmonopol bestellt? Es ist gewiß kein Zufall, daß Lessing sich diese Geschichte ausgesucht und sie auf diese Weise erzählt hat, unabhängig davon, ob er sich der Historie des Motivs in allen ihren Aspekten bewußt war. Nein, Lessing schlägt eine Bresche für die Aufklärung, indem er den Spuren des Gemeinsamen, der Vermischungen folgt.

As personal physician to Henry I, and his most important court scholar, Alfonsi gained literary fame through his publications on a number of different topics. Only one of his books is still known to us now, and it is the only one that serves to entertain rather than to educate. The *Disciplina Clericalis* (*Instructions for Clerics*), completed in 1115, is a collection of 34 stories that he translated from Arabic into Latin: a small, representative selection from the storytelling tradition of al-Andalus, but so impressive that it enthused generations of readers and listeners in Christian Europe. The *Disciplina* is the first collection of stories in the Latin literature of the Middle Ages. Its multicultural significance lies in the manner in which the convert filled his converters with enthusiasm for the culture on which he deliberately turned his back.

The ring parable has numerous fathers, but also originates from within a ring of stories, a series of parables, since all the collections of stories mentioned thus far function according to the same dramatic principle: their disparate parts are set within a framework plot. Chaucer's *Canterbury Tales*, next to the *Decameron* which helped to inspire it one of the most influential narrative works of the late Middle Ages, is structured in this way too. If Lessing also uses this method and if, in the conflict between Saladin and Nathan, a trapdoor to another story opens up, then he is joining a shared storytelling tradition. Not only is the question of who possesses the truth, that is who has the real ring, raised here, but also the question of who is telling the story. Is it Lessing or Boccaccio? Is it the wise Nathan or the beautiful Filomene from Florence's fashionable and wealthy society? Is it Vishnu Sharman or Scheherazade? A Sanskrit court poet or a Jewish scholar from Córdoba? And if they all worked together to create the parable that we still feed upon today, if they, spanning centuries and crossing borders, organised the basic provisions of narrative, who has conclusive authority over interpretation and the monopoly over truth? It is certainly no coincidence that Lessing selected this story and told it the way that he told it, irrespective of whether he was aware of every facet of its history. No, Lessing backs the Enlightenment in that he follows in the tracks of what is shared and intermixed.

Auffällig auch, daß die Ring- und Reigensammlungen stets säkularen Charakters waren. Verschachtelungen bekommen frommen, didaktischen Texten nicht, die Brechungen und die damit einhergehenden Verunsicherungen des Lesers meiden wie der Teufel das Weihwasser. In vielerlei Hinsicht mag die Bibel unser Vademekum gewesen sein, unser Umgang mit Erzählung und unsere literarischen Vorlieben verdanken wir ebensosehr dem *Panchatantra* oder den *Geschichten aus Tausendundeiner Nacht.*

Lessing begnügt sich nicht mit einer Ringparabel, in der die drei abrahamitischen Religionen gleichberechtigt nebeneinanderstehen, er schmiedet zur Verdeutlichung, wie sehr die drei miteinander verflochten und verschmolzen sind, einen weiteren, einen dritten dramaturgischen Ring, nämlich jenen der Blutsbande, der familiären Zusammenhänge, ähnlich den eingangs beschriebenen Filmen *Amar Akbar Anthony* und *Zakhm.* Die Ziehtochter Recha des Juden Nathan heißt eigentlich Blanda von Filnek, und ist eine Christin (auch wenn ihr dies erst gegen Ende des Dramas enthüllt wird). Ihr Bruder, der junge Tempelherr Curd von Stauffen, dessen wahrer Name Leu von Filnek lautet, ist ebenfalls Christ. Der Vater der beiden war ein Moslem namens Assad, der Bruder Saladins, der sich später Wolf von Filnek nannte. Der Sultan ist somit Onkel einer Halb-Christin und Halb-Muslima, die in einem jüdischen Haushalt von einer Christin erzogen wird. Keiner außer Nathan ist der, der er zu sein scheint, aber wie bemerkt der Klosterbruder im Gespräch zu Nathan: 'Doch was man ist, und was man sein muß in der Welt, das paßt ja wohl nicht immer.' So unglaubwürdig und an den Haaren herbeigezogen klingt diese Anordnung, man kann sie nur rezipieren als Illustrierung einer zentralen Position kosmopolitischen Denkens, daß wir die Frucht eines vielfältigen, komplexen und unentwirrbaren Wurzelwerks sind. Christentum und Islam sind durch Abstammung einander verwandt, das Judentum in Gestalt Nathans, der sowohl Recha als Säugling an Kindes Statt annahm, als auch im großen Finale ihren Bruder an sein Herz zieht, durch geistige Nähe, durch väterliche Freundschaft, auch wenn Lessing das Judentum nicht zum Blutsverwandten macht. Da muß dann ein Ausspruch des Klosterbruders die Brücke bilden: 'Und ist denn nicht das ganze Christentum aufs Judentum gebaut? Es hat mich oft geärgert, hat mich Tränen genug gekostet, wenn Christen gar so sehr vergessen konnten, daß unser Herr selbst ein Jude war.'

It is also striking that the story collections I have cited are all secular in nature. Didactic, pious texts are not given convoluted forms; they avoid unsettling their readers like the devil avoids holy water. In many respects while the Bible may have been our vade mecum, when it comes to shaping our approach to narrative and our appreciation of its intracacies we owe at least equal thanks to the *Panchatantra* and the *Tales from One Thousand and One Nights*.

Lessing does not content himself with a ring parable in which the three Abrahamic religions stand side by side on an equal footing, but forges a third, dramaturgical ring to clarify how the three religions are fused together. This third ring is that of blood ties or familial connections, exactly as in the films described at the beginning, *Amar Akbar Anthony* and *Zakhm*. The Jewish Nathan's foster-daughter Recha is actually named Blanda von Filnek and is a Christian (although this is only revealed to her at the end of the play). Her brother, the young Templar, Curd von Stauffen, whose real name is Leu von Filnek, is also a Christian. The pair's father was a Muslim called Assad, Saladin's brother, who later named himself Wolf von Filnek. This makes the Sultan uncle to a half-Christian, half-Muslim girl, who is brought up in a Jewish household by a Christian woman. With the exception of Nathan, no-one is who he seems to be, but, as the Friar remarks during a conversation with Nathan, 'what one is, and what one must be in this world, that is not always the same'. This arrangement sounds so incredible and far-fetched that one can only interpret it as an illustration of a central position of cosmopolitical thought: that we are the fruit borne of multifaceted, complex and inextricable roots. Christianity and Islam are related through their ancestry, Judaism, in the figure of Nathan, who adopts Recha as an infant and embraces her brother in the play's grand finale, is related to both through intellectual proximity and fatherly friendship, even if Lessing does not make a blood link with Judaism. The Friar makes the connection: 'Is it not true that Christendom is built on Jewish faith? I've oft been angered, moved to bitter tears, when Christians could so utterly forget that our Lord Jesus was a Jew himself.'

Diese Wahrheit haben wir inzwischen, nach dem Holocaust und neunzehn Jahrhunderten der Judenverfolgung, akzeptiert. Die andere Verwandtschaft leugnen wir momentan eifrig. Doch Lessing würde heute auf einer judeo-christlich-islamischen Tradition beharren, und das würde die Gralshüter des essentiellen Geistes auf die Palme bringen. Bittet doch schon in *Nathan* Rechas Erzieherin für ihren Schützling: 'Laßt lächelnd wenigstens ihr einen Wahn, in dem sich Jud' und Christ und Muselmann vereinigen; – so einen süßen Wahn.'

Und wer die Verwandtschaftsirrungen und -wirrungen in *Nathan der Weise* übertrieben konstruiert findet, der bedenke folgendes Beispiel, zu dem wir ebenfalls über Boccaccio gelangen: In der ersten Geschichte des fünften Tages gelingt es zwei jungen Zyprioten gegen alle Widrigkeiten ihre Geliebten für sich zu gewinnen. Diese beiden Helden stammen aus *Barlaam und Josaphat*, einer griechisch-christlichen Biographie Buddhas samt Legenden über seine früheren Leben. Diese Geschichten wurden so beliebt, daß Josaphat (eine Verballhornung von Bodhisattva) im 14. Jahrhundert kanonisiert und seitdem als Heiliger der katholischen Kirche verehrt wird, ebenso wie Barlaam, dessen Name von dem Sanskritwort *Bhagvan* abgeleitet ist, dem ersten Beinamen Buddhas (eigentlich wird in dieser Version behauptet, daß Buddha Siddharta, also sich selbst, zur Erleuchtung geführt hat, und zwar als Christ!). Gewinnt die Ringparabel nicht an Glaubwürdigkeit, wenn man sich bewußt macht, daß ein Christ, der am 27. November, dem St.-Josaphat-Tag, des Heiligen gedenkt, gleichzeitig die Gnade Buddhas erbittet?

Leider war Alfonsis *Unterweisung für Kleriker* nicht sein einziges Werk, mit dem er der Zukunft seinen Stempel aufdrückte. Seine Schmähschrift *Dialog gegen die Juden* war noch lange nach seinem Tod im Umlauf. Der Titel ist irreführend, denn es handelt sich nicht um einen Dialog, sondern um eine Polemik gegen das Judentum und den Islam. So kenntnisreich das Werk auch die Glaubensgrundsätze beider Religionen darstellt, so erbittert geht es mit ihnen ins Gericht. Später diente es der antijüdischen und antimuslimischen Propaganda als wichtige Quelle von hoher Autorität, da ihr Verfasser ein zum Christentum konvertierter Jude war, also das Licht der Kirche erblickt und so den Fehler seiner Geburt wiedergutgemacht hatte.

We have in the meantime accepted this truth, after the Holocaust and nineteen centuries of anti-Semitic persecution. The other relationship between Christianity and Islam we deny vehemently at present. But Lessing would persist in claiming a Judeo-Christian-Islamic tradition, which would rile the guardians of the Holy Grail of the essential spirit. Recha's governess in *Nathan* pleads on behalf of her charge: 'Smile and let her keep this one belief, which Jew and Christian share with Muslim too, a sweet delusion, if it be no more!'

Whoever finds the aberrations and confusions of the relationships in *Nathan the Wise* forced should consider the following example, which comes to us again via Boccaccio. In the first story of the fifth day, two young Cypriots succeed against adversity to win the hearts of their beloved. These two heroes make their first appearance in *Barlaam and Josaphat*, a Greek-Christian biography of Buddha which is full of legends about his early life. These stories were so popular that Josaphat (a corruption of Bodhisattva) was canonised in the fourteenth century and has been venerated as a saint in the Catholic church ever since, just like Barlaam, whose name is derived from the Sanskrit word *bhagvan*, the first epithet of Buddha (in fact it is claimed in this version that Buddha led Siddhartha, that is himself, to a state of enlightenment, and that as a Christian!). Does the ring parable not gain in credibility when one realises that a Christian who, on 27 November, Saint Josaphat's Day, commemorates the saint, is simultaneously asking for grace from Buddha?

Unfortunately Alfonsi's *Instructions for Clerics* was not the only work which he left to posterity. His defamatory *Dialogue against the Jews* was still in circulation long after his death. The title is misleading since it was not a dialogue but rather a polemic against both Judaism and Islam. The work portrays the fundamental beliefs of both religions as being well-founded, but takes them to task in the same measure. It later served anti-Jewish and anti-Muslim propagandists as an important and highly authoritative source since its author was a Jewish convert, and so had seen the Church's light and made good the mistake of his birth.

In der ambivalenten Gestalt des Petrus Alfonsi treffen zwei ideengeschicht-
liche Stränge aufeinander, die Europa noch maßgeblich formen sollten:
der wunderbare Reichtum der säkularen Erzählung auf der einen Seite
und das dämonische Vermächtnis des Antisemitismus und Antiislamismus
auf der anderen.

Diese Ambivalenz ist sichtbar in der Version der Ringparabel aus
den *Gesta romanorum*: hier gelten die drei Ringe nicht als gleichwertig,
sondern es existiert der eine gute, wahre, schöne Echte – die anderen zwei
erweisen sich als Fälschungen. Es kann nur eine wahre Religion geben, die
beiden anderen müssen Betrüger sein. Und selbstverständlich ging man
im mittelalterlichen Abendland davon aus, bei der einzig wahren Religion
könne es sich nur um die christliche handeln. Welchen Aufruhr verur-
sachte die angebliche Aussage Kaiser Friedrichs II. anno 1239, alle Welt sei
hintergangen worden von den drei Betrügern Jesus Christus, Moses und
Mohammed. Ob nun dieser Ausspruch nun so fiel oder nicht, er zog die
sofortige Bannbulle Papst Gregors IX. nach sich und ein paar Jahrhundert
später die anonym erschienenen Traktate *De tribus impostoribus* – Bücher,
in denen ebenfalls alle drei monotheistischen Religionsstifter des Betrugs
geziehen werden. Lessing verquickt Ringparabel und Betrügertopos in dem
Satz: 'So seid ihr alle drei betrogene Betrüger, der rechte Ring vermutlich
ging verloren.' Daraus läßt sich auf Lessings eigene Überzeugungen schließen,
die zuletzt maßgeblich geprägt waren von Spinoza und dessen freigläubiger
Metaphysik, dem Glauben an eine alles durchwirkende Kraft.

Wir sollten nicht vergessen, daß es auch zum Programm der Aufklärung gehörte, der seit den Kreuzzügen virulenten Dämonisierung des Islams
entgegenzutreten, was die Operettenaufklärer von heute nicht wahrhaben
wollen, die in unseren aus allen Regalen platzenden Einkaufszentren Mori-
taten vom Untergang des Abendlandes krächzen. Das Wissen über ferne
Kulturen vertiefte sich, die Kenntnisse über die Vielfalt und Differenz
auf einem Globus, dem man nach Belieben wenden und drehen konnte,
auch wenn er noch weiße Flecken aufwies, nahmen zu. Zugleich verlangte
der wissenschaftliche Geist eine Eingliederung dieser Erkenntnisse in ein
universelles Weltbild. Autoren wie Voltaire stellten kulturvergleichende
Überlegungen an, die nicht von der Unterlegenheit des Anderen ausgingen.
So erträumte sich Wieland, Freund und Mitstreiter Lessings:

Two strands in the history of ideas meet in the ambivalent figure of Alfonsi, both of which would play a significant part in shaping Europe: the wonderful richness of secular storytelling, on the one side, and the demonic legacy of anti-Semitism and anti-Islamism, on the other.

This ambivalence is evident in the version of the ring parable in the *Gesta romanorum*. Here the three rings are not considered equal, rather there is one which is the good, the real, the beautiful, authentic ring. The other two prove to be forgeries. There can only be one religion; the other two must be false. And naturally Westerners in the Middle Ages assumed that the sole authentic religion could only be Christianity. What turmoil was caused by King Frederick II's alleged statement in 1239 that the whole world had been deceived by the three impostors Jesus Christ, Moses and Mohammed. Whether this statement was correctly ascribed to him or not, it promptly incurred a bull of excommunication from Pope Gregory IX, as did a few centuries later the anonymous authors of *De tribus impostoribus*, in which the founders of all three monotheistic religions are likewise accused of deception. Lessing combines the ring parable and the topos of the impostor in the sentence: 'O then you are, all three, deceived deceivers! [...] the genuine ring no doubt got lost'. From this we can infer something of Lessing's own convictions, which were, ultimately, shaped to a considerable degree by Spinoza and his metaphysics of free belief, or the faith in a force that pervades everything.

It should be borne in mind that opposing the demonisation of Islam, which had been practised with vitriol since the Crusades, was also one of the objectives of the Enlightenment, something that today's philosophers of Enlightenment lite, who squawk street ballads relating the downfall of the West in our shopping centres, their shelves bursting with goods, are loath to admit. Knowledge of distant cultures deepened, as understanding increased of the diversity and points of difference within a single globe, which one could rotate and turn at will, even if it still showed blank spots. At the same time the scientific mind demanded that these insights be integrated into an universal world view. Authors such as Voltaire considered questions of cultural comparison without assuming the inferiority of the Other. Wieland, friend and comrade-in-arms to Lessing, dreamt of the following:

> Die Kosmopoliten betrachten alle Völker des Erdbodens als eben so viele Zweige einer einzigen Familie, und das Universum als ein Staat, worin sie mit unzähligen anderen vernünftigen Wesen Bürger sind, um unter allgemeinen Naturgesetzen die Vollkommenheit des Ganzen zu befördern, in dem jedes nach seiner besonderen Art und Weise für einen eigenen Wohlstand geschäftig ist.

Das 18. Jahrhundert war in vielem progressiver als das ihm nachfolgende, in dem die machtpolitischen Anforderungen an eine imperiale Ideologie und die Übertragung des Darwinismus auf das Soziale und Kulturelle zu einem hierarchischen Kulturentwicklungsmodell führten, gemäß welchem die westeuropäische Kultur eine derartig hohe Entwicklungsstufe erreicht habe, daß alle anderen ihr unterlegen waren. Je nach Gusto wurde aber auch das Fremde, das reiz- und wertvoll erschien, der eigenen Kultur einverleibt und als Ureigenstes ausgegeben – oder wie es Nathan gegenüber dem Klosterbruder formuliert: 'Denn was mich Euch zum Christen macht, das macht Euch mir zum Juden!' Als ausgetüftelte Systeme, die überall und jederzeit gelten sollten, behaupteten die imperialen Dogmen und Ideologien eine falsche Universalität. Der Tempelherr aus *Nathan* bringt es auf den Punkt: 'Der Aberglauben schlimmster ist, den seinen für den erträglicheren zu halten.' Wann immer das Eine als universelle Wahrheit Gültigkeit beansprucht, widerspricht es der Wahrheit des Vielfältigen.

All das mag ja zutreffend beschrieben sein, aber was hat es mit der Gegenwart zu tun, könnte man einwenden, wie es so häufig geschieht, wenn einem die Lehren der Geschichte mißfallen. Sehr viel, denn ich bin fest davon überzeugt, daß wir als Individuen aber auch als Menschheit keine andere Wahl haben als zu Kosmopoliten zu werden, wenn wir in der Globalität gedeihen und als Gemeinschaft auf diesem ausgelaugten Planeten überleben wollen. Vieles von dem was Visionäre wie Lessing idealistisch postulierten, deckt sich inzwischen mit unserer Erfahrung und Weltkenntnis. Wenn Lessing in der *Hamburgischen Dramaturgie* erklärt: 'In der Natur ist alles mit allem verbunden, alles durchkreuzt sich, alles wechselt mit allem, alles verändert sich eines in das andere', beschreibt er nicht nur eine naturwissenschaftliche Tatsache, sondern auch die Realität unserer gegenwärtigen kulturellen Vernetzungen.

The cosmopolites regard all the peoples of the earth as exactly that number of branches of the same family, and the universe as a state in which they live with innumerable other rational beings in order to advance, in accordance with the general laws of nature, the perfection of the whole, in which each is busily working in their own unique way for their own prosperity.

The eighteenth century was more progressive in many ways than the one which followed, in which the demands of power politics for an imperial ideology and the application of Darwinism in the spheres of society and culture led to a hierarchical model of cultural development, according to which Western Europeans had reached such a high level that all others were inferior to them. Depending on individual taste, foreign elements which seemed delightful and valuable were absorbed into the home culture and passed off as one's own – or as Nathan tells the friar: 'For what makes me for you a Christian, makes yourself for me a Jew!' In the form of invented systems, which were expected to be valid in all places and at all times, the imperial dogmas and ideologies claimed an universality that did not exist. The Templar from *Nathan* puts it succinctly: 'That superstition is worst which takes itself to be of all the most endurable'. Whenever one particular group claims the validity of its truth to be universal, it denies the truth of diversity.

One could object, as is often done when the lessons of the past are found to be displeasing, that all this may be true but has nothing to do with now. But the opposite is the case, since I am convinced that we, as individuals, and also as humanity, have no other choice than to be cosmopolites if we want to thrive in a global world and survive as a community on this depleted earth. Much of what visionaries such as Lessing idealistically postulated corresponds now to what we know of the world and how we experience it. When Lessing declares in the *Hamburg Dramaturgy*: 'Everything is connected in nature, everything intertwines, everything exchanges with other things, everything changes into the other thing', he not only describes a scientific fact, but also the reality of our present cultural interconnectedness.

Galt früher, daß alles mit allem in Verbindung stehen könnte, so wissen wir heute aus eigener Anschauung, daß nicht nur alles mit allem in Verbindung gebracht wird, sondern auch steht. War früher eine Weltsprache Utopie, so haben wir heute das Englische und ein gesteigertes Bewußtsein für universelle Grundregeln. Wir wissen inzwischen, daß der goldene Satz 'Behandle andere so, wie du von ihnen behandelt werden willst' sich bei Konfuzius und in der *Mahabharata*, bei Buddha und im Zoroastrismus, in altgriechischen Texten ebenso wie im Neuen Testament findet – ein universal-globales Prinzip, das sich jenseits aller Religionsgräben findet. 'Sind Christ und Jude eher Christ und Jude als Mensch?' fragte so auch Nathan. Und als letztes Jahr auf Anregung von Karen Armstrong eine 'Charta des Mitgefühls' interaktiv im Internet ausgearbeitet wurde, einigte man sich auf folgende Formulierung: 'Das Prinzip des Mitgefühls liegt allen Religionen, ethischen und spirituellen Traditionen zugrunde und ruft uns, immer alle anderen so zu behandeln, wie wir selbst behandelt zu werden wünschen.'

Gewiß leben wir in Vielsprachigkeit, selbst wenn wir einsprachig agieren. Gewiß ist unser Denken und Schaffen zunehmend migratorisch und immer weniger territorial. Und gewiß werden wir einander zwar nicht gleicher, aber zunehmend verständlicher. Die erträumten Universalien von einst gehören zu unserem globalen Wortschatz. All das erscheint manchen als Chance, anderen als existentielle Bedrohung. Wie Edouard Glissant schreibt:

> In der weltweiten Begegnung der Kulturen, die wir als Chaos erleben, scheinen uns die Anhaltspunkte verloren gegangen zu sein. Wo wir auch hinschauen, nur Katastrophen und Agonie. Wir verzweifeln angesichts dieser Chaos-Welt. Aber der Grund dafür ist, daß wir immer noch versuchen, sie an einer souveränen Ordnung zu messen, die ein weiteres Mal danach strebte, das Welt-Ganze zu einer beschränkten Einheit zu führen. Das Chaos ist schön, wenn man alle seine Bestandteile als gleich notwendig erachtet.

Deswegen brauchen wir ein nicht-systematisches, intuitives, paradoxes, fragmentarisches, zwiespältiges Denken, denn nur dieses wird der Komplexität und Vielfalt der Welt, in der wir leben, gerecht.

As in the past it was accepted that everything could be in connection with everything else, so today we know from observation that not only is everything brought into contact with everything else, but that everything also communicates together. Where previously the idea of a common world language was utopian, we now have English and an increased awareness of universal precepts. We know, meanwhile, that the golden rule, 'Treat others as you wish to be treated by others', is to be found in Confucianism and in the *Mahabharata*, in Buddhism and in Zoroastrianism, in ancient Greek texts and in the New Testament – a global, universal principle that crosses all religious borders. Nathan similarly asked: 'Are Jew and Christian sooner Jew and Christian than man?' And when last year, at Karen Armstrong's proposal, a 'Charter for Compassion' was drawn up interactively on the internet, the following formulation was agreed upon: 'The principle of compassion lies at the heart of all religious, ethical and spiritual traditions, calling us always to treat all others as we wish to be treated ourselves'.

Of course, we live in a multilingual world, even if we operate mono-lingually. Our thinking and doing is increasingly migratory and ever less territorial. And undoubtedly we are becoming, possibly not more similar to each other, but certainly more easily understood. The commonalities once dreamt of now belong to our global vocabulary. All this seems to some to be down to chance, to others it is an existential threat. As Edouard Glissant writes:

> In the worldwide encounter between cultures, which we experience as chaos, the reference points seem to us to have been lost. Wherever we look there is only catastrophe and suffering. We despair in the face of this chaos-world. But the reason for this is that we persist in attempting to measure it by a sovereign order that attempted one more time to lead the world in its entirety to a limited unity. Chaos is beautiful when one considers all its components as equally necessary.

This is why we need non-systematic, intuitive, paradoxical, fragmentary, conflicting thinking, because only that will do justice to the complexity and diversity of the world in which we live.

Der kosmopolitische Bürger sollte für diese Aufgabe, allein schon aus etymologischen Gründen, gerüstet sein. Als Kosmopolit gehört er der größtmöglichen *polis* an, dem Universum und widerspricht der konventionellen Überzeugung, der einzelne gehöre einer bestimmten Gemeinschaft unter den vielen auf Erden an, ihr und nur ihr allein. Als Bürger gehörte er aber durchaus einer bestimmten Burg an, verteidigte sie einst, bewohnte sie dann bzw. lebte in ihrem Schatten in der Stadt. Im 'kosmopolitischen Bürger' finden das Globale und das Lokale als zwei Seiten einer Medaille zusammen. Die Lage ist keineswegs so grimmig, wie uns jene einreden wollen, die im Saft ihrer düsteren Erwartungen schmoren. Der Fundus an kulturellen Universalien wächst, ohne daß wir deswegen unbedingt alle gleich werden. Die freie All-Welt-Kulturschaft (Glissant) funktioniert erheblich besser als die freie Weltwirtschaft, doch merkwürdigerweise schreien gerade die Verfechter der entfesselten Finanz- und Handelsströme nach Protektionismus in der Kultur, um sie zu schützen vor der Fremde, sie in einer Nische zu konservieren. Dieser Kulturkonservatismus ist weltfremd. Er begreift nicht die Dynamik von Verschmelzung und Vermischung, die stets zu kultureller Neuerung führen, und er bildet sich ein, man könne einen Wall gegen das Fremde errichten. Mehr als je zuvor werden Traditionen nach freiem Gutdünken ausgewählt oder neu erfunden. Das Unvorsehbare ist zu einer entscheidenden Kategorie der dynamischen Vernetzungen geworden.

Ein wunderbares Beispiel kosmopolitischer Wertigkeit wird von dem amerikanischen Publizisten Malcolm Gladwell in seinem jüngsten Buch *The Outliers* beschrieben, eine parabelhafte Geschichte von Kultur, Kommunikation, Tradition und Überleben. Jahrzehntelang hatte die Fluggesellschaft Korean Air eine der höchsten Unfallraten weltweit, 17-mal höher etwa als etwa United Airlines. Das galt als Rätsel, denn der aufstrebende Tigerstaat Südkorea investierte in neue Flugzeuge, die Wartung entsprach höchsten Anforderungen, ebenso die technische Ausbildung der Piloten. Das Problem wäre früher gelöst worden, wenn der Vorstand von Korean Air Lessing gelesen hätte:

> Nun, wessen Treu und Glauben zieht man denn am wenigsten in Zweifel? Doch der Seinen? Doch deren Blut wir sind? [...] Wie kann ich meinen Vätern weniger, als du den deinen glauben? Oder umgekehrt. Kann ich von dir verlangen, daß du deine Vorfahren Lügen strafst, um meinen nicht zu widersprechen? Oder umgekehrt.

The cosmopolitan citizen should, solely for etymological reasons, be armed for this task. As a cosmopolite he belongs to the largest possible *polis*, the universe, and rejects the conventional conviction that the individual belongs to one particular community among the numerous that exist on earth, and to that one only. As a citizen he previously belonged completely to a certain castle, which he defended and in which he dwelled, or, as the case may be, in the town that lay in its shadow. The 'cosmopolitan citizen' regards the global and the local as two sides of the same coin. The situation is by no means as grim as those who stew in the juice of their own gloomy expectations would have us believe. The pool of cultural commonalities is growing without us necessarily becoming more equal because of it. The free All-World cultural landscape (Glissant) functions a great deal better than the free world economy, but strangely enough it is the advocates of unrestricted finance and trade flows who are demanding cultural protectionism to shield them from foreign influence, to restrict what is foreign to a niche. This kind of cultural conservatism is unworldly. It does not understand the dynamics of fusion and integration which always leads to cultural innovation, and it imagines that a rampart can be built to keep all foreign elements out. Traditions are freely chosen, or even newly invented, now more than ever before. The unforeseeable has become a pivotal category of dynamic interconnectedness.

A delightful example of cosmopolitan valency is described in the Canadian journalist Malcolm Gladwell's latest book *The Outliers*, an allegorical story of culture, communication, tradition and survival. For decades the airline Korean Air had one of the highest accident rates worldwide, seventeen times higher than United Airlines for example. It was regarded as puzzling, since the aspiring tiger economy state of South Korea had invested in new aeroplanes, the servicing of which complied with high standards, as did the technical training of the pilots. The problem would have been solved sooner had Korean Air's directors been readers:

> Well then, whose faith are we least like to doubt? Our people's, surely? Those whose blood we share? [...] How can I trust my fathers less than you trust yours? Or turn about. Can I demand that to your forebears you should give the lie that mine not be gainsaid? Or turn about.

So spricht Nathan zu Saladin, und so erklärt auch Gladwell die Gründe für die Katastrophenanfälligkeit der Südkoreaner: Traditionsbewußtsein und mangelnde Flexibilität in einer Kultur starrer Autorität und Hierarchie. Der Anthropologe Geert Hofstede, führender Spezialist für innerkulturelle Dimensionen, entwickelte zur Messung dieses Phänomens einen sogenannten Power-Distance-Index. Südkorea als Land, in dem Autorität nicht hinterfragt und Macht demonstrativ ausgespielt wird, stand auf diesem Index weltweit an zweiter Stelle. Die Kopiloten und Flugingenieure trauten sich in Gefahrenmomenten nicht, gegen die eigenen Konventionen zu verstoßen. Als sie beim Anflug auf Guam hätten energisch eingreifen müssen: 'Kollege, wir fliegen direkt auf einen Hügel zu und werden in zwei Minuten aufprallen', äußerten sie statt dessen 'Herr Kapitän, der Wetterradar hat uns bislang oft geholfen', ein verklausuliert untertäniger Hinweis auf die besorgniserregende Anzeige der Instrumente. Der machterfüllte aber übermüdete Pilot überhörte die Warnung, das Flugzeug zerschellte zwei Minuten später am Hügel. Erst als im Jahre 2000 Korean Air einen amerikanischen Außenseiter namens David Greenberg als Verantwortlichen für die Flugoperationen anstellte, wurde das Problem gelöst. Greenberg verschaffte den Piloten eine zweite Identität jenseits der erdrückenden Hierarchie, indem er verfügte, daß nur fliegen dürfe, wer Englisch beherrsche und in den Cockpits nur Englisch gesprochen werden dürfe. Mit der fremden Sprache brachen die Konventionen auf, ein informeller, familiärer, direkterer Stil, der sich aus einem anderen kulturellen Vermächtnis speiste, breitete sich aus. Der fremde Chef zwang die Koreaner, sich mit den Schwächen ihres eigenen Vermächtnisses auseinanderzusetzen, ohne dieses zu verteufeln oder gar abschaffen zu wollen. Er errichtete eine zweite Ebene, auf der die sonstige Untertänigkeit aufgehoben war. Die südkoreanischen Piloten wandelten sich so schnell, daß Korean Airlines heute zu den sichersten Fluggesellschaften der Welt gehört. Aber dazu war ein kosmopolitischer Blick vonnöten. Die Südkoreaner selber konnten den eigenen Treu und Glauben nicht in Zweifel ziehen.

That is how Nathan speaks to Saladin and that is also how Gladwell explains the reason for the South Koreans' propensity for accidents: consciousness of tradition and a lack of flexibility within a culture of rigid authority and hierarchy. The anthropologist Geert Hofstede, a leading specialist in intra-cultural dimensions, developed the power distance index to measure this phenomenon. South Korea, a country in which authority is not questioned and power is demonstratively exercised, claimed second place in the index out of all the countries in the world. During moments of danger co-pilots and flight engineers did not dare to contravene their own conventions. When, during an approach to Guam, they should have intervened with a resolute warning such as, 'Colleague, we're flying directly towards a hill and will make impact in two minutes', they remarked instead, 'Captain, the weather radar has been very helpful so far', a submissive, coded reference to the worrying indications on the instruments. The all-powerful, but exhausted pilot overheard the warning and two minutes later the aeroplane smashed into the hillside. Only in the year 2000, when Korean Air appointed an American outsider by the name of David Greenberg to be responsible for flight operations was the problem solved. Greenberg supplied the pilots with a second identity beyond the constrictions of hierarchy by decreeing that only those who could speak English were allowed to fly, and that English was the only language to be spoken in the cockpits. The foreign language broke down the conventions and a more informal, familial and direct style, fed by a different cultural legacy, was developed. The foreign director forced the Koreans to deal with the weaknesses of their cultural legacy, without demonising it or doing away with it altogether. He built a second level on which the submissiveness that otherwise prevailed was abolished. The South Korean pilots changed so quickly that today Korean Air is one of the safest airlines in the world. But for this to happen, a cosmopolitan perspective was necessary. The South Koreans themselves were not able question their own loyalty and beliefs.

Da wir glücklicherweise nicht zur einstigen Ignoranz und Borniert-
heit regredieren können, müssen wir zum Verstehen voranschreiten. Und
dieses Verstehen ist angesichts der Herausforderungen der Zukunft über-
lebensnotwendig. Die gescheiterte Konferenz von Kopenhagen hat gezeigt,
daß wir eine höhere Konsensfähigkeit entwickeln müssen. Und wer, wenn
nicht Lessing, hat gesagt, daß des Menschen wichtigste Eigenschaft die
Empathie ist, denn 'ohne Zweifel derjenige der beste Mensch ist, der die
größte Fertigkeit im Mitleiden hat.'

Ziel der Empathie ist es nicht, den Anderen auf Teufel komm raus
verstehen zu müssen, denn dies bedeutete, ihm durch das Prisma der eigenen Wahrnehmung eine falsche Transparenz aufzudrücken, ihn zu redu-
zieren und somit zu erniedrigen. Es beinhaltet aber sehr wohl, kulturelle
Differenzen nicht zu verabsolutieren, sondern in ihnen ein wandelbares
Potential zu erkennen. Es grenzt an Wahnsinn, in der heutigen Welt die
Ressource Vielfalt nicht kreativ zu nutzen.

Ich bin dem Thalia Theater sehr dankbar, daß es mich zur Beschäfti-
gung mit Lessing angeregt hat. So durfte ich einen Giganten des Geistes
entdecken, der bei herrschender Glutsonne einen tröstlichen und ermu-
tigenden Schatten wirft. 'Lese jeden Tag etwas, was sonst niemand liest.
Denke jeden Tag etwas, was sonst niemand denkt. Tue jeden Tag etwas,
was sonst niemand albern genug wäre, zu tun. Es ist schlecht für den Geist,
andauernd Teil der Einmütigkeit zu sein.' Diese Zeilen schrieb Lessing in
Hamburg. Als er im Jahre 1781 starb, verfügte der Hanseatische Senat, von
Lessings Ableben sei keine Notiz zu nehmen. Kraft Amtes hat der Hambur-
ger Rat somit die Unsterblichkeit des ungeliebten Theatermachers verfügt.

Since fortunately we cannot regress to a former state of ignorance and narrow-mindedness, we must march on towards understanding. And this understanding is, in the face of the challenges posed by the future, crucial for survival. The failed [climate] conference at Copenhagen has shown that we need to develop a better capability to reach consensus. And who but Lessing was it who said that man's most important characteristic is empathy, since 'the best man is, without doubt, he who is most accomplished in compassion'.

The aim of empathy is not a hell-bent insistence on understanding the other person, since this means impressing upon him a false transparency through the prism of one's own perception, to reduce him and even to demean him. However, it does involve, while not making cultural differences absolute, acknowledging in them a variable potential. To fail to use the resources of diversity in a creative way in today's world borders on lunacy.

I am very grateful to the Thalia Theatre that it has prompted me to engage with Lessing's work. It has enabled me to discover a great thinker who, under a blazing sun, throws a comforting and encouraging shadow: 'Read every day something no-one else is reading. Think every day something no-one else is thinking. Do every day something no-one else would be foolish enough to do. It is bad for the mind to be constantly a part of unanimity.' Lessing wrote these lines in Hamburg. When he died in 1781, the Hanseatic City's Senate decreed that his death was to be ignored. And thus, by the power vested in it, the Hamburg Senate secured the immortality of the unloved man of the theatre.

Bibliography

Petrus Alfonsi, *Dialogue against the Jews*, tr. Irven M. Resnick (Washington, DC: Catholic University of America Press, 2006)

——, *The Disciplina clericalis*, tr. (into German) and ed. Eberhard Hermes, tr. (from Latin and German into English) P.R. Quarrie (London: Routledge and Kegan Paul, 1977)

The Balavariani Barlaam and Josaphat. A Tale from the Christian East, tr. David Marshall Lang (London: Allen & Unwin, 1966)

Giovanni Boccaccio, *Decameron*, tr. G.H. McWilliam (London: Penguin, 1995)

Johannes von Capua, *Directorium vitae humanae* (Klagenfurt: Armarium, 1981)

Geoffrey Chaucer, *The Canterbury Tales*, ed. Jill Mann (Harmondsworth: Penguin, 2005)

Gesta romanorum: Entertaining Moral Stories, trs Rev. Charles Swan and Wynard Hooper (New York: Dover, 1959)

Malcolm Gladwell, *The Outliers: The Story of Success* (London: Penguin, 2009)

Edouard Glissant, *Kultur und Identitat. Ansatze zu einer Poetik der Vielheit*, tr. Beate Thill (Heidelberg: Wunderhorn, 2005)

Kalidasa, *The Recognition of Sakuntala*, tr. W.J. Johnson (Oxford: Oxford University Press, 2008)

Gotthold Ephraim Lessing, *Hamburgische Dramaturgie* [1767–1768], in *ibid.*, vol.2, pp. 121–533

——, *Nathan der Weise* [1779], in *Lessings Werke*, ed. Kurt Wölfel, vol. 1 (Frankfurt am Main: Insel, 1967), pp. 467–594

The Mahabharata, tr. John D. Smith (Harmondsworth: Penguin, 2009)

Soma-deva, [*Katha-saritsagara*] *The Ocean of the Rivers of Story*, 2 vols, tr. Sir James Mallinson (New York: New York University Press, 2008/2009)

Tales from the Thousand and One Nights, tr. N.J. Dawood (Harmondsworth: Penguin, 1973)

Vishnusarma, *The Hitopadesha: A Collection of Fables and Tales in Sanskrit*. ed. Lakshami Narayan Nyalankar Sansk, trs Lakshami Narayan Nyalankar Sansk and Sir Charles Wilkins (Calcutta: Sharsungro Press, 1844).

Visnu Sarma, *The Panchatantra: the Book of India's Folk Wisdom*, tr. Chandra Rajan (Harmondsworth: Penguin, 1995)

Voltaire, 'History of the Crusades', sections 53–9 of *Essai sur les moeurs et l'esprit des nations*, in *Les œuvres complètes de Voltaire*, ed. Nicholas Cronk, vol. 23 (Oxford: Voltaire Foundation, 2010), pp. 269–400

——, 'On the Koran' [1748], 'De l'Alcoran et de Mahomet' in *Les œuvres complètes de Voltaire*, ed. Ahmad Gunny, vol. 20B (Oxford: Voltaire Foundation, 2002), pp. 329–42

Christoph Martin Wieland, 'Das Geheimnis des Kosmopolitenordens' [The Secret of the Order of the Cosmopolitans], in *Aufsätze zu Literatur und Politik*, ed. Dieter Lohmeier (Reinbek: Rowohlt, 1970)

Films

Amar Akbar Anthony (dir. Manmohan Desai, 1977)

Zakhm (dir. Mahesh Bhatt, 1998)

CORNELIUS PARTSCH

Autopol, Prison Privatisation and the Dystopian Turn in Contemporary Sci-Fi

In Ilija Trojanow's oeuvre to date the chilling futuristic thriller *Autopol* stands by itself on account of its generic makeup and literary form. Trojanow's second novel recounts a dramatic prison revolt in the titular high-security prison complex. Its first readers found it characterised sensationally as 'an online road movie: Science-fiction, created as a "novel in progress" on the digital asphalt of the data highway'.[1] This pronouncement refers to an earlier instantiation of *Autopol* in cyberspace, as the second in a series of three so-called 'novels in progress' that were written under the auspices of the well-known culture programme *Aspekte*, at the time a joint venture of ZDF Television and MSN. Along with Joseph von Westphalen's *Lametta lasziv* (1996) and Matthias Politycki's *Marietta* (1998), *Autopol* took shape as an experimental serial novel under the guidance of the ZDF editor and author Gerald Giesecke and graphics specialist Rudi Leitermann, and with the collaboration of co-author Rudolf Spindler and composer Hans Huyssen.[2] The goal of these 'novels in progress' was to spark interest

---

1   From the front matter of the novel, Ilija Trojanow, *Autopol* [in collaboration with Rudolf Spindler] (Munich: Deutscher Taschenbuch Verlag, 1997).

2   See Matthias Politycki, *Marietta – die Idee, der Datensatz und der Strohhut. Schreiben und Schreiben-Lassen im Internet* (Mainz/Stuttgart: Steiner, 2000); Joseph von Westphalen, *Lametta lasziv. Ein kleiner scharfer Roman* (Zurich: Kein & Aber, 2001). Norman Ohler's *Die Quotenmaschine* (Hamburg: Hoffmann & Campe, 1996) has been identified as the very first such literary venture in German. See Thomas Wegmann, 'Verschaltbar statt haltbar? Eine unvollständige Bestandsaufnahme zur Literatur im Internet', in Matthias Harder (ed.), *Bestandsaufnahmen. Deutschsprachige Literatur der neunziger Jahre aus interkultureller Sicht* (Würzburg: Königshausen & Neumann, 2001), pp. 43–62, esp. p. 48. See also Roberto Simanowski, *Interfictions. Vom Schreiben im Netz* (Frankfurt am Main: Suhrkamp, 2002).

among well-known authors for the internet as a space for the creation and dissemination of literature and to explore possibilities for its development. In a number of different online formats, readers could observe the writing process and communicate both with each other and with the authors. Online users could attempt to participate in the writing of the novels by making suggestions for on-screen appearances, alterations, plot developments and hyperlinked textual routes. In *Autopol*, author and editors took advantage of the digital technology by adding images, animations and video. To some extent the project must qualify as a failure, however. In statements about their experiences, the participating authors displayed a sense of ambivalence about cyber-literature. While Trojanow bemoaned a low level of participation from the public,[3] Politycki noted that despite initial enthusiasm he saw no significant differences between the cyber-format and 'normal' literature.[4]

The proponents of 'interfiction' point to several innovations distinguishing literary activity in cyberspace from its manifestations in print. According to them, interfictions are more public, fluid, unfinished, dialogic, and less easily classifiable than texts which readers find ready fixed between the covers of a book. Thus Thomas Hettche, co-editor with Jana Hensel of the cyber-literature collection *NULL*, views interfiction as an attractive alternative to the predominantly product-oriented approach to literary activity and reception in the marketplace: 'Texts on the internet are unfinished and semi-private. They are attractive because of their ephemeral status'.[5] This emphasis on process and malleability that depends on potentially anarchic practices of generic hybridisation, formal de-centring,

---

3   Anne Petersen and Johannes Saltzwedel, 'Absturz der Netz-Poeten', *Der Spiegel* 51 (16 December 2002), p. 178.
4   See Viktor Schlawenz, 'Novel in Progress. Matthias Polityckis Roman *Ein Mann von vierzig Jahren* entstand im Internet', *literaturkritik.de* 2.4 (April 2000) <http://www.literaturkritik.de> accessed 30 August 2012; and Beate Lakotta and Dorothee Stöbener, 'Liebe zum Klammeraffen. Spezial-Gespräch mit Autor Matthias Politycki über das Schreiben im Netz', *Spiegel Spezial* 10 (1 October 1999), p. 44.
5   Quoted in Jobst-Ulrich Brand, 'Gerüstet für das neue Lesen', *Focus* 42 (18 October 1999). See also Thomas Hettche and Jana Hensel (eds), *Null* (Cologne: DuMont, 2000), to which Trojanow made several contributions.

and textual fragmentation afforded by the new medium was reinforced by Trojanow himself when he noted that cyberspace had the potential to generate entirely new literary forms, 'something that does not yet have a name'.[6] In accordance with the serial progression of the novel's assemblage and the hypertextual bifurcations which can lead to non-linear readings, *Autopol* is said to consist of 'text particles' (Mazenauer) and 'countless tiny text morsels' (Balzer).[7] Multiple narrators and movable narrative strands provide for a variety of perspectives on the prison revolt plot. The reader benefits from three main sources: the protagonist Sten Rasin, the TETA corporation, and the media. These viewpoints derive from a variety of narrators (Rasin, a journalist, a third-person narrator, as well as voices in dialogues) and reproduced documents (e-mail messages, memos, newspaper clippings, and transcripts of TV shows). As a result, the plot of *Autopol* is constituted by gaps and narrative components, and nearly devoid of psychological explication. In terms of genre it is similarly hybrid, as it is part science fiction, part hostage drama, part prison escape narrative, and one of a number of types of thriller (action, conspiracy, crime, ecological, political).

By and large, reviewers of *Autopol* took up the novel's status as 'hypertext' and reflected on the possibilities for literary activity in cyberspace. A short review in *Der Spiegel* aptly entitled 'Trojanow's Horse' asserts that *Autopol* conveys disappointing content in an intriguing form.[8] In a more thorough reading, Christa Karpenstein-Eßbach notes that, in order to be readable, the hypertextual, digressive structure of *Autopol* appears to require the use of conventional, highly familiar generic references and linguistic patterns:

> This novel is assembled from a multitude of text particles, but on closer inspection these particles reveal themselves as elements of conventional genres like science-fiction or action literature with their respective stylistic traits and plot patterns. Other constituent parts are imitations of the news. The texts themselves offer no new aesthetic

---

6   During a public symposium in Stuttgart, quoted in Rolf Spinnler, 'Namenloser Thriller im Netz', *Stuttgarter Zeitung* (26 March 1998).

7   Beat Mazenauer, 'Aufstand in der Sonderzone', *Freitag* (20 March 1998); Jens Balzer, 'In antiliberaler Mission', *Berliner Zeitung* (6 December 1997).

8   'Trojanows Pferd', *Der Spiegel* 12 (17 March 1997).

experiences. On the contrary, the formal principle of arbitrary linkage seems to be founded upon the use of conventional, hollowed-out particles, such as readily recognisable plot samples and a spontaneous, topical language made of set phrases.[9]

In his acerbic reading in the *Berliner Zeitung*, Jens Balzer condemns *Autopol* as so much 'multimedia trickery', while taking the editors at Deutscher Taschenbuch Verlag (dtv) to task for recasting an internet novel into a book without restructuring the narrative: 'Evidently, they simply tacked Trojanow's half-finished text files together. This may be interesting to future generations as a sketchbook from the stone age of cyber-literature. As a book among books, to buy, read or to present as a gift, *Autopol* is unusable.'[10] By the close of 1998 the novel had been taken offline and is currently available only in printed form. Overall, the novelty of the multi-media, dialogic parameters of *Autopol*'s production and reception in cyberspace was lauded by critics, but the text itself fared less well. Dorothee Stöbener summed up the reactions: 'The attempt was praised, the result not so much.'[11]

Due to their concentration on the novel's online provenance, none of the reviewers placed *Autopol* into a literary or generic tradition or examined its position within contemporary German literature. Jens Balzer only briefly points to a literary aspect of the text, the use of 'popular motifs from the repertoire of "New Wave" science fiction from the likes of John Brunner or Philip K. Dick'. This presumably refers to a tendency to expand science fiction from its base in the 'hard' sciences to more 'social' concerns, such as politics, ecology, or anthropology. In order to situate *Autopol* in the sci-fi genre, as the publisher has done, one has to assess more precisely the ways in which the novel's fictional world represents an extrapolation of current scientific knowledge and practice. The apparatus that serves both as the

9   Christa Karpenstein-Eßbach, 'Mediale Wirkungsästhetik: Formierungen von Reiz und Gefühl', in Brigitte Häring and Knut Hickethier (eds), *Buchstaben, Bilder, Bytes* (Norderstedt: Books on Demand, 2004), pp. 27–46, here p. 44.

10 From a SF fan site comes a similar verdict: 'As printed book it is a mildly entertaining collection of notes'. Florian Breitsameter, 'Autopol' (21 February 1998). <http://www.sf-fan.de/rezensionen/ilija-trojanow--autopol.html> accessed 30 August 2012.

11 Dorothee Stöbener, 'Dicht am Dichter. Deutsche Autoren schaffen die Literatur ins Internet', *Spiegel Spezial* 10 (1 October 1999), p. 36.

setting and as the resonant symbol for a dystopian vision of a near-future society is the prison. The prison structure itself, its specific spatial and technical characteristics, its functioning, and the people connected with it, as managers, staff or inmates, offer a microcosmic portrait of the larger social system. Like so many other dystopias, the narrative commences with the protagonist's trial, sentencing, and introduction into an inscrutable punitive environment. Erika Gottlieb views the trial scene in such novels as 'a thematically and symbolically central device of dystopian fiction', since it discloses from the outset the hegemonic order's virulent anti-individualism and the duality of law and lawlessness that characterises its actions.[12] Without an immediate spatial or temporal dislocation, such novels thus accomplish for the reader a de-familiarising effect arising from the protagonist's alienation at the hands of the hegemonic order, marking the fictional world as dystopian.[13] Rasin's very first utterance demonstrates beyond any doubt that he is up against a sinister, anonymous power: 'That was that. Now they've shut me down for good' (9). He is kept in solitary confinement during the proceedings against him, for an act of sabotage against the TETA Corporation, but shows little interest in the trial, presumably because he is certain to be found guilty and to be given the punishment of 'AUSSCHAFFUNG' [DEPORTATION]. Rasin defiantly recalls a time not long ago when he beat three guards to a pulp, which is why the prison authority sends six men to administer a sedative before his transfer.[14]

Autopol, the name of the institution where Rasin is to serve his sentence, is not only in the hands of the same corporation against which he committed the alleged transgression, but also sits at the top of the state's carceral pyramid as the most thoroughly rationalised and normalised penal institution in the network. The inmates are housed in constantly

12   Erika Gottlieb, *Dystopian Fiction East and West. Universe of Terror and Trial* (Montreal: McGill-Queen's University Press, 2001), p. 10.

13   See Raffaela Baccolini and Tom Moylan, 'Introduction: Dystopia and Histories', in Raffaela Baccolini and Tom Moylan (eds), *Dark Horizons: Science Fiction and the Dystopian Imagination* (London: Routledge, 2003), pp. 1–12, here p. 5.

14   Stepan ('Stenka') Razin (1630–1671) was a legendary leader of the Don Cossacks who led major uprisings against the Russian nobility and the Tsar.

moving high-security convoys made up of enormous transporters crawl-ing at slow speed along a closed-off stretch of autobahn. These convoys circulate through Europe, from what appears to be Emden in northern Germany eastwards to Poland and south to Slovakia, then back around through the Czech Republic and along Germany's southern and western borders, as a map included in the novel reveals (88). This gigantic circle is dotted with 'Resting Places', logistics centres equipped with medical facili-ties, arsenals, and supply stockpiles. Groups of society's poorest members, who are unemployable and thus least productive – they are known as 'the Useless' – roam outside these stations and alongside the highways, living off the land and scavenging what is discarded from the prison buildings. With Rasin's arrival, the processing of incoming 'objects' into the system is shown to be clinical and impersonal. Their heads are shaven under a mechanical hood while they read their police file on a screen placed in front of them. Automatic sedation awaits anyone not following the procedure to a tee. Rasin notes that he would only understand later that this prison would become 'our – 79fold –new hell' (13), referring to the 79 prison-ers in his unit. In contrast to the other 78 inmates, Rasin is the only man imprisoned for his political activities, having accumulated a long list of treasonous crimes, such as willful damage to property, breach of the peace, incitement to riot, sedition, and the founding of an illegal organisation.

Everyday existence in this prison follows a similarly impersonal, isolat-ing and brutalising path. At night, the prisoners sleep in locked, air-condi-tioned bunks that prevent all the usual illicit night-time prison activities, while making sure that no sense of solidarity and communal purpose devel-ops. Occasionally, guards force prisoners to fight each other and broadcast these events on closed-circuit TV throughout the Autopol network. Rasin, who is pressed into facing off against a massive murderer known as the Monster of Marseilles, calls these televised contests 'the deported form of *Eurovision*' (36). Although comparatively small in stature, he prevails and rises in the estimation of his fellow inmates. During daylight hours, prisoners perform various kinds of labour assignments, mostly in the pro-cessing and disposal of the toxic waste generated in the highly industri-alised European economies. Rasin sums up daily life in Autopol as 'dead for one half of the day, and subhuman for the other half' (24). A turning point, when the narrative focus shifts from the brutal egotistical survival struggle to organised resistance, occurs after Rasin and members of his unit are deployed to clean up the site of an accident which occurred after the driver of a special transport was disoriented by a swarm of bats and overturned his vehicle. While a company memo reveals that toxic waste spilled out during the accident, Rasin observes that six men from the work detail became ill soon after returning from the site of the 'special treatment' and then disappeared without a trace.[15] The realisation that it would likely not take long before the same fate awaits him and the others at Autopol drives Rasin to hatch a daring escape plan which involves overwhelming the prison personnel. The novel picks up speed at this point, unfolding the structural acceleration of the thriller narrative, cutting rapidly between locations and gradually raising the stakes for the characters. At this onset of a counter-narrative, it may be noted that the configuration of Autopol as an institution marked by constant surveillance, extra-juridical modifications of punishment, penal labour, and various techniques of subjection and objectification adheres to a model of the modern prison that Michel Foucault, referring to the Mettray penal colony which opened its doors in 1840, characterised as operating 'well beyond the frontiers of criminal law'.[16]

Rasin's formidable foe, the TETA Corporation, is depicted as a powerful and sinister multinational that exercises censorial control over its employees, uses a private army, provides lacklustre medical care to the inmates at Autopol only sufficient to keep them in shape for work, lies to the government and the public about contamination levels in its prison, and routinely encroaches upon democratic freedoms. In addition, the

---

15   Rasin later learns from a nurse that four of these inmates have died. In one of *Autopol*'s intertexts, Margaret Atwood's *The Handmaid's Tale* (Toronto: McClelland and Stewart, 1985), 'useless' women ('unwomen') are sent off to enormous concentration camps and forced to work and die in contaminated sites. These infamous colonies for ageing, infertile and subversive women are the creation of the neo-fascist, fundamentalist patriarchy of the Republic of Gilead and are 'composed of portable populations used mainly as expendable toxic cleanup squads' (pp. 320–1).

16   Michel Foucault, *Discipline and Punish. The Birth of the Prison*, tr. Alan Sheridan (New York: Vintage Books, 1995), p. 296.

company employs a strategy of media manipulation. A journalist, who suspects wrongdoing, for example, hears from his editor that the newspaper was not likely to publish any critical exposés since TETA was controlling its owner by paying him extravagant speaker fees. Once the truth about the transporter accident and the ensuing rebellion is uncovered by an old-style muckraker, who goes undercover as a member of the cleaning staff and whose newspaper publishes a sensationalist account, very much in the manner of the mass-circulation *Bild-Zeitung*, TETA slips into spin control mode. A spokesman assures the press that the company's response to the hostage situation would be centred on 'the human element' (89), while internally the CEO, speaking in English, expresses his determination to 'mop this up quickly' (77). As the hostage situation unfolds, the media continue to dramatise the events at Autopol and, instead of throwing light on the underlying causes of the rebellion, fill the 24-hour news cycle with human-interest stories, interviews with a self-proclaimed expert, and with the distraught wife of one of the hostages. News coverage reaches fever pitch when the hostages and their captors are on their way to the airport: 'the horrific ordeal that has millions of TV viewers glued to their sets, just like us, has already gone on for half an hour' (168).[17] In the course of the hostage drama, the TETA leadership does not communicate with the rebels in good faith. The company agrees to grant the inmates safe passage to a destination of their choosing on condition that the hostages are released at the airport, but Special Forces in the service of TETA attack the transporter en route. This aggressive strategy entails collateral damage, leaving several prisoners as well as two hostages dead. Sounding very much like a government official, a TETA spokesperson asserts that the company could not have negotiated in earnest with 'terrorists' (181).

An internal TETA memo instructs employees how to respond to inquiries from the press or friends and family, while promising dire

17   Although the journalist and Rasin have a meeting of the minds inside Autopol and tape an interview to be broadcast later, as stipulated by one of Rasin's demands, the journalist cautions that too many powerful forces have an interest in moving on quickly: 'I doubt that anyone will make the effort to investigate everyday operations in Autopol' (150).

consequences for those who stray from the official narrative. In the extensive text, consisting of ten 'exemplary replies', the company praises Autopol in which, through TETA's skillful management, an optimisation of capacities occurs through efficient streamlining and merging of juridical, social, medical, and ecological services. Accordingly, the memo employs the term 'deportation' to apply equally to the hazardous waste and to the convicts, both of them brought to Autopol for 'temporary storage' before possible transport to territories outside Europe, foremost among them the West African nation of Guinea. The euphemisms of technocratic rationalism are drawn from the language of late twentieth-century global capitalism but, at the same time, establish a connection with similar linguistic obfuscations associated with National Socialism. 'Ausschaffen' in particular may be taken as a variation on a whole terminological field employed by the Hitler regime to indicate various processes of removal and elimination, as for example 'aussiedeln' [to move to a ghetto or camp], 'aussondern' [to select], 'ausschalten' [to remove through murder], 'ausmerzen' [to eliminate], and 'ausradieren' [to eradicate]. Numerous other terms used in the novel such as 'Volksverhetzung' [incitement of the people], 'Zwischenlager' [interim/transit camp], 'Endlagerstätte' [final camp], 'Zwangsarbeit' [forced labor], 'Sonderbehandlung' [special treatment], 'Untermensch' [subhuman], 'Lösung' [solution], and 'Transporter' follow similar referential trajectories.[18] Among their many functions, the 'resting places' are also quite literally places for the dead, since each is equipped with a crematorium. The TETA corporation emphasises the socio-economic significance of Autopol, point-

18   See Robert Michael and Karin Doerr, *Nazi-Deutsch/Nazi-German: An English Lexicon of the Language of the Third Reich* (Westport, CT: Greenwood Press, 2002) for further information. The purpose of deception applies in a particularly sinister fashion to 'Endlager' and 'Sonderbehandlung' in National-Socialist usage. The first term was used to suggest falsely that there would be no further deportation of prisoners to death camps, while the second term was employed as code to mark prisoners to be murdered. Today, 'Ausschaffung' is not used in Germany, but in Switzerland it refers to the deportation of illegal immigrants or refused asylum seekers who usually spend time in 'Ausschaffungshaft' (detainment) before being returned to their countries of origin. 'Ausschaffung' is not a translation of 'outsourcing' which is commonly rendered as 'Auslagerung' or 'Ausgliederung'.

ing to the large number of employment opportunities for skilled workers, which includes the area of 'clean-up logistics', and to substantial savings for the public coffers: 'With Autopol, TETA offers the most economical solution to industrial and social problems' (21). The configuration of the Autopol complex itself, the terminology used to mark its various parts and functions, and the equation of crime and contamination in the corporation's official pronouncements all point to the status of Autopol as an analogous construction, a near-future prison labour camp system which the reader is to connect with the *l'univers concentrationnaire* put in place by the Nazis.[19] This prison labour camp system for the age of globalisation, however, is not designed to manufacture munitions but to dispose of the waste generated in unspecified nuclear, bacterial, and chemical branches of first-world industries.

Autopol is set in an unspecified Europe, which is politically organised as a confederation akin to the European Union, in the very near future, possibly the early twenty-first century. The novel provides a few temporal clues, such as mention of the 'Castor time' (17), which is depicted as a bygone time of critical public interest in the transport of radioactive waste to interim storage facilities such as Gorleben in Lower Saxony.[20]

19   The term derives from David Rousset's early study of the concentration camp system (1946), which he described as 'the gangrene of a whole economic and social system.' Rousset's book was never translated into German, but appeared in English as *A World Apart* (London: Secker and Warburg, 1951), trs Yvonne Motse and Roger Senhouse. See Colin Davis, 'David Rousset (1912–1997)', in S. Lillian Kremer (ed.), *Holocaust Literature: An Encyclopedia of Writers and* their *Work*, vol. II (New York: Routledge, 2003), pp. 1048–52.

20   The Castor transports ('Castor' is an acronym for 'cask for storage and transport of radioactive material') galvanised the anti-nuclear movement in Germany which questions the safety of the transports and organises protests to stop them from reaching their destination. Secrecy, corruption, and accidents damaged the cause of nuclear power in general and of this manner of moving radioactive waste out of nuclear power plants in particular. At the German-French border, for example, a train carrying castors derailed on 4 February 1997 between the towns of Perl (Saarland) and Apach (Département de la Moselle in the Lorraine region). The German Federal Ministry for Environment, Nature Conservation and Nuclear Safety swiftly reassured the public

A further indication of the short temporal distance between the fictional events and year of publication comes from the prisoner Schwänchen who tells Rasin about growing up in Karl-Marx-Stadt (now once again named Chemnitz) and about the caesura of German unification. As a narrative which shares generic characteristics with Science Fiction, and the readerly expectations that attend to it, *Autopol* allows readers to apprehend the present as a likely history to a future which lies just around the corner. In *Autopol*, the element of extrapolation, one of the crucial components of science fiction (SF), finds expression not so much in imagining a point of future scientific knowledge and technological practice as in sketching out a later stage of a specific theory of capitalist organisation, its effects on the social sphere and on the environment, and its application to the human body. The political ideas of the governing entity that has established such industrial conglomerations like Autopol dependent on prisoners for labour are those of a utopian neo-liberalism. The consequences of such a possible future unfold in the novel primarily in the particular area of penal policy, which is associated with many taboos and carries much historical baggage in Germany. For these reasons it is as an appropriate site for contrasting the dystopian world represented in the novel with German social democracy of the late 1990s and the early 2000s. In addition, *Autopol*'s central concern with crime and criminological discourses situates it in broader debates about Americanisation and American-style globalisation.

Scholars in the field of criminal justice have for some time studied the differences between penal policy and prison administration in European countries and the United States. The American model has, all in all, not

---

that a release of radioactivity was a virtually impossible ('Zug mit radioaktivem Abfall aus Kernkraftwerk Emsland an deutsch-französischer Grenze entgleist.' <http://www.bmu.de/pressearchiv/13_legislaturperiode/pm/1381.php> accessed 30 August 2012). The Saarland state government then asked that no more transports be routed through its territory. The discovery of 'crying' (that is, leaking) casks has caused the largest scandal to date and has eroded public trust in the ability of the nuclear industry to regulate itself. These incidents were reported exhaustively in the press. See Fritz Vorhols, 'Der Castor-Skandal zeigt: Selbstkontrolle der Atomindustrie ist nicht genug', *Die Zeit* (28 May 1998).

fared well, as displayed in the common descriptors: 'populist', 'macho', 'regressive', and 'fascistic'.[21] Although a so-called 'penal populism' is evident in many affluent societies, the United States is generally considered to have gone the furthest in politicising and outsourcing criminal justice. John Pratt has recently defined the term 'penal populism' as referring to the paradoxical simultaneity of rising prison populations and dropping crime rates, a situation that is both rooted in and perpetuated through a higher degree of social control and corporate influence.[22] Pratt sees a link between penal populism and the collapse of trust in the modern institutions of government, the decline of deference, and the growth of ontological insecurity, along with new media technologies disseminating such unsettling information.[23] A key moment in *Autopol* calls attention to this sort of Americanisation of penal policy and to the need for a systematic procurement of prison populations. In a conversation between the CEO of TETA and an assistant, it is revealed that the company operates within a wider politico-economic scheme to criminalise the underclass and take the lucrative punitive option instead of following the more arduous path of rehabilitation and re-socialisation of offenders. The assistant points

---

21   See Joel Dyer, *The Perpetual Prisoner Machine. How America Profits from Crime* (Boulder, CO: Westview Press, 2000); Nicola Lacey, *The Prisoners' Dilemma: Political Economy and Punishment in Contemporary Democracies* (Cambridge: Cambridge University Press, 2008); and J. Robert Lilly and Paul Knepper, 'The Corrections-Commercial Complex', *Crime & Delinquency* 39.2 (1993), pp. 150–66. On mass incarceration, see David Downes, 'The Macho Prison Economy. Mass Incarceration in the United States – A European Perspective', *Punishment & Society* 3.1 (2001), pp. 61–80; and Vivien Stern, 'Mass incarceration: "A sin against the future"?' *European Journal on Criminal Policy and Research* 4.3 (September 1996), pp. 7–25.

22   For an overview of the history of private involvement in imprisonment in the US, see Malcolm M. Feeley, 'Entrepreneurs of Punishment. The Legacy of Privatization', *Punishment & Society* 4.3 (2002), pp. 321–44.

23   John Pratt, *Penal Populism* (New York: Routledge, 2007), pp. 158–66. Alessandro de Giorgi concurs with this assessment in his discussion of the 'penal state' as an example of American exceptionalism. Alessandro de Giorgi, *Re-thinking the Political Economy of Punishment. Perspectives on post-Fordism and Penal Politics* (Aldershot: Ashgate, 2006), pp. 100–1.

out that the number of inmates has grown exponentially in recent years. He suggests that these figures warrant classifying the prison population as a distinct social group: 'A class of the excluded, the marginalised. And society makes an allowance for this class; it is entered in the balance sheet, so many million for TETA' (148). The CEO does not disagree with this candid assessment and blames the government for having burdened his company with the thankless and unprofitable task of coping with failed social policies:

> We produce, we offer services, but we can't take care of all those for whom there is no piece of the pie. That's why we have this uprising. The government dealt us a really bad hand. The responsibility for those who've fallen by the wayside [...] We're not even making a profit with this business (148).

His jeremiad not only naturalises the rebellion inside the prison as part of a larger struggle for survival and material possession but also hints at the economy of power behind the production of 'delinquency', which Foucault famously analysed as 'a diversion of illegality for the illicit circuits of profit and power of the dominant class' (280).

While some scholars of penal cultures have linked the sharply punitive public attitude in the United States, and the politicians eager to appeal to it, to a similarly voracious appetite for consumption, which leads to scape-goating,[24] others have pointed to a connection between penal excess and the murderous practices of twentieth-century totalitarian states. Nils Christie, whose *Crime Control as Industry: Towards GULAGS, Western Style* is now available in a third edition, begins by citing Zygmunt Bauman's assertion, as made in *Modernity and the Holocaust* (1991), that the societal

---

24   See Simon Hallsworth, 'Rethinking the Punitive Turn: Economies of Excess and the Criminology of the Other', *Punishment & Society* 2.2 (2000), pp. 45–60; Barry Vaughan, 'The Punitive Consequences of Consumer Culture', *Punishment & Society* 4.2 (2002), pp. 195–211; Ian Loader, 'Ice Cream and Incarceration: On Appetites for Security and Punishment', *Punishment & Society* 11.2 (2009), pp. 241–57; and Jonathan Simon, 'Fear and Loathing in late Modernity. Reflections on the Cultural Sources of Mass Imprisonment in the United States', in David Garland (ed.), *Mass Imprisonment. The Social Causes and Consequences* (London: Sage, 2001), pp. 15–27.

conditions that made Auschwitz possible have not disappeared. Christie emphasises that the 'social production of moral indifference in modern societies' endures and that it can be observed in their penal policies and prisons.[25] Christie does not go so far as to claim that the future prisons will look like concentration camps but suggests that they may well resemble the gulags (or work camps) of the former Soviet Union. He predicts that Western Europe may be pressured to follow the path laid out by the United States and Russia in this regard.[26] In a more recent study of the 'global corporate gulag', Michael Hallett finds that the 'war on terror' has set those powerful nations involved in it on an intensified course of punitive excess leading towards a 'supranational carceral state'.[27] In the case of Germany, less alarmist conditions currently prevail. Pratt asserts that there is less penal populism in Germany because of a well-developed belief in the welfare state, trust in the ability of unelected criminal justice experts to manage the process, and far less media attention on crime.[28] One measure of how far a country has proceeded down the path to becoming a 'penal state' is often identified as the degree of privatisation that has been allowed to occur there. In recent times, the idea of privatising prisons was first discussed in Europe in Britain and France during the 1980s, with the American experience already in evidence and under scrutiny. While privatisation was not adopted in France, in Britain The Wolds, the country's first private remand prison, was opened on 6 April 1992. As Jon Vagg notes, the first Prison Inspectorate report published shortly thereafter ranks as 'one of the most damning reports published on any prison to date'.[29] For

---

25 Nils Christie, *Crime Control as Industry: Towards GULAGS, Western style*. 2nd edn (London: Routledge, 1994), p. 163.

26 *Ibid.*, p. 199.

27 Michael Hallett, 'Imagining the Global Corporate Gulag: Lessons from History and Criminological Theory', *Contemporary Justice Review* 12.2 (2009), pp. 113–27, here p. 115.

28 Pratt, *Penal Populism*, p. 168. On the less central status of law and order discourse in Germany, see also L. Zedner, 'In pursuit of the vernacular: Comparing law and order discourse in Britain and Germany', *Social Legal Studies* 4 (1995), pp. 517–34.

29 Jon Vagg, *Prison Systems. A Comparative Study of Accountability in England, France, Germany, and The Netherlands* (Oxford: Clarendon, 1994), p. 302. More recently,

reasons rooted primarily in the National Socialist past, the issue of privatisation came to Germany later and still has not occupied an audience beyond the field of criminology,[30] nor been the subject of national discussion. To this day, 'it is a strongly held principle that the state should never give up its monopoly in the use of force and the control and treatment of deviance',[31] that monopoly being stipulated in Article 33 Paragraph 4 of the German Basic Law or *Grundgesetz*. Nonetheless, the federal state of Hesse pioneered a new approach by entering into a public private partnership with a German subsidiary of the British Serco Group to privatise in part a new prison located in Hünfeld in 2005. A little over two years later, the *Süddeutsche Zeitung* reported that the privatisation bubble had burst in embarrassing fashion for Hesse's CDU-led government of Roland Koch and that the Hünfeld prison was actually costing the state more than the prisons entirely in the hands of the state.[32]

Sim has stated that Great Britain ('the prison capital of Western Europe') has followed closely the American model of prison expansion and rising incarceration rates, accompanied by unchanging crime rates. Joe Sim, 'Militarism, Criminal Justice, and the Hybrid Prison in England and Wales', *Social Justice* 31.1–2 (2004), pp. 39–50. On the earlier debates, see also Mick Ryan, *Privatization and the Penal System: The American Experience and the Debate in Britain* (New York: St Martin's Press, 1989).

30   See Rolf Stober (ed.), *Privatisierung im Strafvollzug?* (Cologne: Heymann, 2001) and Peter Best, 'Die amerikanische Strafkultur und die Privatisierung: Kein Vorbild für die europäische Kriminalpolitik', in Thomas Feltes, Christian Pfeiffer, and Gernot Steinhilper (eds), *Kriminalpolitik und ihre wissenschaftlichen Grundlagen. Festschrift für Professor Dr. Hans-Dieter Schwind zum 70. Geburtstag* (Heidelberg: C.F. Müller, 2006).

31   See Claudius Messner and Vincenzo Ruggiero, 'Germany: The Penal System between Past and Future', in Vincenzo Ruggiero, Mick Ryan, and Joe Sim (eds), *Western European Penal Systems: A Critical Anatomy* (London: Sage, 1995), pp. 128–48, esp. p. 133.

32   See Christoph Hickmann, 'Hinter Gittern ist ein Traum geplatzt', *Süddeutsche Zeitung* (31 March 2008). In the same year, the conservative state government in Baden-Württemberg also resolved to build a new, partially privatised prison in Offenburg. See Ulrich von Schwerin, 'Kann Privatisierung im Strafvollzug Kosten sparen?' *Stuttgarter Zeitung* (April 18, 2008).

Trojanow's dystopian vision of an American-style penal policy discloses the flip side of neo-liberalism's utopian dreams, a world marked by weak government, unchecked turbo-capitalism, and an uninformed and amnesiac public. In this near-future world, the cornerstones of German social democracy have been replaced by an economic order founded upon deregulation and the privatisation of public services, an integral component of the ideology of the pure market that Pierre Bourdieu has likened to the creation of 'a kind of infernal machine'.[33] The inequalities attendant on the prevailing order are given shape in *Autopol* through the extreme cynicism and the harsh Darwinian conditions of the prison-industry conglomerate and its specific organisation of labour. The supply of *Menschenmaterial* is maintained at a level with its consumption, an arrangement that circumvents constitutional and legal frameworks. With the help of docile politicians and acquiescent media, an array of scape-goating mechanisms is deployed to designate the 'other' and to allay middle-class anxieties about globalisation, excess, and exploitation.[34] The Foucauldian explication of the panoptical prison has been realised in Trojanow's vision of central Europe in the early twenty-first century, but without the function of the disciplining 'of the soul' identified in a wide range of enlightened social institutions. Rather, the hybrid structure of Autopol embodies the deployment of rationality to achieve 'solutions' through optimised, multilayered mechanisms of secrecy, profitability, and exclusion. The fictional world of *Autopol* inscribes a social structure that is extrapolated from the present social system, worse only in degree and, at the same time, pointing towards a new, post-Cold-War totalitarianism. As occurs in virtually all of the most influential twentieth-century dystopian novels, such as *Brave New World,*

33   Pierre Bourdieu, 'Neo-liberalism, the Utopia (becoming a reality) of Unlimited
       Exploitation', in *Acts of resistance. Against the tyranny of the market*, tr. Richard Nice
       (New York: The New Press, 1998), pp. 94–105, here p. 100.
34   See also Immanuel Wallerstein's study of the collapse of liberalism after 1989 and, in
       particular, the American backlash against the belief in liberal reformism (called the
       Contract with America), 'a doctrine that combines a fake adulation of the market
       with legislation against the poor and the strangers'. Immanuel Wallerstein, *After
       Liberalism* (New York: The New Press, 1995), p. 3.

1984, *Fahrenheit 451*, and *The Handmaid's Tale*, *Autopol* depicts a miscarried promise of socio-economic improvement.[35] As Gottlieb has shown, these novels voice the fear that Western democracy could fall victim to seductively utopian promises and turn in the direction of totalitarianism, following the precedents established by historical fascism and communism.[36] In a so-called 'post-historical' age, in which neo-liberalism has long propagated itself as the only viable option for ordering the world, a dystopian narrative may elucidate 'both the future of the ideology that controls consciousness in the present and the image of the future as an ideologically determined product'.[37]

Scholars of Anglo-American SF have seen the 1980s as an end of the utopian tendency 'in the face of economic restructuring, right-wing politics, and a cultural milieu informed by an intensifying fundamentalism and commodification'.[38] Authors such as Octavia E. Butler, Kim Stanley Robinson, and Ursula K. Le Guin are viewed as being in the forefront of a so-called 'dystopian turn' which comprises a re-inscription of dystopia as a critically potent form in which a narrative of the hegemonic order and a counter-narrative of resistance are configured in a dialogic relation. Without a dislocating move to an elsewhere, the element of textual estrangement remains in effect since the focus is placed on characters questioning the ruinous, nightmarish social order they inhabit. In German literature, *Autopol* may be seen as part of this development, as another kind of estranged writing that operates between the historical antinomies of utopia and anti-utopia and thus as an exercise in a politically charged form of hybrid textual and generic composition in which the agency of the strong-willed misfit Rasin provides the counterpoint to an oppressive system.[39] The

35 See Keith M. Booker, *The Dystopian Impulse in Modern Literature. Fiction as Social Criticism* (Westport, CT: Greenwood Press, 1994).

36 Gottlieb, *Dystopian Fiction East and West*, p. 10.

37 See Dragan Klaic, *The Plot of the Future. Utopia and Dystopia in Modern Drama* (Ann Arbor: University of Michigan Press, 1991), p. 4.

38 Baccolini and Moylan, 'Introduction: Dystopia and Histories', in *Dark Horizons*, p. 2.

39 For a discussion of the connection between critical dystopias and genre merging, see Jane Donawerth, 'Genre blending and the critical dystopia', *ibid.*, pp. 29–46.

novel rehearses a possible future and on the basis of contemporary evidence
to affect the exposition of a failed utopian vision while resisting closure in
favour of an open ending requiring reflection and inquisitiveness of the
reader and hinting at a utopian residue within its dystopian framework.[40]
As the television cameras capture the bloody ending of the hostage crisis,
Rasin and a few others, who have split from the majority of the inmates,
secretly escape from the prison complex through a network of tunnels
in an old mine. The novel closes with a violent reminder of misdirected
anarchic resistance when it is revealed that one of Rasin's group, a serial
killer aptly nicknamed Zirkel, committed another murder and carried on
the circle of violence which is really a dead end (184).

---

40   For more on the history of this dialogue between SF and utopia, see Gregory
     Paschalidis, 'Modernity as a Project and as Self-Criticism: The Historical Dialogue
     between Science Fiction and Utopia', in Karen Sayer and John Moore (eds), *Science
     Fiction, Critical Frontiers* (New York: St Martin's Press, 2000), pp. 35–47.

CAITRÍONA NÍ DHÚILL

The Hero as Language Learner: Biography and Metabiography in *Der Weltensammler/ The Collector of Worlds*

Es gab nur eine Möglichkeit, sein Leben nicht zu verplempern: Sprachen lernen.

There was only one way for him not to fritter away his life: learn languages.
— *Der Weltensammler*, p. 52.[1]

In the opening disclaimer which, as the second of four short paratexts, precedes the main body of Ilija Trojanow's *Der Weltensammler* (2006), the author succinctly addresses some problems that arise when fiction and biography meet. The novel, he writes, is inspired by the life and work of Richard Francis Burton (1821–1890). The choice of verb (*inspiriert von*) is eloquent, allowing for the flexibility that will characterise the approach to Burton's biography throughout the book. The disclaimer itself suggests a fine balance between the acknowledgement of 'biographische Realitäten' ['biographical realities']² pertaining to Burton, and the creative reworking of, and in places complete departure from, these 'realities' in a narrative which is 'überwiegend ein Produkt der Phantasie des Autors' ['predomi-

---

1 Ilija Trojanow, *Der Weltensammler. Roman* (6th edn Munich: Deutscher Taschenbuch Verlag, 2007), p. 52. Cited as *DW*. Translation: Iliya Troyanov, *The Collector of Worlds*. Translated by William Hobson (New York: HarperCollins, 2009), p. 37. Cited as *CW*.

2 Hobson's – in places rather free – translation renders this as 'biographical fact'.

nantly the product of the author's imagination']. *Der Weltensammler* is thus firmly aligned with an established genre, usually termed 'biographical fiction': the documented life of an historical figure serves as the raw material on which the author draws in the creation of a novelistic text which, in its final form, lays no claim to factual reliability or historical accuracy. The genre allows the novelist to use biography as a resource for fiction; it is widely practised, with notable examples to be found in the work of a range of authors in recent decades, from Penelope Fitzgerald (on Novalis) to Daniel Kehlmann (on Carl Friedrich Gauß and Alexander von Humboldt), and from Colm Tóibín (on Henry James) to Christa Wolf (on Heinrich von Kleist and Karoline von Günderrode).[3]

Biographical fiction stands in a curious relationship to biography proper and constitutes a distinctive form of metabiographical reflection. In the process of exploiting biographical data in the service of a narrative project, the novelist confronts many of the issues also faced by biographers. These are then thematised, with varying degrees of explicitness, in the resulting novel. In the case of *Der Weltensammler*, as I hope to show, the reflection is multi-layered; it encompasses both thematic and formal aspects of the book and accounts for many of its narrative strategies. Problems of biography that are common to both its non-fictional and fictionalised modes include the following: the rationale behind the selection of the subject; the status and reliability of sources, from eye-witness accounts, letters, diaries and interviews, to autobiographical writings and official documents; the elusive nature of the subject's 'identity' or 'personality'; the impossibility of providing a definitive account of another person's life; and, finally, the biographer's own presence in the biography, not to mention stake in the writing of it. These problems are confronted, and reflected on, by Trojanow in his work on Burton; the novel is preceded by the admission that 'Jeder Mensch ist ein Geheimnis; dies gilt um so mehr für einen Menschen, dem man nie begegnet ist' (*DW* 7) ['All individual

---

3   Penelope Fitzgerald, *The Blue Flower* (London: Flamingo, 1995); Daniel Kehlmann, *Die Vermessung der Welt* (Reinbek: Rowohlt, 2005); Colm Tóibín, *The Master* (London: Picador, 2004); Christa Wolf, *Kein Ort. Nirgends* (Berlin: Aufbau, 1979).

lives are mysterious, particularly those of people one has never met'] (*CW* front matter), while the related non-fictional volume *Nomade auf vier Kontinenten: Auf den Spuren von Sir Richard Francis Burton* (2007) opens with the question 'Wer ist dieser Mann, um den es hier gehen soll, und was bringt den Autor dazu, sich mit ihm zu beschäftigen?' ['Who is this man who is to be the subject of this book, and what has led the author to be concerned with him?'].[4]

Biographical fiction and conventional non-fictional biography confront the various aforementioned problems in different ways. Yet despite their obvious differences in approach, these modes of the biographical serve comparable functions, contributing to the construction of cultural prominence and historical visibility and to the canon of biographically available – and viable – historical figures. As Trojanow acknowledges in the appendices to *Nomade auf vier Kontinenten*, Richard Francis Burton was already the subject of a substantial biographical discourse before he 'set out in search of him'. (The search or quest as a metaphor for biographical research is familiar from the work of A.J.A. Symons, Richard Holmes, Eunice Lipton and others, and evoked in the subtitle of Trojanow's second Burton book, *Auf den Spuren*/On the Trail, suggesting as it does that the author has followed a trail of clues and traces in order to find his subject.)[5] Trojanow's fictional narrative persistently casts its protagonist as an enigma, an elusive maverick, a colonist with a difference; yet, in terms of his archival presence, his visibility in historical discourse, and the preservation of traces of his life, Burton is far from being a marginal figure. The *Nomade* appendix lists nine published biographies; this bibliography, while making no claim to be exhaustive (*Nomade* is not, after all, a scholarly work) features some conspicuous omissions, not least the two books by Christopher Ondaatje

---

4   Ilija Trojanow, *Nomade auf vier Kontinenten. Auf den Spuren von Sir Richard Francis Burton* [Nomad on Four Continents. On the Trail of Sir Richard Francis Burton] (Munich: Deutscher Taschenbuch Verlag, 2008), p. 7.

5   Richard Holmes, *Footsteps. Adventures of a Romantic Biographer* (London: Hodder and Stoughton, 1985); Eunice Lipton, *Alias Olympia: A Woman's Search for Manet's Notorious Model and Her Own Desire* (New York: Scribner's, 1992); A.J.A. Symons, *The Quest for Corvo: An Experiment in Biography* (London: Cassell, 1934).

on Burton's Nile explorations and travels in Sindh.[6] Some five further books
on Burton have appeared since the publication of *Der Weltensammler*,
ranging from travel writing and erotica to serious works of scholarship in
postcolonial studies and the history of geography.[7] Burton is clearly big
business in book terms, and his biography a well-traversed field.

Trojanow's books on Burton, particularly the novel, are thus more
fruitfully to be read as an intervention into an existing conversation *about*
his hero than as a portrait or representation *of* him; they form another
piece of the ever-expanding self-referential puzzle that is the biographical discourse on this colonial adventurer, a puzzle moreover that opens
out onto questions of intercultural encounter, transculturation, colonial
and postcolonial discourse, and power relations in the context of British
imperialism. The emerging secondary literature on Trojanow's Burton is
strongly oriented towards postcolonial theory, emphasising the hybridity,
multiplicity and instability of cultural identities, the provisional character
of all subject-positions, and the centrality of strategies and figures such as
boundary-crossing, mimicry and the 'third space' in the colonial encounter.
Michaela Haberkorn writes of *Der Weltensammler*: 'In this novel identity,
memory and cultural belonging are not fixed points of reference. Rather
they are in a state of becoming and are subject to constant change.'[8] Michael
Hofmann addresses related issues:

6   Christopher Ondaatje, *Journey to the Source of the Nile* (Toronto: HarperCollins,
     1998) and *Sindh Revisited: A Journey in the Footsteps of Captain Sir Richard Francis
     Burton: 1842–1849, the India Years* (Toronto: HarperCollins, 1996).
7   W.B. Carnochan, *The Sad Story of Burton, Speke, and the Nile: Or, Was John Hanning
     Speke a Cad* (Stanford: Stanford General Books, 2006); Jon R. Godsall, *The Tangled
     Web: A Life of Sir Richard Burton* (Abingdon: Matador, 2008); Felix Baron, *The
     Persian Girl* (London: Nexus, 2008); Daniel Gilpin, *Burton and Speke's Source of the
     Nile Quest* (Oxford: Heinemann, 2008); Ben Grant: *Postcolonialism, Psychoanalysis
     and Burton: Power Play of Empire* (London: Routledge, 2009); James L. Newman,
     Paths Without Glory: Richard Francis Burton in Africa (Washington, DC: Potomac
     Books, 2010).
8   Michaela Haberkorn, 'Treibeis und Weltensammler: Konzepte nomadischer Identität
     in den Romanen von Libuše Moníková und Ilija Trojanow', in Helmut Schmitz (ed.),
     Von der nationalen zur internationalen Literatur. Transkulturelle deutschsprachige

In spite of all critical misgivings, the historical figure of Burton can serve as a model (*Vorbild*) for us today as participants in a global process of communication, whenever we are concerned with the issues of how to call Eurocentrism into question and to shape intercultural communication in the postcolonial context.[9]

What is missing in the critical literature to date is a sustained reflection on the biographical dimension. *Der Weltensammler* and *Nomade auf vier Kontinenten*, beyond their clear affinities with postcolonial and transcultural literature, as well as with travel writing[10] and the critique of Eurocentric Orientalism, constitute a set of metabiographical reflections in their own right.

To clarify: the term *metabiography* evokes a 'hermeneutics of suspicion' with regard to biography.[11] It would fall beyond the scope of the current discussion to do full justice to metabiography and to the range of forms – some of which are virulently anti-biographical – that it can take. Broadly speaking, it is a postmodern manifestation of the biographical, a necessary complement to the tenacious cultural presence of biography after the dismantling of the genre's founding illusions (which include a model of subjectivity as coherent, individual, and 'narratable'; the notion of a past that

Literatur und Kultur im Zeitalter globaler Migration (Amsterdam: Rodopi, 2009), pp. 243–61, here p. 260.

9   Michael Hofmann, 'Postkoloniale Begegnungen in der globalisierten Welt. Indien und Afrika in der deutschsprachigen Gegenwartsliteratur: Ilija Trojanow: *Der Weltensammler* und Christof Hamann: *Usambara*' (February 2010), 19pp, here p. 17. <http://www.germanistik.ch> accessed 30 August 2012. See also the unpublished dissertation by Andreas Mittermayr, *Kosmopolitische und kosmopolitisch-engagierte Literatur am Beispiel Ilija Trojanows*, University of Vienna, 2011.

10   Gabriele Lotz, 'Historische Reiseromane: Erzählprosa von Christoph Ransmayr und Ilija Trojanow', in Christoph Parry and Liisa Voßschmidt (eds), '*Kennst Du das Land ...?': Fernweh in der Literatur* (Munich: Iudicium, 2009), pp. 75–84.

11   See Wilhelm Hemecker, 'Anton Weberns Tod. Eine Metabiographie von Gert Jonke', in Bernhard Fetz and Hannes Schweiger (eds), *Spiegel und Maske. Konstruktionen biographischer Wahrheit* (Vienna: Zsolnay, 2006), pp. 160–74; Nicolaas A. Rupke, *Alexander von Humboldt: A Metabiography* (Chicago: University of Chicago Press, 2008); and my own 'Widerstand gegen die Biographie: Sigrid Weigels Bachmann-Studie', in Wilhelm Hemecker (ed.), *Die Biographie – Beiträge zu ihrer Geschichte* (Berlin: de Gruyter, 2009), pp. 43–70.

can be reconstructed; and the claim to re-present, to make an absent subject present again and thus knowable). Two quotations will serve to exemplify the anti-biographical end of the metabiographical spectrum. The first is by Sigrid Weigel, in her major study of the Austrian poet Ingeborg Bachmann, where she writes that 'the fundamental methodological dilemma of every biography is the impossibility of posthumously constructing the life story of another person'.[12] A similar view is expressed even more trenchantly by David Nye in his study on the inventor Thomas Edison:

> This study rejects the existence of its subject, Thomas Alva Edison, and will not attempt to recapture him in language. He once existed, but neither he nor any other figure can be recreated. The references in these pages lead not to a hero, but to yellowed papers, restored buildings, old photographs, furniture, cartoons, newspapers, magazines, and museums.[13]

Rather than requiring us to renounce biography altogether, however, critical metabiographical reflections such as these can stimulate a more subtle, disenchanted approach to the traces of past lives and to the stories they generate, thus ultimately enriching our reading and writing of biography.

In what follows, I will try to demonstrate how the narrative techniques of *Der Weltensammler* are informed by metabiographical concepts, suggesting a keen awareness on the novelist's part of the limitations and dubious claims of traditional biography. However, Trojanow's approach cannot be simply endorsed as an instance of critical metabiography. In fact, as I hope to show, *Der Weltensammler* and *Nomade auf vier Kontinenten* present a curious mixture of self-reflexive anti- and metabiography, on the one hand, and unreconstructed biographical protagonism, on the other. The construction of the biographical subject proceeds in awareness of its status as a construction, but does not dispense completely with the mechanisms of characterisation, identification, and stereotyping that are central to the biographical tradition of the heroic 'great man'.

12   Sigrid Weigel, *Ingeborg Bachmann. Hinterlassenschaften unter Wahrung des Briefgeheimnisses* (Vienna: Zsolnay, 1999), p. 294.
13   David E. Nye, *The Invented Self. An Anti-Biography, from Documents of Thomas A. Edison* (Odense: Odense University Press, 1983), p. 16.

The Carlylean Hero

Thomas Carlyle's dictum that 'the History of the world is but the Biography of great men', expounded in his series of lectures, *On Heroes, Hero-Worship, and the Heroic* of 1840, could be taken as the motto of the heroic biographical tradition.[14] The view it expresses shadows the history of biography from its beginnings, underpinning the discourses of greatness, exemplarity and cultural significance that remain implicit in much biography even today. Indeed, Michael Hofmann's comment on Trojanow's Burton, quoted above, nicely illustrates the persistence of the idea that one of the functions of biography is to provide exemplars or role models ('the historical figure of Burton can serve as a model (*Vorbild*) for us today as participants in a global process of communication'). Carlyle's theory of the hero embraces this aspect of exemplarity in all its didactic potential: the *On Heroes* lectures are, according to their author, 'not so much historic as didactic',[15] and the 'Great Men' they discuss are, he promises, 'profitable company'.[16] Carlyle collapses the distinction between history and biography under the sign of greatness, constructing narratives of struggle and leadership in which personality, individual achievement and heroism are the driving forces of history, and the complex structural, material, social and cultural factors underlying historical change are effectively written out. *On Heroes* explores six types of heroism – the hero as divinity, as prophet, as poet, as priest, as man of letters, and as king – and finds their common ground in a courageous non-conformism and a bigness of vision that enables them to break with prejudices and expected behaviours. The defining quality of the Carlylean hero is that he is ahead of his time.

14 Thomas Carlyle, *On Heroes, Hero-Worship, and the Heroic in History* (Berkeley: University of California Press, 1993), p. 26.
15 Quoted in Chris R. Vanden Bossche, *Carlyle and the Search for Authority* (Columbus: Ohio State University Press, 1991), p. 97.
16 Carlyle, *On Heroes*, p. 3.

The troubling political implications of Carlyle's ideology, quite apart from his overblown rhetoric and idiosyncratic style, may tempt us to dismiss his approach as obsolete, the product of a heady mix of Romanticism and counter-revolutionary reaction. Yet to assume that his hero theory has no relevance to the contemporary understanding and practice of biography – a diverse practice which includes biographical fiction – is to assume that today's biographers are no longer susceptible to discourses of greatness and heroism. Carlyle's model of heroic biography may seem alien to today's reader, but it is precisely through its alienating quality that *On Heroes* can provoke reflection on some of the more problematic aspects of biography as cultural practice. By foregrounding greatness and championing cultural heroes as unabashedly as they do, Carlyle's lectures point to biography's role in the construction of culturally prominent elites. While the affirmative notion of 'greatness' may have fallen out of favour, the seemingly more neutral categories to which much modern biography appeals for its legitimation – noteworthiness, uniqueness, contribution, cultural significance, or the idea of being 'ahead of one's time' – draw, at least in part, on a long tradition of honouring the 'great'.

Contemporary biographers may seek to downplay this legacy, or to write against its grain by demystifying their subjects, calling their reputations into question and contextualising and relativising their achievements. Trojanow's decision to narrate large parts of Burton's story from the perspective of the subaltern 'supporting cast' has clear affinities with the counter-tradition of 'post-heroic', debunking biography inaugurated by Lytton Strachey. If 'no man is a Hero to his valet-de-chambre',[17] it surely diminishes Burton's heroic stature to portray him through the eyes of 'valets' or subalterns of the likes of Naukaram and Sidi Mubarak Bombay. Yet as Carlyle himself was well aware when he quoted this aphorism in order to argue with it, its validity very much depends on the valet and on his ability or otherwise to recognise heroic qualities. This ability is one Naukaram certainly possesses: 'So ein Mensch war mein Herr, überall wo er hinging, war er bald mit dem Ort besser vertraut als jene, die ein Leben lang dort

---

17   *Ibid.*, pp. 157–8.

verbracht hatten. Er paßte sich schnell an, Sie würden nicht glauben, wie rasch er lernen konnte' (*DW* 49) ['He was the sort of person, my master, who, wherever he went, would in no time get to know the place better than people who'd lived there their whole lives. He adapted very quickly. You wouldn't believe how fast he could learn things'] (*CW* 34–5). Despite the harsh treatment meted out to him when he follows his master to England, and his clear desire to set the record straight by recounting his version of events, Naukaram remains unstinting in his admiration.

> Er reiste ein Jahr später nach Bombay, und er glänzte in den Prüfungen, in Hindi und Gujarati. [...] Er war fleißig, er hat geschuftet wie ein Ochse in einer Ölmühle. Im nächsten Jahr wiederholte sich alles, er ließ sich in Bombay erneut prüfen, dieses Mal in Marathi und Sanskrit. Er hat erneut bestanden, mit Auszeichnung. (*DW* 64)

> A year later he went to Bombay and shone in his exams in Hindi and Gujarati. [...] He was industrious, toiling away like an ox in an oil mill. And the next year it was the same all over again: he sat more exams in Bombay, this time in Marathi and Sanskrit; he passed again, with distinction [...]. (*CW* 48)

Trojanow's approach, imbued as it is with a postcolonial sensibility, is committed to giving voice to those figures who are marginalised or silenced in traditional biographical accounts of Burton – the figures of the servant, the local observer, the guide. In fact, the runaway success of *Der Weltensammler* needs to be understood within a larger context in which the historical dominance of the dead white European male – not least within the biographical tradition – has been radically contested, and the range of 'narratable' or historically visible lives dramatically expanded. The retelling of the colonial tale involves a privileging of the colonised viewpoint, an approach which seems far removed from the unapologetic elitism of Carlyle's hero theory. Nevertheless, Trojanow's adventurer-protagonist (it is superfluous to mention his gender, race and class at this point) is not dislodged from his central position by the novel's plurality of narrative perspectives and alternative voices. His characterisation retains key features of the Carlylean hero: ready to make sacrifices and to endure harsh discipline in pursuit of his goals, he is fearless, free-thinking, and strong: 'Dem Starken ist jeder Ort Heimat' ['For the strong man every place is home'] (*Nomade* 5).

The Heroic Linguist

To Carlyle's six above-listed heroic types we could add, with reference to Trojanow's Burton, a seventh: the hero as language learner. Burton's (historically attested) linguistic facility is, in the novel, of a piece with his portrayal as generally superior to the other British officers. In keeping with the bigness of vision that typifies the Carlylean hero, Trojanow's protagonist is above the prejudiced and rigid thinking that characterises his compatriots' encounters with other cultures. This makes him extraordinarily adept in negotiating intercultural encounters – although, curiously, less so when these are of a sexual nature. Because the plausible hero needs weaknesses and failures, there is one language Burton is incapable of learning: that of Kundalini's caresses. 'Burton [...] versuchte Kundalini's Fingern zu folgen. Ich möchte ihre Zärtlichkeiten verstehen, dachte er. Die einzige Sprache, die er nicht erlernen konnte' (*DW* 141) ['Burton, stretched out naked on his bed [...], tried to follow Kundalini's fingers. I'd like to understand what they're saying, he thought. The only language he couldn't learn'] (*CW* 115). Yet he is determined to try, and prepared to intensify his studies of Sanskrit in order to gain access to the secrets of the Kama Sutra (*DW* 150, *CW* 123) – a diligence restaged as tragic farce in the episode in which, grief-crazed after Kundalini's sudden death, he parodies the language-learning process with a group of monkeys (*DW* 170–3, *CW* 142–3). The portrayal of his language learning is crucial to his characterisation as a hero: single-minded, driven, and without regard for convention.

The bearers of convention against whom our hero rebels are none other than Burton's fellow Britons, as we see in the advice he receives from them on his arrival in India:

> Am besten – einen ehrlicheren Ratschlag werden Sie nicht zu hören bekommen –, am besten, Sie halten sich von allem Fremden fern! [...] Du sprichst den Dialekt dieser Kerle schon gut, bemerkte der Sanitäter, etwas vorwurfsvoll. Burton lachte: Die Damen von gestern wären entsetzt. Bestimmt denken sie, eine Sprache zu teilen ist wie ein Bett zu teilen. (*DW* 25–6)

All in all – 'now you won't hear a more honest piece of advice than this' – your wisest course of action would be to keep well away from anything foreign. [...] The orderly remarked somewhat reproachfully, 'You speak these fellows' dialect awfully well'. Burton laughed: 'The women from yesterday would be horrified. I'm sure they think sharing a language is the same as sharing a bed'. (*CW* 13–14.)[18]

In a striking passage which imagines the beginning of Burton's intensive study of Indian languages, the learning process itself is curiously bound up with an image of violence and penetration. As it provides a complex metaphor for the interpenetration of the self and the foreign that occurs in language learning, it is worth quoting in full. Having confronted the linguistic limitations of his fellow officers – one of whom erroneously uses the feminine conjugation ('alle wußten, er plapperte seine einheimische Geliebte nach', *DW* 52) ['everyone knew he simply repeated parrot-fashion whatever his native lover said'] (*CW* 37) – Burton sits in solitude, wrestling with an oppressive climate and an unknown vocabulary:

Schweißtropfen rannen über seine Unterarme, seinen Rücken, Fliegen schwirrten um ihn herum, Afghanistan war anderswo und bereits befriedet, und ihm blieb nichts anderes übrig, als Wörter laut auszusprechen, hundertfach wiederholt. Sobald er schwieg, hörte er das Surren der Moskitos, die er nicht loswurde, egal wie oft er durch die Luft schlug und dabei das Wort brüllte, das er sich gerade aneignete. Es gab nur eine Strategie, diese Plage zu besiegen. Er mußte regungslos in seinem Stuhl verharren, die Augen auf das aufgeschlagene Buch vor sich gerichtet, auf das nächste englische Wort, dem wie so oft zwei Entsprechungen zugeteilt waren – die Doppelzüngigkeit der Einheimischen offenbart sich in ihrer Sprache, hatte der weiblich konjugierende Offizier zum besten gegeben. Er war ein hinterlistiges Opfer, das Gehör geeicht auf die heransurrende Mücke, *pratikshaa karna*, die eine Entsprechung, langsam zu wiederholen, jede Silbe ein Schluck Wasser, der Moskito war jetzt nahe, *intezaar karna*, die weitere Entsprechung, die er wiederholte, mehrfach, er spürte, wie sich die Mücke auf seinem Arm niederließ, wie sie hineinstach. Dann schlug er zu. (*DW* 53)

Drops of sweat rolled down his forearms, his back; flies buzzed around him. Afghanistan was miles away and already pacified and there was nothing left for him to do but to say words out loud, repeat them a hundred times. The moment he fell

---

18   Hobson's translation inserts punctuation marks that ascribe speech and thought more unambiguously than those in the original.

silent, he heard the drone of the mosquitoes; no matter how often he beat the air and yelled the word he had just learnt, he couldn't get rid of them. There was only one tactic that worked against that scourge: he had to sit perfectly still in his chair, his eyes fixed on the grammar open in front of him, on the next English word for which Hindi, as so often, had two counterparts – 'the native's duplicity is there, plain for all to see, in their language,' the feminine-conjugating officer had volunteered. He was a cunning victim, his hearing calibrated to the insect's approach as he slowly enunciated the first equivalent, *pratiksha karna*, every syllable a glug of water, then the next, *intezaar karna*, which he repeated over and over until he felt the mosquito land on his arm, felt it bite him – and then squashed it. (*CW* 38)

This is more than just an atmospheric detail. It resonates with the possibility that language learning is a heroic discipline which modifies the
learner's subjectivity and, as with any transformative process, contains an
element of destruction: the speaker of a new language can never revert
to her earlier monolingual self. The patience and tenacity required by
the discipline are further underlined by the fact that the Hindi words
Burton seeks to master at this point are words for 'waiting' or 'awaiting':
the unknown language will only gradually, and never fully, unlock itself to
him. 'Eile, sagte Upanitsche abschätzig, wir müssen sie überwinden. Das
ist das erste, was wir zu begreifen haben' (*DW* 60) ['Haste', said Upanishe
disparagingly, 'is something to be overcome. That is the first thing we have
to be clear about'] (*CW* 45). The protagonist's solitary studies, his lessons
with his teacher Upanitsche, and ceaseless practice in conversation (as
himself or incognito) with native speakers initiate a process of personal
transculturation that goes beyond language to encompass dress, bearing
and habitus, as well as, ultimately, religious practice. A conspicuous trend
in reception and interpretation of the novel has been to see in Trojanow's
Burton a model for the fluid identity of the cosmopolitan, postcolonial
globetrotter; yet the various masquerades, far from being effortless (as the
metaphor of fluidity might imply), are rather the result of a disciplined,
heroic effort which sets the protagonist apart from the other characters.
An overly affirmative response to Burton's intercultural proficiency also
risks overlooking the – ultimately inscrutable, but surely complex – moti-
vations behind it.

Trojanow's Burton: A Metabiographical Perspective

The point of discussing *Der Weltensammler* as metabiography is that it enables us to dispense with the question of whether Trojanow's account is 'right', whether it accurately reflects Burton's experience while 'grasping' or 'capturing' his personality. The metabiographical perspective abandons the detective story model – biography as a 'human mystery to be solved',[19] the biographer reconstructing 'what happened' and 'what the subject was like' out of a mixture of clues and intelligent guesswork. Metabiography acknowledges that the encounter with traces of past lives and the attempt to synthesise these as narrative is an epistemological labyrinth, even a minefield. Indeed, the terrain of metabiography is rife with seductive metaphors: those of portraiture are perhaps the most familiar and widespread, but others such as re-animation, ingestion/digestion, or military engagement offer various ways of conceptualising the biographical enterprise and the relationship between biographer and subject.[20] Lytton Strachey led the charge in 1918 with the veiled homoeroticism of his military imagery in *Eminent Victorians*:

> It is not by the direct method of a scrupulous narration that the explorer of the past can hope to depict that singular epoch. If he is wise, he will adopt a subtler strategy. He will attack his subject in unexpected places; he will fall upon the flank, or the rear; he will shoot a sudden, revealing searchlight into obscure recesses, hitherto undivined.[21]

19 See Richard Holmes, *Footsteps. Adventures of a Romantic Biographer* (London: Hodder and Stoughton, 1985).

20 See Michael Holroyd, *Lytton Strachey: The New Biography* (London: Chatto & Windus, 1994), pp. 475; and my own 'Lebensbilder: Biographie und die Sprache der bildenden Künste' in Bernhard Fetz (ed.), *Die Biographie – Zur Grundlegung ihrer Theorie* (Berlin: de Gruyter, 2009), pp. 473–500.

21 Lytton Strachey, *Eminent Victorians: Cardinal Manning – Florence Nightingale – Dr Arnold – General Gordon* (London: Chatto & Windus, 1918, reprinted 1929), p. vii.

In fact, the modernist rejection of comprehensive, fact-oriented biography in favour of a more impressionistic, polemical approach could be seen as a founding moment of metabiography, a shift in the discourse about past lives from the representationalist question ('what were they like, and how can we best show what they were like?') to the self-reflexive, epistemological question ('how can we know, and why do we ask?'). I would argue that *Der Weltensammler* makes its distinctive contribution at the metabiographical level, rather than at the biographical. As Julian Preece maintains, Trojanow's 'original' novel, read as a portrait of the Victorian colonist-adventure, is in fact riven with Orientalist cliché and 'not original at all.'[22] The originality of Trojanow's intervention into the congested field of Burtonia lies less in its plot, setting, cast of characters and narrative techniques, than in the sheer wealth of metabiographical metaphor it deploys. Each set of relationships the novel depicts offers yet another way of conceptualising the relationship between subject and biographer: as master/servant, teacher/pupil, artist/amanuensis; as parasite/host, colonist/coloniser, criminal/detective. If we read the India chapter as a double biography of *both* Burton *and* his servant Naukaram, the relationships become even richer: the account of Burton's life is interwoven with Naukaram's *curriculum vitae*, and the resulting material in turn inspires the scribe to embark on his first creative project. The dialogues between Naukaram and the lahiya (street scribe) dramatise the unstable power-relations between subject and biographer: while the amanuensis is usually thought to serve the dominant subjectivity which dictates to him, this relationship is unsettled when the scribe takes the narrative into his own hands:

> Durfte er das Leben eines anderen verfälschen? Wozu diese Gewissenhaftigkeit? Er mußte diese Steifheit ablegen, sie ziemte sich nur für Helden auf alten Miniaturen. Bewegung! Biegsamkeit! (*DW* 137)

---

22   Julian Preece, 'Ilija Trojanow, *Der Weltensammler*: Separate Bodies, or: An Account of Intercultural Failure?', in Lyn Marven and Stuart Taberner (eds), *Emerging German-Language Novelists of the Twenty-First Century* (Rochester, NY: Camden House, 2011), pp. 119–32, here p. 124.

Was he allowed to distort another's life? Why such scruples? He had to shrug off this stiffness; it only suited the rigid pose of heroes in old miniatures. Movement! Limberness! (*CW* 112)

So muß es gewesen sein, in etwa. Der Lahiya war sehr zufrieden. Das ist wahre Gewissenhaftigkeit, dachte er, die Geschichte zur Wahrheit zu verfälschen. (*DW* 140)

That's how it must have been, more or less. The lahiya was very satisfied. That is genuine scruples, he thought, distorting a story until it becomes true. (*CW* 114)

The shifting power-balance between subject and scribe-biographer is reflected in the pronouns: mostly, Naukaram is addressed as *Du*, and addresses the scribe as *Sie*, but where conflict arises (*DW* 176–8), this is reversed. Even where the narrative is focalised directly through Burton without the mediating gaze of the minor characters, the text continues to thematise the incompleteness and unreliability of all written, in this case autobiographical, testimony, and the inaccessibility of subjective experience to narrative:

Wenn es etwas gibt, auf das er sich freut, so ist es dieses schriftliche Vergegenwärtigen. Er wird nicht alles aufschreiben, nicht alles dem Manuskript anvertrauen. An äußeren Details wird er nicht sparen [...] Aber seine Gefühle wird er nicht verraten. Nicht alle. Zumal, er ist sich seiner Gefühle nicht immer sicher gewesen. Er will nicht weitere Unklarheit in die Welt setzen. (*DW* 351)

If there is something he is looking forward to, it is this recollection in writing. He won't write everything, confide everything to the manuscript. He won't stint on external details [...] But he won't reveal his feelings, not all of them, especially because he hasn't always been sure of what they are. He doesn't want to bring more uncertainty into the world. (*CW* 300)

If metabiography is the search for an adequate language to describe – and critique – the claims biography seems to make about the knowability of past lives, then *Der Weltensammler* is decidedly metabiographical: the story it (re-)tells serves as an occasion for reflecting on the problems involved in (re-)telling such a story.

The shift in focus from the biographical to the metabiographical by no means entails an indifference to historical accuracy. We can know factual details of Burton's travels, career, acquaintance, living arrangements, in the sense of being able to marshal reliably documented evidence about them. Trojanow's extensive research into Burton's life is evident throughout, and documented in the *Nomade* volume. What *is* impossible, however, is a reconstruction of Burton's intentions and emotions, his effects on others, his personality or character, 'what he was like'; and yet the possibility of such a reconstruction is inevitably implied by any narrative centred on a protagonist. All biography plays with precisely this tension between verifiability and creative reconstruction, a tension which constitutes one of the central themes of biographical theory from Virginia Woolf onwards.[23] The degree of self-reflexivity with which different biographers play this game varies hugely, however. The metabiographical perspective involves a shift in emphasis, away from the ultimately unanswerable question of whether the text 'captures' or 'does justice to' its subject and towards the techniques and narrative strategies used to create a particular sort of biographical protagonist, hero or type.

The Usual Suspects

Resistance to stereotype plays a key role in Trojanow's depiction of his biographical subject as hero: Burton resists the temptation to see the colonial Other through the distorting lens of the coloniser, he has a seemingly endless appetite for knowledge of the foreign, and an almost obsessive willingness to self-transform. Yet for all his refusal of the blinkered thinking of his compatriots, the Burton of *Der Weltensammler* is in fact constructed *through* stereotype. The level of self-reflexivity and irony involved in the novel's deployment of cliché is often difficult to determine. At the centre is the heroic, maverick adventurer, but he is surrounded by a cast of familiar

---

23   See Ira Bruce Nadel, *Biography: Fiction, Fact and Form* (London: Macmillan, 1984) and Fetz (ed), *Die Biographie*.

characters: the dark-eyed, mysterious courtesan, the bigotted members of the British officer class, and the various native informants, who, true to Orientalist form, are subtly or at times not so subtly feminised (Naukaram, for example, waits anxiously at home for his master, and 'should have been born a girl'; *DW* 41; *CW* 26–7; Sidi Mubarak Bombay's loquacious testimony is punctuated by the dismissive and disparaging remarks of his strong, taciturn wife). Trojanow's own fascination (and, as the *Nomade* volume makes clear, identification) with Burton's fascination with other cultures suggests an attitude of openness towards difference, an attitude endorsed in the largely affirmative critical reception of the novel to date. In fact, however, the representation of both cultural and gender differences in *Der Weltensammler* often relies on the reductive shorthand of the Orientalist repertoire, a problem which is compounded rather than offset by the wholesale derision meted out to all British characters save Burton. The maverick is defined with reference to the herd ('er war wie ein alter Elefant, der sich von der Herde zurückgezogen hat und stets allein am Wasserloch trinkt'; *DW* 448) ['he was like an old elephant that has withdrawn from the herd and always drinks alone at the watering hole'] (*CW* 384): the construction of the hero relies on the co-construction of an Other of negative valence, a foil, and this is *not* the 'native', or certainly not only the native, but rather the unenlightened Briton. The very seat of learning – Burton's alma mater – thus becomes a scene of blinkered arrogance: 'Es gab keinen Arabisch-Unterricht in Oxford, keine Alternative zum Latein, falsch ausgeprochen von den Greisen, die sich nichts sagen ließen' (*DW* 248) ['There were no Arabic classes in Oxford, no alternatives to the Latin mispronounced by old men who refused to listen to reason'] (*CW* 209). The 'mispronounced' Latin of the Oxford dons suggests an elsewhere – a utopia? – where Latin is correctly pronounced. The curious idea of mispronounced Latin suggests a binary of falseness and authenticity, distortion and genuineness – strangely jarring in a narrative that is ostensibly concerned with the fluidity and constructedness of identity, its making and remaking through mimicry and masquerade. The slip may or may not be intentional – a deliberate marker of Burton's own impatience with his countrymen, or an effect of the novel's overall tendency to cast Britons other than Burton in an unsympathetic light. Driven by a keen sense of the limitations of his fellow colonists, Burton moves – not effortlessly, but effectively – between worlds; yet for his true colours to shine, the nomad (proficient linguist) needs the non-nomad (ignorant professor) as contrast. The narrative itself, like the critical responses to it so far, emphasises Burton's nomadism and transculturation, his boundary-crossing peripatetics. This has meant that detailed attention has yet to be paid to the spaces inside, and on either side of, the boundaries. In a tale of heroic linguistic proficiency, the mangled Latin of the bigotted British professors is symptomatic of a larger structuring binarism fundamental to the construction of Burton as exemplary *Weltbürger*. The persistent deployment of stereotype in a text that is so decidedly *about* stereotypes – and so clearly aware of, so committed in its opposition to, their negative effects – raises the possibility that they might function as a heuristic device in intercultural encounters: as a way of codifying difference, rendering it recognisable and discussable. In this way, *Der Weltensammler* unsettles any assumption that stereotype is exclusively negative or necessarily pernicious, especially where it is deployed with a degree of self-reflexivity, an awareness that, like biography itself, stereotype is a form of representation arising from, and productive in, encounters with otherness, and that all such representation is bound to entail omissions, distortions and perspectival errors. Just as metabiography enables a critical move beyond pro- or anti-biographical positions, allowing continued engagement with biographical practice alongside a heightened awareness of its epistemological pitfalls, so too does the use of Orientalist and heroic cliché in a novel that thematises prejudice and imperial power suggest the possibility of a meta-stereotypical discourse which might lay bare the role of reductive thinking in intercultural encounters while continuing the search for an adequate mode of engagement with difference.

ERNEST SCHONFIELD

On the Road to Mecca with Trojanow and Burton

Sir Richard Francis Burton (1821–1890) was an influential Orientalist who helped to found the Anthropological Society of London in 1863 and who translated the *Arabian Nights*; he was also a prospector who sought to exploit precious mineral resources, and a diplomat who served the British government for thirty years, working as a consul in Brazil, Damascus, and Trieste. Throughout his life, Burton was on the move. The fact that he never stayed in one place for long suggests an insatiable quality to his voyaging, which anticipates the pathology of tourism as we understand it today. Such 'consuming unrest', according to Alfred Andersch, is the defining feature of the modern tourist, who is 'a hunter of momentary impressions' driven to travel by a desire for the unknown.[1] For Andersch tourists seek out places which they have already read about in books; their experience as tourists is thus mediated by the accounts of previous travellers. As he reports on his journey to Mecca, Richard Burton was certainly a tourist in this respect. His *Personal Narrative of a Pilgrimage*, which was published to popular acclaim in three volumes on his return, frequently refers to the work of his predecessor, the Swiss explorer Johann Ludwig Burckhardt. Unlike a religious pilgrim, who pays homage to a single sacred centre, the tourist usually visits numerous centres or attractions.[2] Again this applies to Burton himself if one considers his career as a whole. Almost as soon as he has 'consumed' a culture by assimilating its language, its beliefs, and its customs, he moves on. As Trojanow's fictional Burton remarks at one

---

1   Alfred Andersch, *Wanderungen im Norden. Mit 32 Farbtafeln nach Aufnahmen von Gisela Andersch* (Zurich: Diogenes, 1970), p. 218 and pp. 217–18.
2   Dean MacCannell, *The Tourist: A New Theory of the Leisure Class* (London: Macmillan, 1976), p. 58.

point in *Der Weltensammler*, Hinduism is now 'passé', which makes it time to turn to Islam.[3] Tourism nevertheless has its origins in pilgrimage. As the historian of tourism John Urry points out, the tourist's experience remains structurally similar to the pilgrim's, in so far as both involve a rite of passage which leads to a modified sense of identity.[4] It is clear that his experiences in Medina and Mecca made a lasting impression on Burton, making him a tourist in this sense too. Towards the end of the *Personal Narrative*, he appears almost reverent: 'I have seen the religious ceremonies of many lands, but never – nowhere – aught so solemn, so impressive as this'.[5] Yet as soon as he has returned from Mecca, he starts planning his expedition to Harar in Somaliland, which becomes his next adventure. As his biographer Fawn Brodie puts it, the swiftness with which the expedition to Harar followed the journey to Mecca suggests that Burton's elation at completing the pilgrimage was 'short-lived, illusory, and substitutive'.[6]

Writers on tourism agree that the tourist's dominant mode of perception is visual. For Andersch, the tourist seeks the fleeting glimpse which may suddenly be beheld, as the landscape 'unveils' itself.[7] For Urry, tourism involves looking at the unfamiliar.[8] In *Pilgrimage* Burton wanted to see and experience the foreign cultures at close range rather than merge himself with them. Trojanow's Burton even wonders whether he is motivated to travel by the difficulty in seeing the unknown: 'Ist es das, was ihn immer wieder in die Fremde zieht – die vorübergehende Blindheit?' (*DW* 245) ['Is this what always makes him take to the road again – this temporary

---

3   Ilija Trojanow, *Der Weltensammler* (Munich: Deutscher Taschenbuch Verlag, 2007), p. 126. Cited as *DW*. Translations are from Iliya Troyanov, *The Collector of Worlds*, tr. William Hobson (London: Faber and Faber, 2008), p. 103. Cited as *CW*.

4   John Urry, *The Tourist Gaze: Leisure and Travel in Contemporary Societies* (London/ Thousand Oaks, CA: Sage, 1990), p. 10.

5   Richard Francis Burton, *Personal Narrative of a Pilgrimage to Al-Madinah & Meccah*, 2 vols, ed. Isabel Burton (New York: Dover, 1964), ii, p. 226. First published in 1855–1856 in three volumes. Henceforth cited as *Pilgrimage*.

6   Fawn Brodie, *The Devil Drives: A life of Sir Richard Burton* (London: Eland, 1986/2002). First published by Eyre and Spottiswoode, 1967, p. 112.

7   Andersch, *Wanderungen im Norden*, p. 218.

8   Urry, *The Tourist Gaze*, pp. 11–12.

blindness?'] (*CW* 206). There is a gendered aspect to this too: Burton wishes to penetrate dark, foreign, feminine secrets with his masculine eyes, just as he wishes to see Kundalini naked while she insists on undressing in the dark. This emphasis on visual perception even extends to the search for religious knowledge: at the end of *Der Weltensammler*, Burton asserts that whereas he has looked everywhere for God, most people 'würden immer wieder in denselben Topf blicken' (*DW* 516) ['are happy just to look in the same pot'] (*CW* 444). The fact that Burton frames religious experience here in visual terms is ironic, given that orthodox Islam forbids religious imagery. Finding pleasure in images poses a potential problem for monotheism because it opens the door to idolatry, even pantheism. When Burton arrived in Mecca and saw the Kaaba, a 'strange, unique' view, he felt no religious enthusiasm, but only 'the ecstasy of gratified pride' (*Pilgrimage* ii, 161).

For a pilgrim to Mecca, visual perception has a dual significance. On the one hand, every Muslim is encouraged to complete the hajj once in their lifetime, if their finances permit. The duty to travel to Mecca and see the Kaaba for oneself is one of the four pillars of Islam. On the other hand, seeing is only one of the many duties which comprise hajj, including the wearing of ihram, the circumambulation of the Kaaba (tawaf), and the many required prayers and recitations from the *Qur'an*. Paradoxically, seeing can denote either respect or dominance. When Burton sees Medina for the first time, after he has embraced his travelling companion Sa'ad, he reverts to the mode of the professional Orientalist, staring, observing, and committing whatever he sees to memory: 'seine Augen beginnen durch den Zauber zu stoßen, sie überfliegen das Städtchen, sie sezieren es, und er prägt sich alles ein' (*DW* 300) ['his eyes begin to analyse the enchantment, scanning the little town, dissecting, memorising'] (*CW* 255). At this point, eyes become instruments of colonial domination; they dissect the landscape in order to process it and assimilate it for Western scientific discourse. John Zilcosky has argued that finding the view from above is one of the gestures of the travel writer of the colonial period. Such elevated perspectives enable travellers 'to gain control over a topography' that might otherwise engulf them.[9] Something rather similar occurs in Trojanow's account of his own hajj.[10] As a compensation for his inability to participate fully in the ritual, Trojanow ascends the terrace of the Haram al-Sharif mosque, and, looking down upon the hypnotic sight of the crowds of pilgrims circling the Kaaba, he attempts to pray with his eyes (*QI* 58; *MM* 66). This passage served as the basis for a similar episode in *Der Weltensammler*:

> Er versucht zu beten, aber bricht bald ab, weil ihm klar wird, daß er das Gebet nur als gemeinschaftlichen Akt akzeptieren kann. Es kann sich nicht zum einsamen Gebet zwingen. Er richtet sich auf und sucht eine erhöhte Stelle, von der aus er über die Köpfe der Kreisenden auf die Kaaba blicken kann. Wenn schon die Zunge sich den Gebeten verweigert, wird er mit den Augen beten. (*DW* 325)

> He tries to pray but soon breaks off as he realises he can only accept prayer as a communal act. He cannot force himself to pray on his own. He stands up and seeks a place higher up from where he can look out over the heads of the pilgrims circling the Kaaba. His tongue has baulked at the prayers, so he will pray with his eyes instead. (*CW* 277)

Trojanow's Burton does not lack linguistic knowledge; instead he lacks the religious faith which would enable him to participate fully in the spoken prayers. And so he seeks 'a place higher up' from which to pray with his eyes. One could argue that in doing so he is behaving like an ethnographer or tourist, preferring observation to direct participation. Praying with the eyes is not the same as praying with the mouth. But in fact most pilgrims climb onto the terrace at some point. Abdellah Hammoudi points out that watching the circumambulation of the Kaaba is a very common practice amongst pilgrims:

---

9   John Zilcosky, *Kafka's Travels: Exoticism, Colonialism, and the Traffic of Writing* (New York/Basingstoke: Palgrave Macmillan, 2003), pp. 54–5.
10   Ilija Trojanow, *Zu den heiligen Quellen des Islam. Als Pilger nach Mekka und Medina* (Munich: Malik/National Geographic, 2009). First published 2004. Henceforth cited as *QI*; Ilija Trojanow, *From Mumbai to Mecca*, tr. Rebecca Morrison (London: Haus, 2007). Henceforth cited as *MM*.

Soon enough, I realized I wasn't the only one watching the spectacle. Other pilgrims, both men and women, came here 'just to see'. [...] They told me that they often came back after evening prayers and went up on the terraces to 'enjoy this extraordinary thing' and observe that 'we're all here.' For the Algerian fellow, this was 'the great thing about Islam,' with all its peoples.[11]

Observing the crowds circling the Kaaba from the terrace is one of the many important stations of the pilgrimage itself. It provides a vision of the umma, the entire global community of Muslims, united in their devotion to God. Towards the end of *Zu den heiligen Quellen*, Trojanow says something similar. In the context of a discussion of Islamic art, the purpose of which, he says, is to facilitate 'einen inneren Sinn' (*QI* 136) ['an inner perception'] (*MM* 171),[12] Trojanow asserts that the sight of the world's Muslims circling the Kaaba is the most beautiful decoration in Islamic culture: 'So kann man die Versammlung der Gläubigen als ein Ornament erfahren, das größte und schönste aller islamischen Ornamente' (*QI* 138) ['the congregation of believers can be perceived as an ornament, the greatest and most beautiful Islamic ornament of all'] (*MM* 173). Further evidence to support this claim is offered by Hammoudi, who attests that the vision of the crowds can give rise to profound emotional reactions:

> The vision had lost none of its bewitching power. I could feel my legs trembling, and Abbas once again started to weep. [...] I recognized the mounting anxiety, the feeling that gripped me at moments of extreme attraction, which I knew was dangerous. Perhaps this was the meaning, forgotten today, of the state of religious awe.[13]

Orthodox Islam prohibits figurative representations, but, as Trojanow points out, the symmetrical beauty of Islamic art can inspire a sense of religious awe which can penetrate and capture people's hearts: 'Die Schönheit ist ein Dieb, der bei uns einbricht, um uns unseren behutsamen,

---

11   Hammoudi, *A Season in Mecca*, p. 152.

12   Trojanow's Burton, too, makes the distinction between external vision and inner sight: 'Nicht das Offensichtliche ist bewegend, sondern die Zeichen, die ein jeder von ihnen mit seinem inneren Auge erkennt' (*DW* 299), 'It's not the outward form that is moving, but the signs each of them recognises with his inner eye' (*CW* 254).

13   Hammoudi, *A Season in Mecca*, pp. 156–7.

kurzsichtigen und engstirnigen Existenz zu berauben' (*QI* 137) ['Beauty is a thief that steals in to relieve us of our cautious, short-sighted and narrow-minded existence'] (*MM* 171).[14] It is therefore clear that visual perception is an important mode of experience for the pilgrims who perform the hajj. They witness the circumambulation of their fellow pilgrims, the beauty of the mosque, and the Kaaba itself. These sights undermine any attempts at detached observation. In this context, seeing can be a legitimate mode of participation, because these sights seem to be capable of challenging even the most resolutely secular gaze.

Der Weltensammler tells the story of three of Burton's most famous exploits: in addition to his pilgrimage to Mecca, these are his activity as a spy in India and his exploration of the sources of the Nile. The Arabian middle section of the novel describes Burton's pilgrimage, performed in the guise of 'Sheikh Mirza Abdullah' who pretends to be a dervish and healer. The two most important intertexts for this part of the novel are Burton's own *Personal Narrative of a Pilgrimage to El-Medinah and Meccah* (1855–1856), and Trojanow's account of his hajj which he undertook in the company of a group of Indian Muslims, *Zu den heiligen Quellen des Islam*. *Der Weltensammler* is, however, considerably more than the sum of its parts. As its preface indicates, the novel is 'eine persönliche Annäherung an ein Geheimnis' ['a personal approach to a secret'], yet the novel stops short of unveiling Burton completely. Instead, it is a highly structured literary work, comprising multiple narrators. In comparison, *Zu den heiligen Quellen des Islam* reads like a preparatory sketch. While the novel does include some material from the earlier travelogue, its treatment of philosophical and religious themes is more refined and considered. *Der Weltensammler* is also more intensely subjective than Burton's own account, notwithstanding Burton called it a *Personal Narrative*. Burton's principal concern is to

---

14   The view of the crowds circling the Kaaba may thus have a similar function to the medieval rose-window in Christian cathedrals, which were also designed to draw hearts closer to God. I am reminded here of Rilke's poem 'Die Fensterrose': 'So griffen einstmals aus dem Dunkelsein/der Kathedralen große Fensterrosen/ein Herz und rissen es in Gott hinein.' Rainer Maria Rilke, *Neue Gedichte* (Frankfurt am Main: Suhrkamp, 1976), p. 30.

transmit geographical, ethnographic, and cultural data. Throughout, he is careful to maintain a posture of scientific objectivity, which is supported by numerous footnotes, maps, appendices, and other scholarly apparatus. As Fawn Brodie points out, compared to that other great British traveller on the Arabian peninsula, T.E. Lawrence, Burton's style is detached: 'where Lawrence wrote a luminous self-portrait that greatly exposed himself, Burton successfully hid himself and exposed the whole Arab world'.[15] Burton's narrative stance in the *Pilgrimage* is ambiguous: whilst he sometimes offers moments of lyrical enthusiasm, the main narrative mode is the detached empirical observation of the ethnographer. Occasionally, he lapses into dismissive, even racist, Orientalist clichés.[16] Throughout he adopts an individualistic rhetoric which owes much to the spirit of the colonial adventurer. For example, he regards desert travel as a trial of manhood: 'What can be more exciting? [...] Man's heart bounds in his breast at the thought of measuring his puny force with nature's might, and of emerging triumphant from the trial. This explains the Arab's proverb, "Voyaging is victory"' (*Pilgrimage* i, 149). Burton's gloss here clearly suggests that what excites him is the thought of conquering new territories. Even the fact that Burton made the pilgrimage disguised as a dervish was unnecessary, since he could have entered Mecca posing as a convert to Islam. The impersonation may have been merely for the benefit of his British audience, who would otherwise have suspected him of having genuinely converted.[17]

The ambiguity of Burton's position was clear to the founding theorist of Orientalism, Edward Said, who explained that 'Burton thought of himself both as a rebel against [...] Victorian moral authority and as a

15 Brodie, *The Devil Drives*, p. 110.
16 By today's standards, some of Burton's comments are certainly racist, for example: 'coldly supercilious as a Turk, energetically avaricious as an Arab' (*Pilgrimage* i, 164) and 'the greedy Arabs' (388). For a discussion of the stark contrast between Burton's 'recurrent expressions of empathy' and 'his sweeping generalizations about Africans as a race', see Dane Kennedy, *The Highly Civilized Man: Richard Burton and the Victorian World* (Cambridge, MA: Harvard University Press, 2005), pp. 151–5.
17 Maya Jasanoff, 'Let in the Djinns', *London Review of Books* (9 March 2006) pp. 34–5, here p. 34.

potential agent of authority in the East.'[18] For Said, even though Burton was incredibly 'knowledgeable about the degree to which human life in society is governed by rules and codes', his prose radiates 'a sense of assertion and domination over the all the complexities of Oriental life.'[19] Thus, according to Said, Burton's idiosyncrasy is undermined by the fact that his writing echoes imperialist ideology which asserted Europe's superiority over the Orient. Burton's language studies were actively encouraged by the army as a means to promotion. And his thirty-year career as a diplomat was anything but counter-cultural. In a recent biography, Dane Kennedy reminds us that Burton was in many ways a product of the establishment against which he occasionally rebelled. Burton's projects involved constant collaboration with fellow Orientalists.

The searching, fragmentary style of Trojanow's *Zu den heiligen Quellen des Islam* is very different to the positivist accumulation of observed detail in Burton's *Pilgrimage*. One of the central themes of Trojanow's memoir is the sociability of Islam, as symbolised in the huge encampment of pilgrims in the valley of Mina:

> In den großen, zentralen Strömungen des Islam gibt es keinen Platz für Eremiten, für Einsiedler, für einen lebenslang weltabgewandten Weg; weder Klöster noch Mönche sind vorgesehen. Wie das Tal von Mina symbolisiert, ist Islam der Versuch, eine soziale Ordnung aufzubauen, indem sich die Gemeinschaft an ein göttliches Gesetz hält und ein spirituell wahrhaftiges Leben inmitten des Gewusels führt, inmitten des Menschen Überschuß. (*QI* 92–3)

> In the central currents of Islam there is no place for hermits, for solitary figures, for a life lived with one's back to the world, neither monasteries nor monks are catered for in an Islamic context. As the valley of Mina symbolises, Islam is the attempt to build up a social order in which the community upholds the word of God and leads a spiritually truthful life in the middle of the throng, among an overflow of people. (*MM* 113)

18   Edward W. Said, *Orientalism* (London: Penguin, 2003), p. 195. First published 1978.
19   *Ibid.*, pp. 195–6.

Trojanow respects Islam for its egalitarianism and for its emphasis on shared religious practices. To a greater extent than Christianity, which teaches love of one's neighbour, Islam enjoins believers to engage in communal solidarity. The Prophet himself was a social reformer, who gave the city of Medina the world's first written constitution and who emphasised the equality of all believers in his farewell sermon. One of Islam's most important values is *adl* (justice). The concept of *adl* implies social justice and the duty to resist all kinds of oppression. In a recent interview, the historian Eric Hobsbawm has drawn attention to Islam's egalitarian character:

> Islam [unlike other religions] does seem to me to have great assets for continuing to expand – largely because it gives poor people the sense that they're as good as anybody else and that all Muslims are equal. [...] a Christian doesn't believe that he's as good as any other Christian. [...] The structure of Islam is more egalitarian and the militant element is rather stronger there. I remember reading that slave-traders in Brazil stopped importing Muslim slaves because they kept rebelling.[20]

The unity of all Muslims is symbolised by Mecca itself, which is both the direction of prayer and the goal of the hajj, which assembles all Muslims in the same place. Trojanow, much like previous hajjis from the West such as Malcolm X,[21] is impressed by the strong feelings of comradeship and fraternity which prevail. In *Zu den heiligen Quellen* he emphasises this communal aspect: 'For the Hajj is not only an individual pilgrimage, it is a communal congregation, an entreaty of the Ummah' [the global community of Muslims] (*QI* 15; *MM* 14).[22] Trojanow too underlines that the social inequalities which exist in most Muslim countries are in stark contrast to the fundamental egalitarianism of Islam itself:

---

20   Eric Hobsbawm, 'Interview – World Distempers', *New Left Review* 61 (2010), pp. 133–50, here p. 145.
21   Malcolm X, *The Autobiography of Malcolm X* (New York: Grove Press, 1966), p. 338.
22   Trojanow also points out that the Haram al-Sharif in Mecca is the only mosque in the world where men and women are not physically separated (*QI* 55; *MM* 63).

Ein jeder verneigt sich vor Gott unmittelbar hinter den Sohlen seiner Mitmenschen, egal wer der Höhergeborene oder der Bessergestellte ist. Die Gleichheit aller Menschen wird im gemeinsamen Gebet angemahnt. Wenn aber ein Prinzip so zentral ist im Ritual, wenn es so kompromißlos inszeniert wird, wie kann es dann außerhalb des Gebets völlig mißachtet werden? (*QI* 55)

Everyone bows down to God directly behind the soles of a fellow human, regardless of who is higher-born or better situated. The equality of all people is emphasised in common prayer. When a principle is so central to ritual, when it is performed with no degree of compromise, how can it then be so totally ignored outside of prayer? (*MM* 62)

Trojanow's insight – that Islam and the striving for democracy are essentially compatible – has been confirmed by the Arab Spring of 2011. Even if in many cases the demands for democratic reform have not yet been met, the events of 2011 showed that is what most people in the Middle East want.

Trojanow's texts are typical of modern accounts of the hajj in so far as they focus mainly on personal impressions. Modern authors tend to emphasise the individual experience of the narrating pilgrim, putting the hajji rather than the hajj centre stage.[23] Their main concern is no longer to supply external information, but to explore the pilgrim's inner experience. This is the case with Abdellah Hammoudi's recent *A Season in Mecca*.[24] Born in Morocco, Hammoudi is now a professor of anthropology at Princeton. His hajj memoir contains a fascinating reflexion on what it means for pilgrims to wear the two white ceremonial cloths known as ihram. For Hammoudi, the state of wearing ihram – and its associated prohibitions – signifies a clear break with one's everyday self and one's everyday life, in favour of a commitment to a path and a narrative which transcends selfhood: 'ihram [...] modifies the limits of bodies and identities. It was

---

23   Barbara D. Metcalf, 'The Pilgrimage Remembered: South Asian Accounts of the Hajj', in Dale F. Eickelman and James Piscatori (eds), *Muslim Travellers: Pilgrimage, Migration and the Religious Imagination* (London/New York: Routledge, 1990), pp. 85–107, here p. 91.

24   Abdellah Hammoudi, *A Season in Mecca: Narrative of a Pilgrimage*, tr. Pascale Ghazaleh (Cambridge: Polity, 2006).

testimony to a condition I didn't comprehend.'[25] Because Hammoudi is a non-practising Muslim and a professional ethnographer, he was forced to question his own motives for travelling to Mecca. The modern narrative of the hajj tends to pose the question of the meaning of the pilgrimage for the individual. Answering it requires the individual to reflect upon his or her expectations and assumptions. This feature is not unique to writing about the hajj, however. Travel writing as a genre allows an individual personality to emerge: 'the formal structure of the travel account [...] makes it particularly appealing to a certain kind of modern personality which prefers not to resolve but to sample and explore'.[26] Travel writing can accommodate reportage, autobiography, anecdote and ethnography. As such, it offers an important mode of reflection about the hajj.

However, the genre of fiction is surely even richer than travel writing, because – as well as mixing genres – it enables a multiplicity of perspectives to coexist simultaneously. Travel writing is inevitably bound to an individual perspective: for example, Burton's account of the hajj, despite its ambivalences, is clearly the product of a dominant personality which lays claim to empirical, objective truth. In contrast to this, *Der Weltensammler* is narrated by a large number of mainly indigenous characters. The use of multiple narrators effectively calls Burton's own truth claims into question.[27] Much of the story is told from the point of view of Burton's servants. This restores the previously marginalised, non-European characters to the centre of Burton's story. The narrative principle of the book is summed up when the Catholic priest who performs the last rites for the dying Burton decides to question the servants about their master's character: 'Wenn er die Diener ausfragte? Diener wissen doch alles' (*DW* 509) ['What if he asked the servants? Servants know everything'] (*CW* 444). What interests me about the Arabian section of *Der Weltensammler*, however, is that it is not narrated by servants. It is narrated by Burton's travelling companions and hence, to

25   *Ibid.*, p. 148.
26   Metcalf, 'The pilgrimage remembered', p. 87.
27   Stephanie Catani, '(Re-)Thinking History: Ilija Trojanows *Der Weltensammler*', *Angermion* 2 (2009), pp. 91–108, here p. 98 and p. 104.

a certain extent, by his equals. Hamid al-Samman becomes Burton's host in Medina; and Saad Al-Dschinni, 'the Demon', is a born traveller like Burton himself. Their interpretations serve to accentuate the ambiguity of Burton's position: on the hajj, Burton was simultaneously taking part and playing a part. The difficulty of interpretation is underlined when the narrative tells us that Burton himself was unsure of his own feelings: 'Aber seine Gefühle wird er nicht verraten. Nicht alle. Zumal, er ist sich seiner Gefühle nicht immer sicher gewesen' (*DW* 351) ['But he won't reveal his feelings, not all of them, especially because he hasn't always been sure of what they are'] (*CW* 300). The fact that the main protagonist is uncertain about his feelings seems to call for the interpretations which the multiple narrators provide. The Arabian section is structured in the form of an official investigation carried out by three different investigators, each one with his own political agenda: the Ottoman satrap who governs the province of Hijaz; the Kadi of Mecca and the Sharif of Mecca. As Trojanow points out in an essay on the narrative procedure used in *Der Weltensammler*, these official interrogators act out the interpretive dilemmas faced by the readers themselves.[28] In doing so, they provide a level of meta-narrative reflexion.

Trojanow's Burton seems to prefer the egalitarianism of Islam to the hierarchies of the British class system and the Hindu caste system. Burton's relationships in the hajj section of the novel may be somewhat idealised, however.[29] Whereas Burton admits that he gave money to his travelling companions in order to buy their friendship (*Pilgrimage* i, 165–6); in *Der Weltensammler*, these financial transactions are barely mentioned. And, whilst the Burton of the *Pilgrimage* is scathing about the avarice of his companions, Trojanow presents these same companions as loyal to Burton when they are interrogated by the Ottomans. In particular, the character of Saad [spelled Sa'ad in Burton's text], the African former slave, acquires

---

28   Ilija Trojanow, 'Komplot(t) – Wie plant der Autor den perfekten Plot', *Wespennest* 149 (November 2007), pp. 6–10, here p. 9.

29   Julian Preece, 'Faking the Hadj? Richard Burton Slips between the Lines in Ilija Trojanow's *Der Weltensammler*', in Preece, Frank Finlay, and Sinéad Crowe (eds), *Religion and Identity in Germany Today: Doubters, Believers, Seekers in Literature and Film* (Oxford: Peter Lang, 2010), pp. 211–26.

a significance in *Der Weltensammler* which he did not have for Burton. For once in Trojanow's novel, Burton encounters someone who is as well-travelled as himself and whose wanderlust is comparable to his own. Saad's principal characteristic is also his love of travel: 'Es was sein erklärtes Ziel, kostenlos zu reisen, und er kam seinem Ideal beachtlich nahe' (*DW* 281) ['It was his avowed aim to travel free and he came pretty close to his ideal'] (*CW* 238). Trojanow's description of Saad is faithful to Burton's account: '[Sa'ad] wandered far and wide, to Russia, to Gibraltar, and to Baghdad. [...] he has resolved, cost what it will, to travel free.' (*Pilgrimage* i, 162). However, Trojanow's narrative tactfully omits the racist elements of Burton's description of Sa'ad: 'He is the pure African [...] unscrupulous to the last degree' (*Pilgrimage* i, 162). Like Burton, too, Trojanow's Saad is a determined practical joker, with a devilish side to his personality, and even a potential for mental instability (think of the monkeys whom Burton invites as house guests in Baroda). In *Der Weltensammler*, these shared qualities serve to motivate a friendship which is far from apparent in Burton's *Pilgrimage*, which focuses on the man's volatile character and his cruelty to Mohammed. Burton's references to Sa'ad are mainly pejorative; he continually uses the epithet 'Sa'ad the Demon', for instance in comments such as 'Sa'ad the Demon was especially vicious' (*Pilgrimage* i, 223). The principal interaction between the pair of travellers in the *Pilgrimage* is financial: Burton forces Sa'ad to repay a debt, which increases Sa'ad's estimation of him (*Pilgrimage* i, 276). This is very different from the relationship portrayed in *Der Weltensammler*. It is almost as if Trojanow has portrayed Burton as he would have wanted him to be – or perhaps projected some of his own experience of the hajj onto Burton's.

The main conversation between Burton and Saad in *Der Weltensammler* takes place in the middle of the night, when the rest of the caravan is asleep. It is Sheikh Abdullah's (i.e. Burton's) turn to keep watch, and, like Burton, Saad has trouble sleeping. Soon the two men realise that they have a shared passion – travelling:

> Wieso so düster, Saad? [...] es drängt micht zum Aufbruch. Ich weiß, sagte Sheikh Abdullah, das Glück des Weges. Ja, der Weg, er ist unersetzbar. Trotz aller Mühsal, er ist es, der mein Herz höher schlagen läßt. Wir sind Reiter zwischen Stationen, es ist unser Schicksal, anzukommen und aufzubrechen. (*DW* 295)

'Why so sombre, Sa'ad?'
'[...] I feel the urge to set off again.'
'I know the happiness of the way,' said Sheikh Abdullah.
'Yes, the way, nothing can take its place. Despite all the tribulations, it is what makes my heart knock louder. We are riders between staging posts; it is our fate to arrive and set off again.' (*CW* 251)

This conversation is structurally important in the novel because it is the only time that Burton encounters another person who truly shares his love of travelling, and who is almost as well-travelled as he is. For the first time, Burton seems to find a man who comprehends him, even if Saad cannot penetrate his disguise. The second high point of their friendship occurs when the two men behold their destination – Medina – for the first time. If we compare the accounts by Burton and Trojanow of this moment when the pilgrims reach their destination, important differences emerge. The sense of comradeship in Burton's text is fleeting: 'It was impossible not to enter into the spirit of my companions, and truly I believe that for some minutes my enthusiasm rose as high as theirs. But presently when we remounted, the traveller returned strong upon me: I made a rough sketch of the town' (*Pilgrimage* i, 280). In Trojanow's version Burton embraces Saad: 'umarmt er Saad heftig, versinkt in den Armen dieses riesigen Mannes und murmelt ehrliche Worte der Dankbarkeit' (*DW* 299) ['he suddenly falls into Sa'ad's arms and hugs this huge man tightly, murmuring words of genuine gratitude'] (*CW* 255). The combination of close physical contact and mumbled words makes this scene one of the emotional high points of the novel. At this point, Trojanow's Burton even seems to be on the verge of making a fervent declaration of Islamic faith (*DW* 299; *CW* 255). After this significant divergence from the Pilgrimage, though, the novel soon returns to Burton's own narrative: the detached, analytical side of Burton's character regains control.

As Burton gets closer to Mecca, he begins to grow tired of his companions. He longs for solitude; even Saad has begun to bore him: 'Auch Saad sucht unterwegs seine Gesellschaft, er hat seine Wortkargheit zugunsten einer unermüdlichen Geschwätzigkeit abgelegt' (*DW* 314) ['Even Sa'ad seeks out his company, his taciturnity superseded by an inexhaustible chattiness'] (*CW* 267). At this point, Burton's interest only becomes aroused when he hears an Egyptian tell the story of the great lakes of East Africa. Burton hurriedly takes notes of everything he hears, in case it should become useful. It is almost as if Burton is planning his next adventure, even before the current one is finished. Here, Trojanow's narrative effectively shows Burton's restlessness, the insatiable curiosity which kept driving him onwards. Even the friendship with Saad is not enough to fix his attention for long: for such a man, it seems that even friendships will be transitory. The parallel between Burton and Saad concludes when Saad is interrogated and tortured by the Ottoman authorities. This parallels Burton's torture by the British in the previous section of the book. It shows that methods of violent coercion are used by both Oriental and Occidental states. However, while Burton stubbornly refuses to talk, Saad tells his interrogators whatever he thinks they want to hear. Burton, it seems, has a force of will which his African counterpart lacks.

Trojanow's Burton does not just collect worlds; he participates in them and moves between them restlessly. In highlighting Burton's mistrust of colonial and religious dogma, and, simultaneously, his experimentation with religion, Trojanow gives us Burton as a postmodern hero, a deracinated nomad who thrives in the space between cultures. Trojanow celebrates Burton's non-conformity, his ability to be at home everywhere, and his talent for improvising a new identity based upon a dialogue with different cultures. And yet Trojanow also shows how Burton is shaped by his contacts with Islam, and by his connections with the imperial authorities who employed him. The novel shows how Burton, never entirely independent, is caught in a web of multiple interests and allegiances. For example, Trojanow describes Burton's cordial relations with General Napier in India and the ailing British consul in Zanzibar, even if it also shows that the Royal Geographical Society chose John Hanning Speke rather than Burton to lead the second Nile expedition. Even nomads are defined to a certain extent by the communities from which they come, and the communities between which they move. Anthropologists know that people are formed through their interactions with other people, socialised and reshaped by the culture(s) in which they participate. As Hammoudi puts it: 'I knew that my being, like all beings, went beyond itself – through the senses, language, dreams, passion, need, desire – the list goes on.'[30] The hajj or pilgrimage is a paradigmatic case of a ritual framework which bonds participants by means of a shared religious experience, and, in doing so, irrevocably alters their identity.[31] The completed pilgrimage marks the transition to a new identity, which is signified by the acquisition of the new epithet hajji.

Did Richard Francis Burton collect worlds, or did worlds collect him? Geographical locations can sometimes 'lay claim' to an individual. Memories of places – secular or sacred – can return to haunt people in the most unexpected contexts. Surely this is the case with Burton in *Der Weltensammler*. Each world Burton passes through – Europe, India, Arabia, Africa – leaves indelible traces upon his consciousness. Trojanow represents Burton at the end of his life reciting a Muslim prayer. But when he contemplates the Kaaba in Mecca, it is the words of his Hindu guru Upanitsche which come back to him: 'Zeige mir die Richtung, in der Gott nicht weilt' (*DW* 320) ['Show me the direction where God is not'] (*CW* 273). This implies that the divine principle can inhabit multiple places, multiple faiths and ideologies. *Der Weltensammler* shows that there is a plurality of marvellous places and, at the same time, it affirms the plurality and hybridity of the individual, embodied in the contradictions of Burton himself. The multiple narrative technique of the novel, which permits contradictory possibilities to coexist, is therefore appropriate to its theme. Indeed, Trojanow clearly respects Burton for his ability to accommodate multiple contradictions within his texts: 'Ich kenne keinen anderen Autor, der so entspannt und unverkrampft die Widersprüche im eignen Text duldet' ['I do not know of any other author who tolerates the contradictions in his own work in such a relaxed way').[32] On the one hand, Burton was a moral relativist who refused to accept fixed doctrines: his epic poem *The Kasidah*

---

30   Hammoudi, *A Season in Mecca*, p. 173.
31   The standard work on ritual is still: Victor Turner, *The Ritual Process: Structure and Anti-Structure* (Hawthorne, NY: de Gruyter, 1995). First published 1969.
32   Ilija Trojanow, *Ein Nomade auf vier Kontinenten. Auf den Spuren von Sir Richard Francis Burton* (Frankfurt am Main: Eichborn, 2007), p. 17.

(1880) declares 'There is no God';[33] 'There is no Good, there is no Bad'.[34] On the other hand, he was always willing to assert his own authority as an Orientalist. On the one hand, he was an adventurer and a self-serving publicist, on the other hand a committed student of other languages and cultures. Perhaps Burton is interesting precisely because of his contradictions and multiple allegiances. He was – for the most part – a loyal servant of the British Empire, employing his linguistic abilities in the service of colonialism. The British government recognised his services and rewarded him with a well-paid position as a consul. And yet Burton often defined himself in terms of his identification with Islamic civilisation. As he once remarked to Frank Harris, 'Arabic is my native tongue [...] I know it as well as I know English.'[35] Perhaps the Kadi's supposition in *Der Weltensammler* is correct: 'Zweifellos hat er auf seiner Reise einiges erlebt, was ihn berührt, was ihn verändert hat. Gewiß hat er die unendliche Gnade Gottes erfahren' (*DW* 349) ['there is no doubt that he will have experienced many things on his journey that will have touched him, and changed him. He will have experienced God's infinite grace'] (*CW* 298). Perhaps, even if Burton was an unbeliever, he was truly touched on his pilgrimage; perhaps he did experience 'Gnade' after all.

33   Burton, *The Kasidah* (1880), reproduced in Trojanow, *Ein Nomade auf vier Kontinenten*, p. 203.

34   *Ibid.*, p. 213. On this point, see Maya Jasanoff, 'Let in the Djinns', [see footnote 13], p. 35: 'In the mock-Oriental epic poem *The Kasidah* (1880), Burton delivered himself of the opinion that "there is no God." And that "there is no Good, there is no Bad." It is hard to get more relativist than that.'

35   Brodie, *The Devil Drives*, p. 329.

EVA M. KNOPP

Letting the Subaltern Laugh – How Humour Works in *Die Welt ist groß und Rettung lauert überall/* The World Is Large and Salvation Lurks Around Every Corner and *Der Weltensammler/* *The Collector of Worlds*

> Jokes occur because society is structured in contradiction; there are no jokes in paradise.[1]

In both his first partly autobiographical novel *Die Welt ist groß und Rettung lauert überall/*The World Is Large and Salvation Lurks Around Every Corner and *Der Weltensammler/The Collector of Worlds* Ilija Trojanow taps into literary traditions of humorous fiction, with its trademark garrulous narrators and trickster figures, as well as ironic and parodying modes of representation. This may be one reason that the novels have proved popular with readers. I will suggest, however, in this essay that Trojanow sets out not only to entertain his readers, but also to subvert cultural hierarchies and to transgress hegemonic discourses of cultural and religious identity. He does this in a number of ways which have a long literary tradition, on various narrative levels, and through a number of perspectives, which is partly why the novels are structurally so complex. Despite the fact that the novels deal with far-from light-hearted issues, such as political oppression

---

1   James F. English, *Comic Transactions. Literature, Humor, and the Politics of Community in Twentieth-Century Britain* (Ithaca, NY/London: Cornell University Press, 1994), p. 9.

and ethnic or religious segregation, Trojanow often presents the tense transcultural encounters humorously. Narrating 'jokers', such as Bai Dan in *Die Welt ist groß und Rettung lauert überall* and Sidi Mubarak Bombay in *Der Weltensammler*, have a mainly subaltern social status and can be understood as trickster figures who question power structures.[2]

Comedy can be used to disclose incongruities within a given society by playing with and thus transgressing norms and conventions.[3] We may consider something funny because it defies our expectations or undermines the dominant social norms and values. Comic transactions can also be powerful social 'in- and out-grouping' mechanisms and a means of constructing individual subjectivity and collective identities. We may laugh at people in order to deride them and deny them their positions or we may laugh with someone else about a third party in order to bond with him or her and thereby affirm a shared identity. Depending on the viewpoint of the narrator in a novel, the results can either transgress or affirm hegemonic discourses: '[L]aughter is always caught up in the kinds of distinction between centre and margins every society employs to establish and stabilise its identity.'[4] What makes this conceptualisation of humour and laughter even more fitting for the portrayal of power hierarchies in transcultural settings is that 'funniness involves at once [...] transgressing *and* recognising the rules.'[5] In order to mock the norms of a certain class, culture, or religion, we need to understand and distance ourselves from them at the same time.

---

2   Ilija Trojanow, *Die Welt ist groß und Rettung lauert überall* (Munich: Deutscher Taschenbuch Verlag, 1999). Cited as *Die Welt*. Ilija Trojanow, *Der Weltensammler* (Munich: Deutscher Taschenbuch Verlag, 2007). Cited as *DW*.

3   For an overview of recent cultural theories of humour and its textual and political functions, see Stefan Horlacher, 'A Short Introduction to Theories of Humour, the Comic and Laughter,' in Gaby Pailer, Andreas Böhn, Stefan Horlacher and Ulrich Scheck (eds), *Gender and Laughter. Comic Affirmation and Subversion in Traditional and Modern Media* (Amsterdam/New York: Rodopi, 2009), pp. 18–42.

4   Cf. Manfred Pfister, 'Introduction: A History of English Laughter?', in Pfister (ed.), *A History of English Laughter. Laugher from Beowulf to Beckett and Beyond* (Amsterdam/New York: Rodopi, 2002), vi.

5   Susan Purdie, *Comedy. The Mastery of Discourse* (Hemel Hempstead: Harvester Wheatsheaf, 1993), p. 3.

Trojanow's novels promote flexibility of perspective on political, cultural and religious identity. His technique of juxtaposing different narrative perspectives creates comic situations that reveal cultural inconsistencies, double standards, and injustice. His humour often depends on trickster figures who are part of the marginalised, subaltern social groups.[6] By making them versatile jokers, who can play by the rules and simultaneously transgress them, Trojanow gives the subaltern a voice and, thus, a measure of authority. On the other hand, Richard Burton's fate in *Der Weltensammler* demonstrates the limitations of such play with norms and values, as his endless deferral of identity and the concomitant indeterminacy of perspective leave him an unhappy loner.

In *Die Welt* an authorial, extra-diegetic, and omniscient narrator alternates with the central character Alexandar Luxow who narrates in the first-person and various other third-person focalisers. The narrative is thus unstable, its centre of gravity ever shifting. At times the changes occur so gradually that the reader has difficulty in determining the narrative voice. In *Der Weltensammler* typographical signposts help the reader to follow the frequently alternating narrative perspectives more easily. The novel's multiplicity of voices has been identified as one of the author's main poetological principles.[7] In the first part of *Die Welt* the omniscient narrator's preference for digression is reminiscent of Lawrence Sterne's

6   In this essay I am referring to Antonio Gramsci, who coined the term 'subaltern' to refer to 'those groups in society who are subject to the hegemony of the ruling classes' (Bill Ashcroft, Gareth Griffiths and Helen Tiffin, *Post-Colonial Studies. The Key Concepts* (New York/London: Routledge, 2000), p. 215) and Gayatri Spivak's transposition of the concept to the postcolonial context. She questions whether subaltern groups of society will actually be able to develop an alternative perspective and voice for themselves that is not dependent on the dominant discourse of the colonial ruler (cf. Gayatri Spivak, 'Can the Subaltern speak?', in Cary Nelson and Lawrence Grossberg (eds), *Marxism and the Interpretation of Culture* (Basingstoke: Macmillan, 1988), pp. 271–313).

7   Michaela Haberkorn, 'Treibeis und Weltensammler: Konzepte nomadischer Identität in den Romanen von Libuse Monikova und Ilija Trojanow', in Helmut Schmitz (ed.), *Von der Transnationalen zur Internationalen Literatur* (Amsterdam/New York: Rodopi, 2009), pp. 256–7.

The Life and Opinions of Tristram Shandy, Gentleman (1759–1767), often regarded as the prototype of the English comic novel. Trojanow's first novel oscillates between the classic pattern of the coming-of-age story (or *Bildungsroman* in the German tradition) and a parody of it, just as *Tristam Shandy* does. Magic realist moments, garrulous digressions and an a-chronological sequence of narration disrupt classic patterns of origin. Through the happy ending, however, the novel conforms ultimately to traditional patterns when portraying the hero's re-education and revitalisation with the help of his godfather Bai Dan.

The first-person narrator, who – as it soon turns out – is none other than Bai Dan himself,[8] is not immediately involved in the story. He has a wider and more distanced perspective in comparison with the other characters. This creates an ironic distance between narration and plot that, for Henri Bergson, is a prerequisite for ridicule and laughter[9] and in many instances can be considered a strategy to 'stand back from our pain, rationality, seriousness and fear'.[10] At one such point the pomposity of the Bulgarian communist state authorities is ridiculed. The account of the president's death starts out with a sarcastic fairy-tale parody: 'Eines Tages starb der greise König, und alle waren sehr traurig und weinten' ['One day the aged king died and everyone was sad and cried'] (*Die Welt* 59), and ends with the slap-stick account of how the burial is sabotaged by a flood that washes away corpse and coffin. The pompous fairy-tale diction here serves as an alienation device to distance the reader from this politically unsettling situation and – as we soon find out – helps us to understand that the official discourse contradicts the true feelings of the Bulgarians suffering under the regime, such as the Luxow family.

---

8   Cf. 'Schon wieder ist es passiert: Man hat uns nicht vorgestellt! Erlauben Sie, man nennt mich Bai Dan' ['It has happened once again. We have not been introduced. Allow me: they call me Bai Dan'] (*Die Welt* 18).

9   Cf. Henri Bergson, *Das Lachen. Ein Essay über die Bedeutung des Komischen*, tr. Roswith Plancherei-Walter (Darmstadt: Luchterhand, 1998), p. 15. First published in French in 1900.

10   Paul Lewis, *Comic Effects: Interdisciplinary Approaches to Humor in Literature* (New York: State University of New York Press, 1989), p. 21.

The authorial or omniscient narrative is also used to point out dramatic ironies in the plot. At times this is done in meta-narrative digressions that underline the stories' fictionality, which is a hallmark strategy of magic realism. One such moment is the episode when Jana, Vasko, and Alexandar try to cross the Iron Curtain in the form of a border-wall between Yugoslavia and Italy. Surprised by a patrol, Vasko throws Alexandar over the wall before helping Jana and himself to scale it. At exactly this moment, the narrator stops and annihilates the illusion of realism with a humorous digression. He describes in slow-motion Alex's literal flight into a hay-cart which happens to be passing by at just that moment and takes the opportunity to juxtapose Eastern and Western perspectives on this event. Whereas the flight is a dangerous but life-changing event for the Luxow family, it is merely its curiousness that raises attention among the local Italians on the other side. To them illegal border traffic is merely a bothersome everyday experience: 'Es ist ein Fluch mit dieser Grenze. [...] Man muß damit leben, was soll man machen?' ['This border is a curse [...] We have to live with it, what can we do?'] (*Die Welt* 84). However, the fact that this child seems to have fallen from the sky like an angel makes his arrival worth mentioning: 'jetzt fliehen bei denen schon die Engel' ['now even angels over there are running away']. Later on in the story, the discrepant relevance of the border for the Eastern refugees and the Western locals is underlined when we find out that due to pure ignorance the family tried to cross at the only point in the whole area where it is actually protected by a wall and guarded by a patrol.

Similarly, Trojanow uses the authorial narrator to laugh away the unbearable circumstances which refugees in Western Europe endure. When Alexandar and his parents arrive in the Italian refugee camp of Pelferino, the narrator compares the unmanageability of masses of Eastern European refugees during the holiday-season with Western European traffic congestion during the same period: 'Auch die Flucht kennt Hochsaison: Sommer, wenn Ungezählte durch die Ferien strömen. Im Westen mehr Staus, im Osten mehr Schlangen' ['Even running away has its high season: in summer the crowds flowing through the holidays are countless. In the west there are traffic jams, in the East, queues'] (*Die Welt* 102). The fall of the Iron Curtain, however, has not improved the situation for the refugees. Through Bai Dan's

eyes, we watch a mock-television game show 'ASYLANTENROULETTE
[...] den Wettstreit der Flüchtlinge um Asyl in der EG' ['ROULETTE
FOR ASYLUM SEEKERS [...] refugees compete for asylum in the EEC']
(206), where the non-European contestants answer ridiculous questions or
fulfil pointless tasks, such as pronouncing the word for imperial Germany's
ruling family: 'Nahaufnahme Rajith Bipitham. Er versucht zum siebten
Mal das Wort *Hohenzollern* auszusprechen. Seine Zunge weigert sich, die
Klasse lacht. [...] Wie wollt ihr denn nach Europa kommen, wenn ihr nicht
einmal *Hohenzollern* aussprechen könnt' ['Close up on Rajith Bipitham.
He tries for the seventh time to pronounce the word *Hohenzollern*. His
tongue refuses, the class laughs [...] How can you want to come to Europe
if you cannot even pronounce the word *Hohenzollern*'] (207–8). The con-
testant is humiliated and fails to earn German citizenship.

In *Der Weltensammler* Trojanow generates humour by juxtaposing
different narrative perspectives. In the first part of the novel he intercuts
third-person narration through Burton's own eyes with the narrative of his
naive Indian servant and confidant, Naukaram. The illiterate servant has
fallen out of favour with his master and hopes that the composition of a
letter of reference by a professional writer – the Lahiya – will support his
search for new employment. Most episodes are presented both through
Burton's and Naukaram's eyes and the incongruities between their two
perspectives, one the domineering, yet inquisitive foreign master, the other
the naive, yet culturally knowledgeable servant, expose many of the ironies in British colonial rule in India. As an additional perspective, the sly
Lahiya or scribe ridicules Naukaram's futile undertaking and questions
the authority of the narrative undertaking as a whole. We witness a sheer
endless, at times rather amusing, battle of wills between Naukaram and the
Lahiya concerning the nature of their project. Naukaram has instructed
him to write up an account of his true work and devotion to his master
that will put right Burton's own worthless reference that merely certifies
the dates of his employment. The Lahiya becomes interested in the story
for its own sake and loses sight of the original purpose of the endeavour.
He postpones the letter's completion until Naukaram is heavily in debt
to him, which means that he loses money on the commission. The Lahiya
freely interprets Naukaram's account to fit his own fabrication of a romantic

story of a love-triangle between Burton, Naukaram, and their shared mistress Kundalini. 'So muß es gewesen sein, in etwa. Der Lahiya war sehr zufrieden. Das ist wahre Gewissenhaftigkeit, dachte er, die Geschichte zur Wahrheit zu verfälschen' ['That is how it must have been, more or less. The Lahiya was quite satisfied. That shows true conscientiousness, he thought, falsifying the story to make it true'] (*DW* 140).

It is the last section of *Der Weltensammler* that presents the most outright humour by means of contrasting perspectives. The account of Burton and Speke's exploration of Eastern Africa in search of the source of the Nile alternates between third-person narration, mostly focalised through Burton, and the retrospective account of Sidi Mubarak Bombay. Bombay's light-hearted, exaggerated counter-narrative points out 'wie lächerlich die Wazungu sein können' ['how ridiculous the Wazungu [i.e. the Whites] can be'] (*DW* 398). Bombay acquires, however, more and more authority, whereas Burton's voice fades more and more. However, Trojanow does not grant Bombay unchallenged authority over the story. From time to time, his bragging is affectionately lampooned by his wife: 'Spuckst du wieder große Töne, du alter Schwadroneur. Trägst du wieder mal dick auf? [...] Wenn du irgendwann in deinem Leben auf etwas anderes achten würdest, als auf deine eigenen Geschichten' ['Are you making out you were so important, you old show-off. Are you laying it on with a trowel again? [...] If only you would think about something else in your life than your stories'] (*DW* 394–5). In this way Bombay's already subaltern voice is ridiculed by an even further marginalised member of society, the African woman, whose perspective has been virtually ignored in most accounts of the great race of African exploration. At the end of the chapter, it is this couple's jovial and simultaneously self-ironic attitude which wins through and demonstrates the reconciliatory powers of humour. After having lampooned each other for some time, they enjoy a reconciliatory meal and make love: 'Es bedarf einiger Anstrengung, dieser Tage, aber danach empfinden sie noch immer Glück' ['Nowadays, they need to exert themselves to do it but afterwards they still always feel happy'] (*DW* 505).

Bai Dan and Sidi Mubarak Bombay are both also comic characters in their own stories. Despite apparent differences, they share a number of characteristics and narrative functions with the transcultural trickster figure, as

Burton does too. The trickster has been identified in contemporary Native American literature as 'a marginal figure, a mediator who breaks down any hard distinctions,'[11] whose 'medium is words. A parodist, joker, liar, con-artist, and storyteller, he fabricates believable illusions with words – and thus becomes the embodiment of a fluid, flexible, and politically radical narrative form.'[12] Trojanow's tricksters emphasise humour's subversive powers under oppressive systems. This goes for a number of the political refugees in Pelferino, who are persecuted for their comic transgressions, as the fate of Iwailo demonstrates: '[Er] saß im Gefängnis, weil er Witze erzählt hat. Die mögen sowas nicht.' ['he was in jail because he told jokes. They don't like that sort of thing'] (*Die Welt* 129). Bai Dan too is margin-alised for deriding authority in his native Bulgaria. As a young man he is expelled from the Christian Orthodox seminary for the blasphemous act of writing satirical 'Thesen zur Nichtexistenz GOTTES' ['Theses on the non-existence of GOD'] and subsequently leads a life on the edge: 'Du machst hier mal was, dort mal was, treibst dich mal im Ausland herum, und sitzt mal im Gefängnis' ['You do a bit of this or that in one place and a bit of this or that in another place, mess about abroad, and then spend time in jail'] (54). Bai Dan himself does not consider his resistance to comply as problematic and – in a witty aside – extends Alex's christening oath to ensure that his godson will inherit this scepticism from him: '*vertreibe aus ihm Dummheit und Ignoranz, die ihm andere eingeben*' ['drive stupidity and ignorance which he will get from others out of him'] (57).

The same comic verbal versatility that marginalised those tricksters also saves them in precarious situations from persecution. The same anti-communist jokes that brought Iwailo into trouble in the first place, finally facilitate his escape from the Serbian border police to the West: '[I]ch hab ihnen einige Witze erzählt, Stalin- und Chruschtschowwitze, die kamen bombig bei denen an, die Stimmung wurde immer besser, war kein Problem,

---

11   Kimberly M. Blaeser, 'Trickster: A Compendium', in Mark Lindquist and Martin Zanger (eds), *Buried Roots and Indestructible Seeds: The Survival of American Indian Life in Story, History and* Spirit (Madison: University of Wisconsin Press, 1995), p. 51.
12   Smith, Jeanne Rosier Smith, *Writing Tricksters: Mythic Gambols in American Ethnic Literature* (Berkeley: University of California Press, 1997), p. 11.

aufs Klo zu gehen, alleine, hab dort das Fenster aufgemacht und bin rauf-
geklettert, aufs Dach' ['I told them some jokes, Stalin and Khrushchev jokes,
which they thought were brilliant, the atmosphere got better and better, it
was no problem to go to the toilet, by himself, I opened the window and
climbed up on to the roof'] (*Die Welt* 129). Trojanow's tricksters' verbal
power helps them to find solutions out of hopeless situations. When Bai
Dan arrives in Germany to find his godson, his charm helps him to track
him down. In the end his talent teases Alex out of the deep depression he
has been experiencing since his parents' death.

Trojanow's tricksters, like their Native American counterparts, occupy
positions between worlds and their knowledge of more than one language
makes them mediators between cultures. In *Die Welt* we get the impression
that it is actually the translators and not the managers, who best understand how things work in the Italian refugee camp. Bogdan's translations
and intercultural explanations not only help the Luxow family endure the
hardships in Pelferino, he also makes them aware of their rights as asylum
seekers and advises them to take matters into their own hands and escape
the camp for Germany. This liminal position endows Trojanow's tricksters
with a wider perspective that enables them to reveal discrepancies and
absurdities in their societies. As he knows the local language and customs,
Burton whiles away his time by disguising himself as a native Indian in
front of his fellow officers. He thus mocks his fellow officers' ignorance
of the native Indians, as Naukaram recalls to the Lahiya:

> Er machte sich einen Scherz daraus, vor der Regimentsmesse herumzulungern und
> die anderen Offiziere anzubetteln. Wenn sie ihn wegscheuchten, richtete er seine
> empörte Stimme zum Himmel und beschwerte sich im reinsten Englisch über die
> Herzlosigkeit seiner Landsleute. (*DW* 101)

> He made a joke out of hanging around in front of the regimental mess and begging.
> When the officers chased him off, he raised his voice to the sky in anger and com-
> plained in the purest English about the heartlessness of his compatriots.

Burton also mocks the cultures he encounters on his journeys. As a pilgrim
on the hajj he displays the same distance towards Islamic regulations and
rituals. Trojanow also shows tricksters like Burton or Sidi Mubarak Bombay

using their multilingualism to fool their adversaries. While Burton picks up languages in order to entertain himself by fooling his fellow British officers, Bombay plays a formidable linguistic trick on Speke. After he has become aware of the fact that the British explorers enquire the native names of geographical features but tend to disregard them and replace them with English ones, such as 'Lake Victoria' instead of the original 'Nyanza', he and his companions decide to take revenge by making up obscene names for features in the landscape, which mockingly throw back the imperialists' understanding of African culture in the faces of the British. Yet Sidi Mubarak Bombay is realistic enough to know that his joke exerts only temporary ridiculing powers. He knows that European exploration and subsequent exploitation of the African continent is an irreversible fact. Humour may temporarily transgress traditional power-relations, but is not guaranteed to have a long-term effect on the incongruities it exposes.

Along with their verbal playfulness, Trojanow's tricksters enjoy masquerade and demonstrate playfulness in assuming various identities without losing their sense of self. Bai Dan is the perfect example of such a *homo ludens*.[13] To him games are figurative for dealing with life in general. He cheers up Alex by playing backgammon with him. He is also a virtuoso gambler who does not believe in fortune, but only in skill and positive thinking. He demonstrates the same confidence and playfulness when it comes to describing his multi-facetted, ever-changing identity. He is happy to redefine himself according to what the circumstances require without losing his sense of purpose. This tolerance of ambiguity helps him when dealing with the German border control: 'Um gewisse Hürden zu überwinden, muß man Mißverständnisse zulassen' ['In order to get over certain barriers, you have to permit some misunderstandings'] (*Die Welt*, 181).

Through Burton and Bombay, *Der Weltensammler* compares and contrasts two trickster figures who playfully handle their cultural and religious identities. Throughout the novel, Burton is portrayed as a jack of all trades, who learns languages and changes identities like clothes. He enjoys pretending to be a native Hindu, a Muslim Pakistani, a Persian sufi

---

13   Cf. Horlacher, 'A Short Introduction', p. 23.

and doctor and consequently makes use of this talent to serve a number of purposes: to fool his fellow officers in India, to spy on behalf of the British army in the Sindh, to earn money and esteem as a Persian doctor, or to be accepted as a proper Muslim in order to perform the hajj. Even if many of his deceptions are the cause for humorous episodes, they also evoke discomfort about the unscrupulousness Burton exhibits. Naukaram expresses this unease early in the narrative:

> Es war ein Spiel, gewiß. Aber es war mehr als das. [...] Er steigerte sich hinein. Bald bildete er sich ein, er könne denken, sehen, fühlen, wie einer von uns [...]. Ich war keineswegs überzeugt, im Gegensatz zu ihm, daß man seine Rolle im Leben wechseln kann.' (*DW* 101–2)

> It was a game, certainly. But it was more than that. [...] He grew into it. Soon he imagined that he could think, see, feel, like one of us. [...] In contrast to him, I was by no means convinced that you can change your role in life.

At the end of the novel, we tend to agree with Naukaram. Burton's trickster existence seems to have been mostly a strategy to attain the status of a famous explorer for the British Empire, but when this goal vanishes beyond his reach, he will not stand for any nonsense. It turns out that his masquerading has estranged Burton too much from himself. His non-conformist handling of cultural differences and his assuming and discarding of cultural identities as if they were clothes has failed to win or keep him friends, either in colonialist British society or the Indian, Arabian, and African societies which he explores. In the end it will be Speke, whose simplemindedness Burton constantly lampooned during their trip, who receives all the plaudits for their joint expedition. This leaves Burton full of self-pity. It is here that the reader realises that unlike other tricksters in the novel, Burton has difficulties in applying ironic distance to his own person and fate, despite the fact that he so admires this capacity in others and expects it of them when he comically exposes their peculiarities.

In this respect, Sidi Mubarak Bombay represents the positive counterpart to Burton. He also uses his playful attitude to lampoon the colonialist 'Other'. However, he does not undermine his own manifold cultural identities, even if his experiences as a subject of various colonial regimes and cultures have made him suspicious of any religious or cultural essentialism. He does not masquerade as someone else, but instead conceives himself as multi-facetted.[14] Furthermore, he displays the same self-ironic attitude that Burton admires in his Indian teacher Upanitsche. When he argues with his wife, he takes her degrading lampoons in good part: 'Einmal, [...] traute sie sich, ihn auf seine Körpergröße anzusprechen. Er lachte. Dafür bin ich stark und nicht so leicht umzuwerfen. Ich bin ruhelos, aber nicht zu entwurzeln' ['Once [...] she dared to mention his physical size to him. He laughed. That's what makes me strong and not so easy to knock over. I am restless but you cannot uproot me'] (*DW* 505). In contrast to Burton, Sidi's trickster existence allows him to '*bend rather than break*'.[15]

I have tried to show how humour and ironic distance in Trojanow's two novels are a means to establish self-determination against socio-cultural prescriptions and dominant discourse. Particularly his narrating tricksters Bai Dan and Sidi Mubarak Bombay, who are shown as positive role models, are influential political and cultural commentators and act to determine their own fates. From the margins of society, they shape their own identity by exposing authority and/or re-inscribing themselves into discourses of power through linguistic versatility or by playing games. That way they handle the complexities of communal and individual identities, while keeping their agency by appropriating language and humour to serve their own purposes. Yet Trojanow also shows that humour and masquerading only work at certain points in time to make hardship bearable or to expose the ironies, inequalities, and absurdities of cultural norms. Comic disclosure does not automatically result in their disappearing. Letting the subaltern laugh does not also necessarily result in the long-term change of power hierarchies. In order for this to happen, deeds will have to follow the comic words.

14   See Haberkorn, 'Treibeis und Weltensammler', p. 259.
15   Lewis, *Comic Effects*, p. 21 (his italics).

JULIAN PREECE

Mr Iceberger Runs Amok: The Aporias of Commitment in *EisTau*/Melting Ice

> Ich bin immer wieder entsetzt, wenn ich gefragt werde, ob ich denn Literatur für ein Instrument der Aufklärung erachte. Ja, was denn sonst? Der Fernseher etwa? Literatur muss gegenwärtig sein in dem Sinne, dass sie den Irrsinn der eigenen Epoche spiegelt und zu überwinden trachtet. Ansonsten gilt immer noch: Die Hoffnung liegt in dem Aufbruch des Einzelnen aus seiner selbstverschuldeten Unmündigkeit.[1]

> I am always horrified when I am asked whether I consider literature to be an instrument of the enlightenment. Yes, I do. What else is there? Television? Hardly. Literature has to be contemporary in the sense that it reflects the folly of its own epoch and tries to overcome it. Apart from that, I still maintain that hope lies in the liberation of the individual from his or her own self-imposed immaturity.

Ilija Trojanow, so much should be obvious by this stage of this book, has always been attracted by the big topics. His second novel *Autopol* (1997) was, as Cornelius Partsch argues in his essay, about the skewed relations between the citizen and the contemporary state. His account of his return visits to post-communist Bulgaria in *Hundezeiten*/Dog Times is an angry indictment of the corrupt elite's retention of power after the simulated revolution of 1989. After addressing the anti-Islamic fall-out from the '9/11' attacks on New York in a series of public interventions through the 2000s, Trojanow turned his sights once again on the state's increasing

---

[1]   Ilija Trojanow in conversation with Stefan Gmünder, 'Vor der Katastrophe', *Der Standard (Album)* (27 August 2011).

disregard for its citizens in a pamphlet written jointly with the novelist Juli Zeh, *Angriff auf die Freiheit: Sicherheitswahn, Überwachungsstaat und der Abbau bürgerlicher Rechte*/Attack on Freedom: Security Mania, the Surveillance State and the Demolition of Citizen Rights.[2] Zeh (b. 1974) has been credited with reviving the modern tradition of writers' political commitment, which flourished in the Federal Republic in the second half of the 1960s and early 1970s but has been deemed pretty much *démodé* since then.[3] Like Zeh, Trojanow is in many ways an old-fashioned committed writer who wants to change the world – or at least the ways that we think about it.

By the year 2011, climate change had been a major topic of discussion for a number of years. It was the source of public scandals and political controversy, as well as the subject of a welter of books. Some of these were campaigning tracts, others debunking conspiracy theories, but there were also novels, television series, and films. None reached a bigger audience than Davis Guggenheim's insistently haunting documentary *An Inconvenient Truth* (2006) on the subject of former American vice-president Al Gore's efforts to inform his fellow citizens about what was happening.[4]

Climate change is also the subject of Trojanow's fourth novel, *EisTau*/ Ice Thaw, which was published in August 2011 after some three years of research and writing. This short novel is set in the present on a cruise ship which sails from the southern tip of Argentina past such evocatively named landmarks as Mount Misery, Fury Island, and Last Hope Bay, with stopoffs on the Falklands, King George Island, and South Georgia. Its central character and principle narrator is a former academic glaciologist called Zeno Hintermeier alias 'Mr Iceberger', recently promoted from on-board lecturer to expedition leader on board the *MS Hansen*. He is passionate about ice to the point of obsession and cannot accept that there should be

---

2   Munich: Deutscher Taschenbuch Verlag, 2010.

3   See Stephen Brockmann, 'Juli Zeh, *Spieltrieb*: Contemporary Nihilism', in Lyn Marven and Stuart Taberner (eds), *Emerging German-Language Novelists of the Twenty-First Century* (Rochester, NY: Camden House, 2011), pp. 62–74, esp. p. 62.

4   *An Inconvenient Truth* (dir. David Guggenheim, 2006, USA). For a critical point of view, see also Bjørn Lomborg, *Cool It: The Skeptical Environmentalist's Guide to Global Warming* (New York: Knopf, 2007).

less of it in the world. He abandoned his professorship in despair once the Alpine glacier he had observed, explored, and monitored for more than forty years melted completely away. He is attracted now to the Antarctic because it still has plenty of ice; only on the peninsula which sticks out northwards from the continental land mass is it beginning to diminish.

One of the first questions for a contemporary novelist writing about climate change may be this: what can he or she say about the topic in a work of fiction that has not been said already? If a novelist wants his readers to change their habits, as Zeno Hintermeier wants people to change theirs, what can he tell them to do in a work of literary fiction that they are not regularly told by writers or broadcasters in other media? A novelist can give abstract facts a human shape by showing how they affect the ways his invented characters lead their lives, but even that has surely been tried many times by others, at least in other media. Posing this question, of course, assumes that the initial response to *EisTau* was correct and that the novel is designed to be read as an intervention which changes behaviour. Reviewers in Germany and Austria were certainly inclined to see it in this way. Some criticised Trojanow for the usual failings of didactic literature or *agitprop* by saying that he was lecturing his readers and that his message was too obvious and got in the way of a narrative that would be exciting if it were not encumbered with so much extraneous ballast.

Trojanow acknowledged that his ability to exert influence on events, policy, or patterns of individual behaviour was limited, but he presented *EisTau* in advance of publication as just such a public intervention. In an interview with Vienna's leading daily *Der Standard* he sounded every bit as impassioned and despairing as his central character. In a lecture delivered in English to a Dutch audience the previous year, he recalled his own research voyage on a Norwegian cruise ship to the southern oceans:

> 'If the Antarctic goes, the human race will go with it', declared an unidentified source in the ship's planner. I realized that, if it was to succeed, my novel had to convince readers to take this sentence literally and to identify with the glaciologist's radical zeal (or delusion, whichever you will). Ideally the readers should see themselves and their destructive potential differently after reading my novel. Such ambition![5]

5   Conversation with Stefan Gmünder, 'Vor der Katastrophe'.

Speaking as a fellow campaigner, Trojanow calls Zeno's implacability 'radical zeal'; speaking perhaps as a novelist, he concedes that this zeal may be a 'delusion'. He ends the lecture with a more modest rhetorical question: 'What can literature do except describe someone who resists?'[6] Through his final desperate action when he hijacks the empty ship, Zeno is arguably a resister. Because it is designed to draw attention to the problem of melting ice, his action could be called 'propaganda by deed'. That would make the novel itself a kind of manifesto for the deed because it accounts for Zeno's motivation, mostly in the first-person. According to the narrative conceit, Zeno's leather bound notebook which is discovered on the abandoned ship after he has jumped into the ocean constitutes ninety per cent of *EisTau*'s narrative. The rest is mainly made up of interludes of prose collage, snippets of advertising jingles and everyday speech which are interspersed with snatches of news reports of the ship's hijacking or conversations between survivors or investigators. These sections present the context in which his action has taken place and demonstrate reactions to it. In the performances of *EisTau*, in which Trojanow played the role of narrator, reciting his own novel by heart, and was accompanied by three musicians, these sections were pre-recorded and played back to the audience as snatches of speech from a series of random radio programmes, sounding as if they had been picked up by a listener slowly turning a radio dial. The dramatic effect was arguably greater than that experienced by a reader, who is likely at first to be confused. Not all the phrases sound as if they have been broadcast: some are downright obscene and sound like notices from the brothels that Zeno frequented. One reviewer thought they were 'noise pollution'.[7] Whether from paper or broadcast sources, however, the snippets of speech represent a contemporary cacophony.

For Zeno the relationship between man and glacier is erotic, personal, emotional, and – so Zeno had understood – for the long term. He behaves

6   'Requiem for the Future. Writing a Novel about Catastrophic Climate Change', lecture delivered in Groningen <http://www.vanderleeuwlezing.nl/sites/default/files/LectureTrojanow.pdf> accessed 30 August 2012. The German version 'Requiem auf die Zukunft' was published in *Der Standard (Album)* (26 November 2010).
7   Rüdenauer, 'Der Weltbesserwisser'.

as lover, husband, and doctor to the ice, which is his mistress, wife, and patient. Others, in contrast, have violent intentions towards the object of his love which remind him of rape. The first iceberg that the expedition encounters is described as showing 'ovale Öffnungen' which he sees as 'gewaltige Vulven' ['oval-shaped openings like huge vulvas).[8] Zeno appears always to have felt in this way. His relationship with his Alpine glacier was like 'eine arrangierte Ehe, die sich über die Jahre in Leidenschaft verwandelte, als sei jede Messung eine Bestätigung seiner Einzigartigkeit' ['like an arranged marriage, which over the years turned into a passion, as if each time I took a measurement it confirmed the glacier's uniqueness'] (*ET* 51). His PhD supervisor (in German, *Doktorvater*) acted as the intermediary or marriage broker between research student and the material of his scientific enquiry. As the German word for glacier ('Gletscher') is masculine, Zeno's passion acquires homoerotic overtones.

> Ich tastete ihn jedesmal aufs neue ab, mit meinen Augen, mit meinen Füßen. Bei jedem Innehalten berührte ich ihn, legte meine Hände an seine Flanken und strich mir dann mit den Händen über das Gesicht. Sein eisiger Atem, seine belebende Kälte. Vertraut war mir ein jedes seiner Geräusche, das Knarzen und das Scheppern, das Krachen und das Platzen, jeder Gletscher hat eine eigene Stimme, wenn ich zu anderen Gletschern reise, verglich ich das Hörbild des unbekannten mit dem mir vertrauten. (*ET* 51)

> I felt up and down [him] afresh each time, with my eyes, with my feet. Every time that I paused I touched [him], I laid my hands on [his] flanks and then ran my hands down my face. [His] icy breath, [his] invigorating coldness. I was familiar with [his] sounds, [his] groans and rattles, [his] roars and explosions, every glacier has [his] own voice and whenever I travelled to other glaciers I compared the sounds which they made with those which were familiar to me.

When the glacier 'falls ill', its noises change as the melt water flows to underground lakes, hollowing out the structure from the inside. When the glacier disappears, Zeno grieves.

---

8   Ilija Trojanow, *EisTau* (Munich/Vienna: Hanser, 2011), p. 65. Cited as *ET*.

Zeno's more conventional erotic relationships take second place. He also has no sympathy for the human victims of apparently man-made disasters in the natural world. His wife Helene used to put up with his crockery-smashing fits of temper but left him for good after he whooped with excitement at television reports of a massive avalanche in a faraway country which swallowed up an entire village. Helene's compulsive clothes buying may in his eyes be a symptom of out-of-control consumerism but it may also be a sign of the same melancholy which afflicts him. After her departure and the breakup of their marriage come the succession of whores whom Zeno encounters on his brothel visits and finally on the *MS Hansen* the young Philippino waitress Paulina. Zeno is capable of friendship, a man called Hölbl, who never appears in person, plays an influential role in his life, and he enjoys the respect of his fellow lecturers on the cruise ship, but when it comes to humanity in general, especially western humanity, he is a self-confessed misanthrope. In the message that he leaves after his jump into the southern ocean, he says that he has had enough of being human. The loss of the ice may be also a metaphor for the passing of the good or true world. Zeno is nostalgic because there used to be more beauty on earth, but he is also conflicted in numerous interlocking ways and lives inside a set of morally painful contradictions, which I aim to explore in this chapter. Zeno's troubled self-awareness makes him the novel's hero.

One problem is that nothing that Zeno is doing by working on board the *MS Hansen* is reducing the rate of the ice's disappearance. On the contrary, transporting wealthy passengers to view the frozen wonders of Antarctica is an element of the problem that he wishes to combat. The elderly barkeeper in the southern Patagonian port of Ushuaia, where the ship sets sail and *EisTau* begins, loses patience with him at the end of the first chapter:

> – Du fährst wieder mit und läßt alles geschehen. Du entehrst dein eigenes Heiligtum.
> Er reibt sich die Hand übers Gesicht, über seinen Bart.
> – Ich habe dich beobachtet. Du bist nur Gerede. Deine Empörung ist ein Furz. Du läßt Luft ab, du stänkerst herum, ansonsten bist du wie alle anderen, nein, schlimmer noch du weißt Bescheid, und du läßt dir dein Wissen versilbern.
> Ich wiederspreche nicht, und das facht seine Rage noch mehr an.
> – Jeder, der das Vermeidbare hinnimmt ist ein Schuft.
> Fast schreit er. Und dann weist er mir die schwere Tür. (*ET* 17)

'You're going along again, just letting everything happen. You dishonour what is holy to you.'

He rubbed his face and his beard with his hand.

'I have watched you. You are just talk. Your anger is not worth a fart. You get it out of your system, you go around in a bad temper, but apart from that you are just the same as all the others, except you are even worse than them, you know what is going on and you make money out of it.'

I do not contradict him, which just makes him more furious.

'Everyone who just lets happen what could be avoided is a shit.'

He is almost screaming. And then he gestures for me to leave.

EisTau is about someone who can no longer carry on doing nothing.

In this chapter I hope to show that *EisTau* can be read in a number of ways. If it does depict a case study in resistance, Zeno Hintermeier no more shows readers how they should act in the face of global warming than Richard Burton was a role model for intercultural communication by the end of *Der Weltensammler*. Indeed, it could be argued that both leading characters behave in ultimately self-defeating ways as they fail to rise to the challenges that they set themselves. On his third and final foreign expedition to find the source of the river Nile, Richard Burton reached a point of failure, behaving like the sort of imperialist whom he despised as a younger man. Burton's problem is that it is not as easy to elude the contradictions of his position as he at one time envisaged and he now seems unsure whether he even wants to do so. Zeno is caught in a similar dilemma. He profits from the modern form of imperialism known as tourism, which he quietly despises on account of the tourists' ignorance and their contribution to the destruction of the habitat that they have come to admire. If *Der Weltensammler* was less about an idealised vision of intercultural understanding, as its first readers were inclined to believe, and more about failure and pretence, then first impressions of *EisTau* as evinced in the reviews may also be deceptive. Trojanow's hint that Zeno may be delusional is surely an invitation to see through him and to subject his stance to a critique. If this reading is right, then *EisTau* depicts a character grappling with the dilemma of wanting to halt humanity's destruction of its own living space but who does not know how to go about achieving this goal, even though he is ready to die trying.

There are a number of links between *EisTau* and *Der Weltensammler*. Zeno has travelled with his friend Hölbl to the region of Ladakh in Indian Kashmir. There he heard of a man who spent twenty years reading the same book and when he got to the end of it, began again from the beginning. Zeno tried to concentrate in a similar fashion on a single text. When he had finished, he bought the notebook in which the main narrative of *EisTau* is written. 'Zen and the Art of Glacier Observation' would thus be an appropriate subtitle for the novel. Its hero Zeno was impressed too by the rituals in the Ladakh temples and compares his sixty laps around the *MS Hansen* every morning with the religious practices they encountered there. Like Burton on the pilgrimage to Mecca, they also participated:

> Um mich herum kreisen die Gewässer um die Antarktis, der Ozean und ein Aufgeweckter drehen ihre Runden, im Uhrzeigersinn, wie Hölbl und ich vor Jahr und Jahrzehnt in den Tempeln von Ladakh, frühmorgens, bevor der Arbeitstag begann, das Heiligtum umrundeten, nicht um uns bei den Einheimischen einzuschmeicheln, wie uns manche vorwarfen, stets bereit, jede Horizonterweiterung als Anbiederung an die Fremde abzutun, sondern weil uns die Idee einleuchtete. (*ET* 95)

> All around me the waters are circling the Antarctic, the ocean and a woken-up person are doing their laps, clockwise, as Hölbl and I years or decades ago walked around the holy sites in the temples of Ladakh, early in the morning, before the working day began, not to curry favour with the natives, as some accused us of doing, ever ready to dismiss any extension of our horizons as an attempt to ingratiate ourselves with foreigners, but because the idea made sense to us.

EisTau is an encircling meditation on its subject. Zeno the scientist clearly has a religious sense, but he does not say that the temples in Ladakh, a region of India bordering on Tibet, are Buddhist, any more than he explains that the cold ocean currents circulating around the Antarctic land mass prevent the ice on its surface from melting. He thinks of Ladakh, however, for a third and final time shortly before his death after he has hijacked the ship. The reference is even more cryptic for readers with little knowledge of the Himalayas, as he recalls how he learnt to steer a ship from Vijay the navigation officer: 'wir unterhielten uns, über Ladakh und Tibet [...] über Kailash und Gangotri' ['we talked, about Ladakh and Tibet [...] about Kailash and Gangotri'] (*ET* 166).

EisTau is the same length and scope as one of the three sections in *Der Weltensammler*. It too is multi-voiced to the extent that Zeno's chapters are intercalated with the briefer anonymous sections which are printed in italics. This babble of unattributed utterances functions as a kind of chorus to the tragedy of the main action. Unlike a classical chorus, however, these voices have no focus and unlike Naukaram or Sidi Mubarack Bombay, they do not articulate a coherent scale of values. Zeno's affair with Paulina, whom he abandons with the other passengers and crew to an uncertain fate, is something of a re-run of the much-discussed liaison between Burton and the temple courtesan Kundalini. As Hölbl advises him before he takes up his post, Zeno will have opportunities for holiday romance in his role as lecturer on a cruise ship: what happens on board will stay on board. While their relationship is sustained over three seasons of voyages it does not work (shades of Naukaram following Burton back to Britain) when they leave the special environs of the ship. This is not so much because they are not accepted as a couple in the social contexts of their respective countries: despite being old enough to be her father Zeno is considered a good catch by her family in the Philippines; and back in Germany, he is admired for finding himself such a youthful and attractive mate. The problem is that off ship they have to confront other people's clichéd understanding of a love affair between a male European in fairly late middle-age and a young Philippino woman. Rather than do so, Zeno ducks out by restricting himself to seeing Paulina at sea, when she tends to their shared cabin and caters to his need for sex and companionship. At the centre of *EisTau* is thus a relationship between representatives of two different, in some respects opposing cultures: the First World and the Third World; the 'old continent', whose whole way of life may be as moribund as the Alpine ice, and Asia, whose people, despite their relative poverty, have confidence in the future. Climate change is not a concern for Paulina or her compatriots. 'Sie ist in ihrer erfrischenden Ehrlichkeit und Direktheit meine Lieblingsfigur' ['in her refreshing honesty and directness, she is my favourite character'], Trojanow has said.[9]

9   Conversation with Stefan Gmünder, 'Vor der Katastrophe'.

The *MS Hansen* is either a ship of world state (there are many nationalities on board) or a ship of fools. Trojanow cites Sebastian Brant's 'morality play cum satire' *Das Narrenschiff/The Ship of Fools* published in 1494 as one of his inspirations, adding that 'Ships have always been the paradigmatic setting for escalating tragedy, isolated as they are on the perilous high seas, far from life's usual tamed rivers; they are closed spaces, in which representatives of humankind can indulge their folly'.[10] *EisTau* is a moral novel. The characters are specimens of fallen humanity, each with more or less conspicuous failings, such as pride or vanity. Power relations between socioeconomic and racial groups in the wider world are reflected and accentuated on board. As fas as Zeno is concerned, the passengers are all 'Notare[n], Unternehmensberater[n], Geschäftsführer[n] und Finanzanalysten' ['lawyers, management consultants, chief executives, and financial analysts'] (*ET* 164). This could be a hit list of the world's least favourite professions following the financial crisis which began in 2008. They are the neo-liberals who have propelled the world to the brink of catastrophe, in other words. The Philippino crew are preferred to other nationalities by the captain on account of their pliant temperament: 'they handle better' than Chinese workers, he explains, seemingly mangling German and English, as Zeno finds himself often doing (the German *handeln* means to act or to behave). The passengers include a number of self-indulgent egos and misguided do-gooders. The journalists among them are not much better than freelance advertisers for the shipping company, which values them because they will produce a travel feature which will attract future custom. The lecturers such as Zeno are more independent minded and are united by their sense of wonder, which is demonstrated when they watch for albatrosses together at the beginning of the voyage, but they resemble a troupe of itinerant intellectuals, more knowledgeable and reflective, but also more cynical than the passengers who pay their wages. They face the dilemma of intellectuals in the modern age by being economically dependent on the same forces that they want to criticise.

10   Trojanow, 'Requiem for the Future'.

As a piece of literary writing rather than an exercise in moral exhortation, *EisTau* invites comparisons with other works of literature and, in particular, with literary accounts of voyages. The most obvious of these, especially given the prominence of the disused whaling station on South Georgia, is Herman Melville's *Moby-Dick* (1851). This epic of the oceans also concerns a self-destructive, life-and-death quest, pitting man (representing science, reason, and civilisation) against nature in the shape of the great white whale. In *Moby-Dick*, nature wins. Trojanow contends that when he looked for specific literary antecedents, he found little which featured the Antarctic – although there is a rich body of writing on the 1911 race between Amundsen, Scott, and Shackleton to be the first to reach the South Pole (not to mention a magnificent documentary film on Scott's failed expedition).[11] Zeno Hintermeier none the less is given a distinguished literary pedigree. The original Zeno was a pre-Socratic philosopher to whom a number of mathematical paradoxes are attributed. He shares his name with that most stay-at-home hero in Italo Svevo's psycho-analytical novel, *Zeno's Conscience*, first published in Italian in 1923.[12] Some of the outward similarities between the central characters in Svevo and Trojanow's two novels are striking: they are roughly the same age (57 and 63 respectively), childless, and discuss their relationships with their fathers. Trieste, where Svevo lived all his life, was the European border city par excellence, poised between Italy and Slavic Croatia, at that time governed by Habsburg Austria-Hungary. Richard

---

11   *The Great White Silence* (dir. Herbert Ponting, 1924).
12   Italo Svevo, *Zeno's Conscience*, tr. William Feaver (London: Penguin, 2002), also widely known as *The Confessions of Zeno*, tr. Beryl de Zoete (London: Putnam, 1948). See also Ulrich Rüdenauer, 'Der Weltbesserwisser', *Süddeutsche Zeitung* (21 September 2011), who writes: '*La Conscienza di Zeno* – this could be Trojanow's title for his novel too. The glaciologist's conscience gnaws away at him as the ocean current does at the ice'. Stefan Neuhaus, 'Kein ewiges Eis. Ilija Trojanows neuer Roman: Eine Anklageschrift gegen die Zerstörung der Welt' (*Die Furche*, 1 September 2011): 'The main character is not called Zeno Hintermeier for nothing: according to the Greek origin of his first name, the former professor is a "gift of Zeus", while his surname indicates his rootedness in the regional.' 'Meier' (often as Meyer or Mayer) originally meant grocer or shopkeeper and is one of the most common German names; the prefix 'hinter' (behind) gives the sense of 'back of beyond' or provincial.

Burton served in Trieste as British consul, which is why *Der Weltensammler* begins and ends there. The family in the *Die Welt ist groß und Rettung lauert überall* cross the Yugoslav-Italian border near to the city. Italo Svevo, meaning 'Italian Swabian', is the pen-name of the Jewish Italian Aron Ettore Schmitz, whose own in-between identity recalls those of both Trojanow himself and his novel hero Burton. Through the indirect connection with Trieste, Zeno Hintermeier in *EisTau* picks up where Richard Burton in *Der Weltensammler* leaves off. The ship shares its name with a key character from Thomas Mann's *Tonio Kröger*, which features a northerly voyage from Germany to Denmark and beyond to Sweden. Like *EisTau*, Mann's novella is concerned with binary oppositions, subsumed under the categories of 'artist' and 'bourgeois'. Hans Hansen is Tonio's blond, blue-eyed school-friend: respectable, practical and unimaginative in his apparently untroubled way, he is the intellectual Tonio Kröger's opposite in sensibility. Zeno stands apart from his contemporaries like Mann's Tonio on account of a heightened awareness, which prevents him from behaving as if he does not know that the natural world is being destroyed.

EisTau is structured around a series of traditional binary oppositions: male and female; North and South (or First and Third World); and, most importantly, civilisation, which is associated with masculinity, reason, and dominance, and nature, which is associated with femininity, vulnerability, and beauty. Zeno and Paulina's affair stands at the heart of the novel by dint of its rich field of metaphorical meanings. As a scientist Zeno is aligned with reason, but his conflicted character is a result of his representing a phenomenon that he has come to loathe: civilisation itself. This comes to the fore at the abandoned whaling station, which is a visual representation of rapacious human consumption. The whales and other creatures such as penguins were used up on an industrial scale to make various products for Europeans, frivolous items such as stays for corsets and destructive ones such as explosives. Zeno admits, however, that at times he exaggerates the effect that human beings have on the natural world. He relates that he always tells his listeners that the Falklands war between Britain and

Argentina in 1982 was the first that resulted in more animals than human beings getting killed. 'Keine Ahnung, ob das stimmt. Tiere kommen in Kriegsberichten selten vor, aber es schockiert die Passagiere' ['No idea if that is right. Animals rarely feature in war reports, but it shocks the passengers'] (*ET* 47). This surely alerts readers to the fact that Zeno cannot always be relied on. Sometimes he makes things up. He is teasing his passengers in this episode, of course, by playing up to their own sense of outrage and their (by his lights) superficial love of nature. He knows that he can shock them by highlighting human beings' supposed disregard for other species, but he is also telling them something that he too perhaps wishes were true.

Some of the differences between this entirely fictional voyage and Trojanow's account of his own voyage with a similar itinerary that he undertook on a similar ship (the *MS Nordnorge*) reveal some of the distinctly literary qualities in *EisTau*. In particular, they help in our understanding of its narrator and central character. In an article entitled 'Antarktis. Die letzte Leere'/Antarctica. The Last Emptiness, published in *Die Zeit* in December 2008, Trojanow reports that the 'outstanding lecturers', all scientists or academics of one kind or another, are on a mission to educate their passengers, but he acknowledges that some found their would-be teachers' approach too didactic. While Trojanow shares Zeno's sense of wonder when surrounded by walls of ice as the ship sails through a narrow channel, he is matter of fact in his description of the abandoned whaling station on South Georgia. He goes so far as to claim that the evidence of past human activity even enhances the natural beauty: 'Hier treffen wir zum ersten Mal auf Pockennarben menschlicher Besiedlung, die später der ansonsten unberührten Landschaft der Antarktis noch mehr Zauber verleihen und auf dem Rückweg unseren Eindruck von Südgeorgien prägen werden' ['Here for the first time we come across the pockmarks of human settlement, which later lend the otherwise untouched landscape of the Antarctic yet more magic and on the return journey will determine our impression of South Georgia'].[13] For Zeno, in contrast, the landscape could not speak more eloquently of human beings' lack of respect for the natural

13   Ilija Trojanow, 'Antarktis. Die letzte Leere', *Die Zeit* (12 December 2008).

environment. The differences may in part be explained by the requirements of the two distinct genres, one a travel report in a newspaper, the other a work of fiction. But an authorial polemic is surely more at home in a newspaper than in a novel. If we are looking for Trojanow's own views, which *EisTau*'s reviewers believed were identical with Zeno's, then he is more likely to have expressed them in his own voice in a newspaper.

EisTau ends with Zeno's hijack of the empty *MS Hansen*, when he leaves the other passengers and crew standing on some unnamed icy ground. They have been arranged in the shape of the letters SOS under the direction of a publicity-minded installation artist named Dan Quentin, whom Zeno considers a fraud. Quentin's objectives, however, are ostensibly identical with Zeno's own. According to Quentin, the SOS installation is also intended to wake up the world to the fact that the ice is melting. The problem with Quentin's spectacular work of art is that it is self-seeking and draws attention only to itself. As a stunt it may make the participants feel better about themselves for a little while but that is all that it will do before its memory is drowned in the media cacophony. But as it inspires Zeno to perform his own stunt it has an unintended impact.

There are a series of incidents which lead up to Zeno's self-destructive action that ends the novel. Zeno gets into trouble with the ship's captain for the manner in which he reprimands a Chilean soldier for smoking a cigarette as he goes ashore on King George Island. Zeno is concerned that he will pollute the territory by discarding the butt when he has finished. Zeno is either applying strict standards for the unspoilt landscape or losing his mental grip, depending on your point of view. There is no doubt about the captain's opinion: 'Du bist dumm' ['You are stupid'] (*ET* 120). The soldier ignores Zeno's cries and pulls his gun on him when he persists. The discrete narrative incident is presented to the reader in semi-Brechtian fashion, inviting us to judge the behaviour of each individual and the legitimacy of the action and reactions to it.

At the next island stop some of the passengers alight in order to observe penguins from close quarters. They do so out of love of the natural world and concern for the preservation of these highly distinctive birds which are only found in the Antarctic. They discover that nature does not live by the same rules as civilisation, however, and that penguins cannot understand the nuances of human gestures. When a scavenger bird swoops to take a penguin egg, the American Mrs Morgenthau, upset at the bird's actions, wants to help the brooding penguin by returning the other egg that she has lost. From Zeno's lectures she knows that penguins, aiming to hatch a single chick lay and incubate two eggs. The penguin unfortunately only sees her as another potential predator and pecks violently at her hand, wounding her badly and drawing blood. Mrs Morgenthau's deed is a lesson in liberal interventionism into the natural world: her intentions are good, her lack of knowledge nearly fatal, and the results of her action the very opposite of what she wanted to bring about. There is another narrative layer to the incident because Zeno himself as leader of the expedition is at fault in at least two ways. Not only has he allowed one of his passengers to injure herself, he has failed to pack the regulation first-aid kit and cannot treat her wound which as a consequence becomes infected. Contrary to their cuddly appearance, penguins are dangerous; human antibodies cannot resist the bacteria they carry. Again, Zeno is reprimanded by the captain. By the end Mrs Morgenthau has another reason to feel angry with her expedition leader, as, hidden away in the ship's sickbay recovering from the penguin attack, she is the only passenger on board the *MS Hansen* at the time of his hijack. The third incident is Dan Quentin's human art installation, but by this point Zeno's mind is made up. For the first time in a long while he wakes up from a dreamless sleep, having suffered no nightmares.

EisTau thus demonstrates a series of attempts either by the central character or other figures from the developed world to intervene in events to make the world a better place, in particular to halt the changes in the planet's ecosphere brought about by the rise in temperatures. These episodes enact variations in miniature of what the novel itself purports to do. They all fail. One reason is given in the italicised sections of text which are intercut with the chapters from Zeno's narrative. The *Zivilisationskritik* is located in the form, rather than the content. The modern media treat all subjects in the same way, in the same voice, and in the same style. As readers or listeners we have a short attention span, hopping from channel to channel, or flicking from page to page. All information is commodified and exchange monetised. The most serious questions are debated in the same breath that transmits the most trivial news. As a 'breaking news' story, Zeno's ship hijack gets submerged in a sea of other stories and will be quickly forgotten.

CHRISTINA KRAENZLE

Rewriting Colonial Travelogues: Cosmopolitan Visions and Colonial Legacies in *Nomade auf vier Kontinenten*/Nomad on Four Continents

Given the international success of *Der Weltensammler*, it is not surprising that the novel has eclipsed Ilija Trojanow's other literary endeavours. In particular, his numerous travelogues have received little attention, doubtless in part due to the persistent tendency to regard travel writing as a literary subgenre. While countless studies have investigated the historical role of travel writing in Western encounters with the world and representations of it, contemporary travel writing is less often deemed an equally rich source for the study of representations of identity, difference, and 'transculturation'. This may well be a result of the long-held notion of the 'end of travel', a sense that as global networks of tourism, transportation, and technology make formerly remote areas of the globe increasingly accessible to more and more people, there can be no more 'real' journeys, no new locations to 'discover', simply pre-packaged tourist destinations that nowadays, with the help of internet applications like Google Earth, can even be explored virtually from the comfort of home.

Yet as recent studies have shown, the so-called end of travel has not meant the end of travel writing.[1] On the contrary, since the 1980s popular travel writing has enjoyed a particular boom, attesting to its continued potential not only to reflect but also to shape our understanding of self and

1   See in particular Debbie Lisle, *The Global Politics of Contemporary Travel Writing* (Cambridge: Cambridge University Press, 2006), or Patrick Holland and Graham Huggan, *Tourists with Typewriters. Critical Reflections on Contemporary Travel Writing* (Ann Arbor: University of Michigan Press, 1998).

world and to document the socio-cultural, economic, and environmental implications of mass mobility. Trojanow's travel writings thus provide useful case studies for our understanding of the influence and function of travel and travel writing in our current global moment. More specifically, they can be regarded as representative of a postmodern, transnational turn in travel writing at a time in which models of national culture have lost their credibility and identities are increasingly acknowledged to cut through geographical locations. Born in Bulgaria, educated in Germany and Kenya, and a long-term resident of Mumbai and Cape Town, Trojanow can be counted amongst numerous authors of hybrid cultural backgrounds (such as Pico Iyer, Vikram Seth, Amitav Ghosh, Yoko Tawada, to name but a few) who speak many languages, call several places home, and have sought to explore complex networks of enduring transculturation through travel writing. For some, the emergence of postcolonial or transnational authors marks a phase in the democratisation of travel writing which, at its best, can prove a useful document of diaspora and post-nationalism. In Pico Iyer's view, this development marks a rejection of the colonial legacies of the genre in favour of more cosmopolitan visions of intercultural exchange:

> I think [travel writing has] evolved a great deal. Partly because even when I was grow-ing up, travel writing was mostly white, nearly always male, often from England, and about going to Africa and Kenya and surveying the strange customs of the natives. And I think now it is more and more about a half-Thai, half-German girl living in Iowa City, going to an Afghanistan full of German aid workers and Japanese businessmen. And what used to be a very simple discussion between, in some ways, colonizer and colonized, is now a dialogue between a multi-cultural society and a multi-cultural person. All of which has made the texts much more interesting.[2]

Scholars of recent travel writing are, however, more sceptical. Advancing more critical understandings of cosmopolitanism, they follow investiga-tions undertaken in the wake of Edward Said's *Orientalism* (first published in 1978) that reject simple models of domination and subordination in

---

2   Pico Iyer, cited in Mathew Davis, 'On Travel and Travel Writing', World Hum (30 November 2006) <http://www.worldhum.com/features/travel-interviews/ pico_iyer_travel_writing_20061104/> accessed 19 July 2011.

cross-cultural encounters, highlighting instead the complex and often ambivalent relationships between the cosmopolitan and (neo-)colonial visions they locate in contemporary travelogues. In her recent book, Debbie Lisle argues that the emergence of more multicultural authorial perspectives in no way guarantees a break with travel writing's colonial and patriarchal heritage. On the contrary, constrained by readerly desires for sufficiently exotic locales, contemporary travelogues more often show continuities between a colonial past and a supposedly postcolonial present:

> All travel writing requires the production of difference – it requires the author to discriminate between what is familiar and what is exotic so that readers are satisfied that they are encountering people and places that are sufficiently foreign. Those practices of discrimination do not simply disappear when travel writers realize it is unacceptable – even taboo – to make negative judgments about cultural difference in an era of global diversity and multiculturalism.[3]

Her close readings of popular English-language travelogues reveal how generic conventions and the very act of writing about travel engender particular constructions of difference that are haunted by traces of Orientalism, exoticism, and empire. Her study suggests that a successful jettisoning of imperial models of difference and encounter requires more than self-reflexive shifts in attitude; it necessitates a reworking of narrative convention.

It is within this critical debate that I wish to situate Trojanow's travel writing. Much has been made in the promotion of Trojanow's travel books about his own status as a Burtonesque 'collector of worlds', a polyglot, cosmopolitan world citizen who has travelled, lived in, and written about multiple locations. In this regard, Trojanow's writing provides a productive example with which to investigate further the emergence of more 'transnational' travel writers and their development of the genre. Moreover, a study of Trojanow's German-language travelogues helps broaden contemporary travel writing studies which have, to date, been dominated by investigation

---

3   Lisle, *The Global Politics of Contemporary Travel Writing*, p. 71.

of Anglophone texts.[4] In this essay, I have chosen to single out one travelogue in particular, namely *Nomade auf vier Kontinenten. Auf den Spuren von Sir Richard Francis Burton*/Nomad on Four Continents: On the Trail of Sir Richard Francis Burton. While its subtitle and itinerary through the same locales that provide the setting for *Der Weltensammler* may lead prospective readers to dismiss the book as merely a compendium of field notes taken during research for the 'real' work of the novel, I suggest that it warrants critical attention in its own right. Of all Trojanow's travelogues it is formally the most experimental and most self-reflexively engages with some of the key questions that have been raised about contemporary travel writing: for example, to what extent and in what ways might authors who claim more culturally hybrid perspectives escape the logic of essential cultural differ-ence and exoticism that still taints the genre? More provocatively, are old 'colonial' visions and more 'cosmopolitan' perspectives necessarily mutually exclusive – and how might the contemporary travelogue become a key site for investigating their complex intersections? Unlike Trojanow's more con-ventional travel books, *Nomade auf vier Kontinenten* is, I argue, an attempt to come to terms with not only the ambiguous figure of Richard Burton, but with the ambivalent nature of contemporary travel writing that strives to overcome centuries of European prejudice in the very literary genre most associated with exoticism, imperialism, and the manufacturing of Otherness.[5]

4   As Loredana Polezzi observes, the fact that British and American studies of travel writing tend to ignore texts written in languages other than English is 'particularly paradoxical in the case of a genre which is so clearly concerned with the idea of transfer and mobility'. See Loredana Polezzi, *Translating Travel: Contemporary Italian Travel Writing in English Translation* (Aldershot/Brookfield: Ashgate, 2001), p. 1. Polezzi's work on contemporary Italian-language travel writing offers an exception to this trend as does scholarship on recent French-language travel writing. See, for example, Charles Forsdick, Feroza Basu and Siobhán Shilton, *New Approaches to Twentieth-Century Travel Literature in French: Genre, History, Theory* (New York: Peter Lang, 2006) or the special issue *Contemporary Travel Writing in French: Tradition, Innovation, Boundaries* of the journal *Studies in Travel Writing* 13.4 (2009).

5   See Barbara Korte, *English Travel Writing. From Pilgrimages to Postcolonial Explorations*. tr. Catherine Matthias (New York: Palgrave Macmillan, 2000). As Korte notes 'some scholars consider the travelogue an essentially imperialist mode of representation' (p. 153).

Burton Revisited: *Nomade[n] auf vier Kontinenten*

Nomade auf vier Kontinenten is curiously hybrid,[6] juxtaposing excerpts from Burton's writings with Trojanow's accounts of his own travels to stations along Burton's journeys through India, to Mecca and Medina,[7] across East Africa, as well as to Utah and Trieste. Woven into the mix is Menno Aden's German translation of Burton's *The Kasidah*, which is placed alongside the English original, and numerous photographs and drawings from both Burton's and Trojanow's archives. Although colour-coded (Burton's original writings appear in green, Trojanow's in black), the authors' texts are at times so complexly intermeshed that readers may momentarily fail to distinguish between the narrative voices. The text, like the two travellers, is thus constantly on the move, shuttling between the centuries to offer comparative views of various locations across four continents. The result is a reflection on the changing nature of travel and the enduring legacies of Empire.

By invoking the figure of Burton, Trojanow brings with him on his journey a considerable amount of colonial baggage, a legacy he frankly acknowledges in the opening pages of his travelogue:

> Das 19. Jahrhundert ist in hohem Maße gegenwärtig. [...] Wir sind weiterhin konditioniert von der Weltsicht des imperialen Zeitalters (wie selbst ein kursorischer Blick in die Medien und ihre Berichterstattung über Indien, Arabien und Afrika aufzeigt), weil wir sie nie umgeworfen, sondern nur korrigiert haben. Und heute,

6   Sigrid Löffler characterises the work as simultaneously a 'Nach-Reisebericht', 'Burton-Reader', (auto-)biography, and 'zweistimmige[r] Roman transkultureller Bewegungen'. Sigrid Löffler, 'Verschmelzungsgeschäfte auf vier Kontinenten', *Literaturen* (July/ August 2007), p. 54. Trojanow is, of course, not unique, but representative of a number of recent authors who have taken more experimental approaches to travel writing. As Peter Hulme notes, generic hybridisation is not new and has 'periodically reinvigorated travel writing throughout its history'. Peter Hulme, 'Travelling to Write (1940–2000)', in Peter Hulme and Tim Youngs (eds), *The Cambridge Companion to Travel Writing* (Cambridge/New York: Cambridge University Press, 2002), pp. 87–101, here p. 95.

7   The chapters concerning Trojanow's undertaking of the hajj are are in part taken from his previously published account. See Ilija Trojanow, *Zu den heiligen Quellen des Islam. Als Pilger nach Mekka und Medina* (Munich: Malik, 2004).

da imperiale Positionen mit einer frischen Frechheit bezogen werden und manch ein Intellektueller sich beeilt, sie mit seiner Bildung abzufüttern, ist es lehrreich, nachzuvollziehen, wie das 'viktorianische Archiv' gefüllt wurde, von Männern – und einigen wenigen Frauen – wie Richard Burton.[8]

The nineteenth century is to a high degree with us today. [...] We continue to be conditioned by a view of the world from the age of imperialism (as even a cursory glance at the media and their reporting on India, Arabia, or Africa will show) because we have never cast it off but merely adapted it. And today as imperial positions are adopted with renewed effrontery and intellectuals hurry to bolster them with their erudition, it is instructive to follow how the 'Victorian archive' was filled up, by men – and a few women – like Richard Burton.

Here Trojanow rejects the notion of a clear break with the colonial past and instead points to virulent forms of neo-colonialism that persist through global politics, media, mass tourism, and not least in the genre of travel writing.

Confronting the ways in which travel has been implicated in the colonial past has become a staple of the contemporary travelogue. But Trojanow's focus on the multifaceted and controversial Victorian traveller and explorer is most compelling, particularly because of the ways in which Burton could reconcile curiosity and sensitivity towards other cultures and religions with the often brutal realities of the imperial project. On the one hand, Burton famously learned as many as twenty-five languages during his military and diplomatic career and translated works from languages including Sanskrit, Arabic, and Portuguese (e.g. the *Kama Sutra*, *The Thousand and One Nights or Arabian Nights*, Camões' *Lusiads*) to bring them to the attention of English-speaking audiences. He was an accomplished ethnographer who took pains to master the codes of behaviour of the peoples he encountered to gain better insight into their culture and he often assumed false identities to travel incognito (his journey to Mecca disguised as a

8   Ilija Trojanow, *Nomade auf vier Kontinenten. Auf den Spuren von Sir Richard Francis Burton* (Munich: Deutscher Taschenbuch Verlag, 2008), p. 16. Cited as *Nomade*.

Muslim pilgrim would earn him fame and notoriety back in England);⁹ his celebrated travels and his expeditions to places including India, Arabia, East and West Africa, South and North America are documented in over twenty travelogues. Most remarkably, his encounters with religious, cultural, and sexual difference led him to write defences of practices and traditions from around the globe as well as critiques of various aspects of his British society that caused scandal amongst his Victorian readers.

On the other hand, however, Burton's lifelong engagement with questions of difference cannot be considered simply as a benign intellectual pursuit. As Edward Said has noted, while Burton's extensive knowledge of other languages and religions may have made him a remarkable exception to many of his peers, he was not simply a rebel against Victorian authority, but in many ways its most effective agent.¹⁰ Burton was keenly aware of how his linguistic and cultural knowledge and his ability to amass information under the cover of various disguises had the power to advance both his own career and British colonial endeavours. As biographer Dane Kennedy puts it, Burton's achievements made him 'a man who contributed more than most to the vast body of knowledge about other peoples and practices that constituted the Victorians' "imperial archive"'.¹¹ Most disturbingly, Burton's admiration for other religious and cultural practices did not extend to the peoples of sub-Saharan Africa where, contrary to his previous encounters in Arabia and India, he was unable to establish close relationships with the local residents. Influenced by emerging mid-nineteenth-century notions of race, Burton would become a proponent of

9 See Dane Kennedy, *The Highly Civilized Man. Richard Burton and the Victorian World* (Cambridge: Harvard University Press, 2005), p. 90. There is some controversy regarding the extent to which Burton's disguises actually fooled the Muslims he encountered on the hajj and also in other locations where Burton and later his wife Isabel liked to don local dress in their travels. Kennedy suggests there is considerable evidence to suggest that Burton's (and Isabel's) masquerade was detected, but for various reasons humoured, so that 'we are left to wonder [...] who was deceiving whom.' For Kennedy's assessment, see especially his chapter 'The Impersonator', pp. 58–92.
10 Edward Said, *Orientalism: Western Conceptions of the Orient* (New York: Vintage, 1979), pp. 195–7.
11 Kennedy, *The Highly Civilized Man*, p. 8.

polygenist theories that placed Africans in a separate and inferior species of humanity and legitimised European colonial rule. And while he at times voiced scathing criticism of British society, Burton did not object to the atrocities committed in its name in the colonies.[12]

Burton thus remains such an intriguing figure because he points to the ambivalent nature of travel, encounter, and engagement with difference which both served the imperial enterprise well and simultaneously led to subversive results which could threaten to call the validity of European cultural superiority and, ultimately, the entire colonial project into question. But rather than see Burton as merely the paradoxical product of the transition from the Victorian to the modern era, Trojanow seeks to explore the consequences of the contradictory paradigms of difference that he maintains still lie at the heart of our understandings of self and world.

The focus on Burton not only allows Trojanow to explore continuities and disjunctures between Burton's era and the present, it also allows him to consider what postcolonial theorists have termed the 'palimpsestic' nature of place that is never simply material, but socially constructed through the multiple – and often conflicting – stories produced by the various cultures that have inhabited it. If, in this 'itinerant age',[13] there are no new places left to explore, then there is an acute sense in contemporary travelogues that there can only be 'zones of repetition',[14] belated journeys to locations already travelled by countless others. Nowhere is this sense of belatedness more apparent than in the kind of project that Trojanow undertakes, namely the retracing of the steps of a famous explorer like Burton. Such a journey necessitates not only a physical quest, but also textual ones: Trojanow's pursuit of Burton becomes above all a confrontation with the 'archive', the collection of travelogues, stories, myths, and images that document previous journeys. While Burton's voice is most conspicuous,

---

12   Burton was a witness to and advocate of the torture and brutal public executions in the Sindh, where convicts were tied to the mouths of canons before these were fired. Trojanow notes: 'Er [Burton] begrüßt diese Bestrafung, weil er sie für abschreckend hält, denn Moslems glauben, daß der Mensch mit seinem sterblichen Körper in den Himmel aufsteigt', *Nomade*, p. 152.

13   Korte, *English Travel Writing*, p. 168.

14   Holland and Huggan, *Tourists with Typewriters*, pp. 67–9.

Trojanow's travelogue is rich with other intertextual references. Trojanow thus reminds us how travel has historically been associated with the act of collection and presents himself as a *Weltensammler* in his own right, not simply a collector of impressions gained through his own travels, but an archivist of numerous representations of the stops along the journey. *Nomade auf vier Kontinenten* thus walks a fine line: on the one hand, it evokes nostalgia for a lost age of travel and exploration, when men like Burton could claim to be the first to travel to unknown territories. On the other hand, it simultaneously attempts to interrogate the enduring myths and fantasies deployed by such travellers that continue to shape our understanding of place.

Authenticity, Authority and the Archive

Travel writing's ambivalent status has always been complicated by its generic hybridity. Located at the crossroads of fiction, non-fiction, reportage, ethnography, and autobiography, travelogues not only present highly personal visions of actual places, people and events, but also have a long tradition of incorporating anecdotes and sources of dubious veracity. The travelogue's potential unreliability, Holland and Huggan argue, has always been one of its main sources of entertainment and appeal.[15] While many writers may go to great lengths to establish their own authority and the accuracy of their travelogues, it is not uncommon for postmodern travelogues to underscore their more fictional qualities. Playing with the traditions of the 'travel liar,'[16] such overt attempts to reveal their own fictitiousness undermine what Mary Louise Pratt has termed the trope of the 'monarch-of-all-I-survey,'[17] in which authors assume the authority to uncover an incontrovertible truth

---

15 *Ibid.*, p. 16.
16 *Ibid.*, p. 37.
17 Mary Louise Pratt, *Imperial Eyes. Travel Writing and Transculturation* (London/ New York: Routledge, 1992), pp. 201–24.

about other (often non-Western) cultures. In *Empire of Signs*, for example, Roland Barthes makes no claims to truth; he explains his project as the creation of a 'fictive nation', not the quest for some other cultural reality.[18] His goal is instead an act of wilful alienation – 'a revolution in the propriety of symbolic systems' – in which to disturb his person and to 'undo our own "reality" under the effect of [...] other syntaxes'.[19] Barthes thus mocks the ethnographic tone of travel writing which adopts a seemingly objective stance and professes to achieve insight and truth about essential cultural differences. He points instead to the artifice of both foreign and familiar cultural conventions that can be revealed in acts of travel and encounter. Authors as diverse as Michael Ondaatje, Amitav Ghosh, Yoko Tawada, and W.G. Sebald have engaged in similar projects, blending fact and fiction in the travelogue form.

Fiction, myth, and unreliable narrators play important roles from the very start of *Nomade auf vier Kontinenten*. The travelogue begins in the Himalayas with the incredible tale of Trojanow's visit to an antiquarian bookshop in Shimla that is eerily empty of customers, but brimming with rare volumes. The colonialists who retreated to Shimla to escape the blistering summer heat, Trojanow muses, must have been 'eifrige Leser' ['busy readers'] (*Nomade* 31). A cursory glance reveals early editions of seventeenth-century travelogues, such as Thomas Coryate's *Coryat's Crudities* and Leo Africanus' *The History and Description of Africa*, first editions of Rudyard Kipling, and Mirza Muhammad Hadi Ruswa's Urdu classic, *The Courtesan of Lucknow*. With this brief catalogue, Trojanow references examples of travel writing and fiction that have helped shape enduring impressions and myths of place.

It is the encounter with the shop's peculiar owner that provides an initial impetus for Trojanow's travels. Producing a mysterious index that purports to catalogue the world's destroyed manuscripts, the shopkeeper raises Trojanow's hopes that some of Burton's diaries may still exist. Thus

18   Roland Barthes, *Empire of Signs*, tr. Richard Howard (New York: Hill and Wang, 1982), p. x.
19   *Ibid.*, pp. 3–6.

begins a quest for Burton's missing manuscripts that brings him into contact with various individuals en route who provide guidance, documents, and personal accounts of their own family connections with Burton. The traces (*Spuren*) referred to in the travelogue's subtitle are therefore from the outset marked as textual ones; although the quest for Burton involves a physical journey, material traces are sought primarily through Burton's (missing) diaries. Trojanow's travelogue becomes its own archive of excerpts from Burton's surviving writings, drawings, and photographs, along with anecdotes, impressions, and opinions about Burton provided by Trojanow and his various interlocutors. Significantly, though, the archive remains incomplete: 'Trotz großer Anstrengung und der Hilfeleistung einer Vielzahl von Burtoniern auf vier Kontineneten habe ich sie [Burtons Tagebücher] nicht finden können' ['Despite my best efforts and the assistance of numerous Burton afficianados on four continents I have not been able to find them [Burton's diaries]'] (*Nomade* 413). And while the details of Trojanow's quest for Burton's missing notebooks may be pure invention, this only serves to prove the larger point, namely that all history is speculative, comprised of scraps of information and incomplete records. The likely fiction of the bookseller thus constitutes a deliberate blurring of boundaries that recalls the inevitable presence of fictional elements even in those genres that aim to present themselves as purely factual.

The emphasis on fiction and unreliability persists as Trojanow continues his journey. After selling him a first edition of Burton's *The Book of the Thousand Nights and a Night* for a breathtaking ten thousand dollars, the shopkeeper provides him with a name and address in Goa: Carlo da Cunha – grandson of Burton's acquaintance Gerson da Cunha – will no doubt supply more information, the shopkeeper assures him. In Goa, da Cunha and his wife indeed prove gracious hosts, inviting the author into their home and introducing him to prominent members of Goan society, but not before da Cunha submits Trojanow to a test of his gullibility. Recounting a dubious story of his family's lineage, Carlo claims to be a direct descendent of the sixteenth-century Portuguese explorer and soldier Tristan da Cunha. Carlo relates how his ancestor fell in love with the local Rajah's wife and how, after the death of her husband, she was destined to perish on her husband's funeral pyre in the Sita ritual. With the help of local co-conspirators, Carlo alleges, the explorer succeeded in saving the woman and the da Cunha line was born. When Carlo breaks into operatic song to embellish his story with dramatic commentary, Trojanow's initial suspicions about the truth of the account are confirmed. In response to Trojanow's utter disbelief, da Cunha explains the motive for his tall tale: 'Ich wollte prüfen, ob Sie zu jenen Europäern gehören, die nur nach den Geschichten schürfen, die ihre eigenen Landsleute im fernen Boden vergraben haben' ['I wanted to test whether you were one of those Europeans who are only scratching away for stories which your own compatriots have buried in faraway soil'] (*Nomade* 57).

Although the source of Carlo's story is never revealed, the plot and verses he sings stem from Louis Spohr's 1823 opera *Jessonda*. Representative of what James Parakilas terms the 'Age of Discovery' operas of the nineteenth century, *Jessonda* deploys the common trope of an interracial love story between a famous explorer and an exotic female.[20] Set in the Age of Columbus, Europe's first period of overseas expansion, operas like Spohr's *Jessonda*, Gaspare Spontini's *Fernand Cortez, ou la conquête du Mexique* (1809), Giacomo Meyerbeer's *L'Africaine* (1865), or Félicien-César David's *La perle du Brésil* (1851) showed Europeans as occupiers and colonisers and offered parallels to European colonial pursuits of the nineteenth century.[21] As Parakilas demonstrates, these operas explored the possibilities of lasting relationships between coloniser and colonised, relationships which could only be deemed acceptable by European audiences when constructed through the erasure of difference. A common obstacle in these operas is religion, which is depicted as incomprehensibly threatening: in Jessonda's case Hindu custom has condemned her to death. The exotic female's abandonment of her native culture is thus presented as reasonable; religious difference is overcome on European terms, while the conqueror is transformed into a saviour. In operas like *Jessonda*, the European colonial presence could be cast as a benevolent, civilising influence, a notion that well

---

20   James Parakilas, 'The Soldier and the Exotic. Operatic Variations on a Theme of Racial Encounter', *The Opera Quarterly* 10.2 (1993), pp. 32–56, here p. 36.
21   *Ibid.*, p. 37.

suited imperial designs (*Nomade* 36–8). The insertion of da Cunha's yarn thus references an entire repertoire of exoticism in the Western musical tradition that – much like the many volumes in the Shimla bookshop – can be counted among the European archive of representations of Otherness. It also can be seen as a kind of warning to the traveller himself and, consequently, to the reader. As da Cunha suggests, while travel may offer the promise of first-hand experience and encounter, travellers may all too often 'discover' what they set out to find, namely the myths and fantasies of previous journeys, both factual and fictional.

Imagining Place: Colonialism, Conservation, and Tourism

While Da Cunha's story may be immediately detectable as the product of Orientalist fantasy, *Nomade auf vier Kontinenten* also explores how the persistent consequences of colonial visions of place and landscape may not always be so obvious. Experiences of place, Trojanow reminds us, are never uncomplicated perceptions of reality, but are always mediated through a long history of representations. Despite their obvious materiality, places and landscapes are always, to some degree, permeated by individual and collective imaginings that often go unnoticed in the wake of centuries of aesthetic tastes, scientific paradigms, patterns of use and ownership, and political or economic interest. In the East African episodes, Trojanow invites reflection on the ideological implications of particular ways of looking at landscape and on how many contemporary practices of conservation and tourism need to be understood in the larger historical context of European colonialism.

Like so many journeys, Trojanow's retracing of Burton and Speke's Nile expedition begins with a map. In preparation for their trip, Trojanow and his travel companion visit the Maps and Survey Office in Darussalam to consult maps based on old colonial surveys; during the course of the actual journey these are revealed to be purely fictional, full of non-existent routes and inaccurately charted terrain. Trojanow's experience corroborates the countless postcolonial studies that have revealed the omissions, misrepresentations, and distortions of colonial maps that often had more to do with the expansionist desires of imperial observers than with the material realities of the landscapes observed. A common feature of what J.B. Harley terms the 'unconscious distortion of map content' is the omission of spaces inhabited by indigenous peoples.[22] Colonial visions often cast space as empty, a *terra nullius* devoid of human presence awaiting European inscription through the act of 'discovery,' mapping and naming. Trojanow references this cartographic zeal when he cites John Hanning Speke's description of East Africa as 'eine riesige Landkarte des ewig Gleichen' ['a giant map of the eternally same'] (*Nomade* 327). Speke's assessment reduces the living landscape to a map, lacking diversity and devoid of culture or civilisation. Trojanow notes how this notion dominated the British and European press which reported on Burton and Speke's progress through allegedly unknown territory and failed to acknowledge that the expedition was in fact following long established caravan routes that facilitated trade in goods such as gold, ivory and, more disturbingly, slaves. Trojanow suggests that while England may have long abolished slavery, the British expedition nevertheless continued to benefit from the spoils of the slave trade: 'Die Sklavenhändler haben Afrika aufgeschlitzt, wie den Bauch einer Schwangeren. Männer wie Burton und Speke sind diesen Blutweg entlanggegangen, sie haben von ihm profitiert' ['The slave traders slit Africa open, like the belly of a pregnant woman. Men like Burton and Speke travelled along this road of blood and profited from it'] (*Nomade* 307). Speke and Burton's comments about sparsely populated landscapes on the route to Lake Tanganyika need to be seen in the context of a region depopulated by human trafficking.

Trojanow's visits to several of Tanzania's national parks and protected areas raise disquieting ethical questions about the complex intersections between contemporary conservation and tourism and the ideological

---

22   J.B. Harley, 'Maps, Knowledge and Power', in Denis Cosgrove and Stephen Daniels (eds), *The Iconography of Landscape* (Cambridge: Cambridge University Press, 1988), pp. 277–312, here pp. 289–90.

underpinnings of notions of pristine nature that have their roots in the colonial past. Considering the history of the Selous Game Reserve (a UNESCO World Heritage site since 1982), he notes how the German colonial administration designated the first wildlife preserves at the end of the nineteenth century in response to the threats posed by commercial and recreational hunting. Models of an untouched wilderness that could be distinguished and separated from land transformed by human presence (exemplified by the late nineteenth-century development of US national parks like Yellowstone or Yosemite) continued to inform conservation policy under British colonialism, with often devastating consequences for indigenous populations who were involuntarily relocated or whose access to ancestral lands was otherwise restricted.[23] In what Trojanow terms the 'Tragik des edenischen Afrikas' ['tragedy of Edenic Africa'], 'wildernesses' like the Selous Game Reserve had to first be created before they could be protected (*Nomade* 329). For example, the development of the Selous reserve entailed the displacement of approximately 40,000 people.[24] Trojanow argues that the colonial ideologies that informed wilderness creation in formerly inhabited lands have persisted well into the twenty-first century; he criticises conservationists such as the Frankfurt zoologist Bernhard Grzimek who continued to advocate the restriction of human access – including the access of indigenous populations – to protected areas:

> Nachdem die ersten 'Entdecker' (das Getötete ist endgültig entdeckt) die Fauna erlegt hatten, begann die nächste Generation, voller Scham und Sentimentalität, sich um den Naturschutz zu kümmern. Zoologen aus der nördlichen Hemisphäre fühlten sich auserwählt, riesige Gebiete von der Größe etwa der Serengeti nicht nur vor ihren blutrünstigen Artgenossen zu schützen, sondern vor den Afrikanern selbst, die seit Jahrtausenden im Einklang mit der Natur gelebt hatten. [...] Die Nationalparks und Tierreservate Afrikas sind durch und durch *white man's country*, geprägt von einer Fiktion der Unberührtheit. (*Nomade* 327–8)

---

23 William H. Adams and Jon Hutton, 'People, Parks and Poverty. Political Ecology and Biodiversity Conservation', *Conservation and Society* 5.2 (2007), pp. 147–83, here pp. 152–5.
24 *Ibid.*, p. 155.

> After the first 'discoverers' (anything dead is well and truly discovered) had killed the fauna, the next generation, full of shame and sentimentality, began to worry about protecting the environment. Zoologists from the northern hemisphere felt themselves to be chosen to protect great areas the size of the Serengeti not only from the bloodthirsty members of their own species but from the Africans themselves, who had lived for millennia in harmony with nature. [...] The national parks and wild animal reservations of Africa are through and through white man's country, marked by a fiction of that they are untouched.

Throughout his African travels, Trojanow considers how Western myths of the African landscape persist through the popular exoticism of the global media with a force that never existed in Burton's time: 'Ich bin erstaunt, wie viele verniedlichende Visionen durch meine Phantasie geistern. In den Schriften von Richard Burton, John Hanning Speke und anderen frühen Reisenden sind sie nicht existent' ['I am astonished how many belittling visions haunt my imagination. They are not there in the writings of Richard Burton, John Hanning Speke and other early travellers'] (*Nomade* 347–8). He laments the circulation of clichés like the anthropomorphic wildlife of Walt Disney or the romanticised landscapes of Sidney Pollack's film *Out of Africa* (1985) that caused a boom in safari tourism to places like Kenya and Tanzania. He contends that the environmental damage from subsequent development far surpasses any harm that might have been done from the continued residence of indigenous populations. Nor is there much ethical difference, he suggests, between the contemporary tourists who pay tens of thousands of dollars for the license to kill wildlife in the game reserves and the likes of J.A. Hunter, Theodore Roosevelt, or Captain Richard Meinertzhagen who came at the turn of the twentieth century to experience the hunt and kill 'wild' nature, except that the contemporary tourist enjoys far more modern conveniences. While safaris and eco-tourism have become a major source of income, Trojanow points to how this wealth is distributed unequally to a small group of elites. And whereas the costs of this increased tourism have historically been borne locally, the more intangible benefits of the enjoyment of the African landscape accrue to wealthy Western tourists: 'Die Weißen erfanden eine menschenfreie Ursprünglichkeit, in der sie ihre zivilisationsmüden Sinne reinigen konnten. Kein anderer Kontinent bietet so viele Möglichkeiten, die Wildnis als Themenpark, als historisches

Museum, neu zu konzipieren' ['The Whites invented a pristine realm free of people in which they could cleanse their senses made weary by civilisation. No other continent offered so many ways to rethink the wilderness as a theme park or an historical museum'] (*Nomade* 329–30).

Trojanow likewise criticises 'das museale Konzept' of conservation when he visits another UNESCO world heritage site at Hampi, India, where he questions the conflicting desires to preserve the site's archaeological record and to develop it, in part to cater to the tourism which has increased since the site was inscribed on the UNESCO World Heritage list in 1986. Trojanow notes the paradox of mass tourism which can attract investment to help save endangered sites like Hampi, but at the same time creates overcrowding and environmental damage that threaten to destroy them. Here, too, the local population appears to receive little benefit from the proceeds of heritage tourism: while large landowners and developers reap the financial rewards, local farmers work the land for a minimal daily wage. Trojanow's general critique of tourism is a running theme and unsavoury package tourists are a conspicuous presence in *Nomade auf vier Kontinenten*: drunken British holiday makers disturb other guests in a Goan resort; visitors to Hampi obliviously disturb a local wedding ceremony; European tourists in Zanzibar are compared to invading armies; Tanzanian tour operators lament the ignorance of foreign visitors who have difficulty locating Tanzania on the map and, confusing Zanzibar with Zimbabwe, cancel their trips when political tensions in Zimbabwe run high. The risks travel poses to both the traveller and local populations is underscored in Trojanow's journey along the so-called 'Aids-Highway' and during a sojourn in a popular truck stop, Mlindizi, where prostitution flourishes and doctors estimate at least half the population is HIV-positive.

Trojanow's negative appraisal is not exceptional in contemporary travel writing where the criticism of mass tourism has become a mainstay, especially where the developing world is concerned. In *Nomade auf vier Kontinenten*, revelations about the provincialism of Western tourists often function to invert the historical conventions of imperialist travel writing that touted the superiority of European society over allegedly backward populations elsewhere. In Zanzibar, Trojanow marvels at the multilingual, well-travelled residents and notes the long history of cosmopolitanism in the region when he cites Burton's reflections on the Portuguese encounters with Zanzibar at the close of the fifteenth century. Burton writes about how the Portuguese, expecting to find wild, uncultivated natives, were astonished to find a wealth and culture beyond their imagination: 'Die bescheidenen Geschenke der Europäer an diese wohlhabenden Prinzen, deren Ehefrauen sich mit Perlen und Edelsteinen schmückten, müssen einen sehr geizigen Eindruck von der portugiesischen Zivilisation hinterlassen haben' ['The modest gifts of the Europeans to these prosperous princes whose wives adorned themselves with pearls and precious stones, must have left a mean impression of Portuguese civilisation'] (*Nomade* 286). Trojanow tracks the syncretism that marks the many destinations along his travels, noting the connections between global cultures that can be seen in the migration of music, language, cultural or religious traditions across continents. He thus historicises cosmopolitanism, both questioning the tendency to see it as a primarily contemporary phenomenon and voicing doubt over whether first-world, privileged hypermobility necessarily leads to more enlightened cross-cultural encounters.

But like so many travel writers, Trojanow also uses unsophisticated tourists as a foil for his own position as a worldly traveller. Debbie Lisle locates the tendency to maintain the spurious traveller/tourist division as a strategy to project difference not onto locals, but rather onto the increasing numbers of fellow tourists who threaten to usurp the travel writer's unique status. The repeated denigration of tourists, she suggests, helps to create an authorial persona of confidence, solitude, masculinity and expertise exclusive to an allegedly superior 'traveller'.[25] That Burton engaged in a similar practice is evidenced when Trojanow cites a letter he wrote to the Secretary of the Royal Geographical Society, Dr. Norton Shaw, in which he complains about the 'Menge kleiner Touristen', the '[u]nzählige Herren, die Tagebuch schreiben' and, most contemptuously, the female American missionary, 'die Autorschaft anstrebt' ['the crowd of little tourists', 'the innumerable gentlemen who keep a diary', 'aspiring to authorship'] (*Nomade* 279). In his letter to Shaw, Burton attempts to distinguish his own writings from

25   Lisle, *The Global Politics of Contemporary Travel Writing*, p. 77.

the scribblings of mere tourists, thereby claiming the superior quality and accuracy of his own accounts. Certainly, Trojanow also sets himself apart from fellow travellers: he is not duped by Carlo da Cunha's unbelievable story; his mastery of multiple languages, lengthy residences in India and Kenya and intense study of Islam in Mumbai offer him insight into local cultures that his fellow travellers often do not possess. At the very least these episodes suggest a hierarchy of informed, 'authentic' and/or ethical travel; however Trojanow is not afraid also to show himself occasionally himself as a tourist, likewise benefiting from the services of agencies, tour guides and the general infrastructure of the tourist industry.

This is especially true in the section that relates his undertaking of the annual Muslim pilgrimage. Here Trojanow must abandon the figure of the solitary traveller since, unlike in Burton's time, the pilgrimage can now only be performed through travel agencies approved by the Saudi Arabian government. Trojanow calls attention to the many details of the package tour experience: the ubiquitous Cosmic Travel luggage carried by each member of the tour group, the pre-arranged transportation, accommodation and meals, and the attentive presence of Hamidbhai, the group's tour guide. Trojanow juxtaposes his own experience with Burton's, citing Burton's complaints about the lack of amenities for the pilgrims. But even here Trojanow can't resist contrasting his contemplative journey with that of some of his fellow pilgrims: while he sits in meditation and prayer, putting into practice the religious lessons learned from Islamic scholars during his sojourn in Mumbai, others play games on their cell phones, deliver ill-informed lectures on the tenets of Islam, or worry about the score in the latest match involving Manchester United.

Trojanow may not relinquish the prevailing traveller/tourist dichotomy, but he nevertheless takes care to acknowledge the privilege of unfettered movement, pointing out that not everyone travels across borders willingly or easily. The story of a family of young children forced by poverty and hunger from their home in Bijapur recalls the dire conditions of involuntary displacement. In Zanzibar Trojanow's admiration for the multilingual, well-travelled locals is heightened by his recognition of the ways in which obstacles to mobility – travel costs, visa requirements, etc. – affect them more adversely than Western travellers. Even his own plans to travel to Pakistan are repeatedly thwarted by political or personal circumstances, belying notions of a borderless world. Pakistan thus remains one of the stations on Burton's journey that Trojanow is unable to visit; he can only contemplate the country 'lesend und nachdenkend' ['reading and contemplating'] (*Nomade* 153) and filtered through Burton's writings. Trojanow furthermore considers how socio-economic borders impinge on the traveller's journey on his flight from Mumbai to Jeddah. Securing one of the more comfortable seats on the upper deck prompts contemplation of the ways class and wealth play out in the allegedly classless experience of the hajj. Finally, an anecdote about how he and the only other two white travellers on a broken-down bus in Zambia were rescued by a passer-by shows at least an awareness of the ambivalence of his own position and the ways in which race, nationality and wealth affect the possibilities and experience of mobility. These episodes contradict more celebratory theories of cosmopolitanism that obscure the socio-economic privilege of 'world citizens' who, like Trojanow himself, move relatively effortlessly across borders, free to consume other cultures and places and to claim multiple identities.

Travel and Translation

While Burton may be best known for his sensational travels, he is also well remembered for his endeavours as a linguist and translator; his translations of the *Kama Sutra* and *Arabian Nights* remain authoritative. Indeed, Burton is a good reminder of how travel and translation have long been connected, a fact underscored by *Nomade auf vier Kontinenten* which itself combines travelogue with translation: embedded in Trojanow's accounts of his own travels are his German-language translations of Burton's travel writings and Menno Aden's translation of Burton's *The Kasidah*, an epic poem asserting the relativism of religious faith. Acts of translation are everywhere visible in the travelogue as Trojanow considers his own movement across linguistic borders as well as Burton's lifelong pursuit to master the languages he encountered on his journeys. Visual images such as the photograph of Burton working on his translation of *Arabian Nights* or facsimiles of Burton's marginal, handwritten notes to translations of Ariosto recall Burton's achievements as a translator; untranslated chapter subtitles recall the various scripts and languages of locations visited by both travellers. Translation is however not always linguistic: in Mumbai Trojanow attempts to decipher the significance of the behavioural codes of female dancers and male patrons in one of the city's *ladies bars*; in Tanzania Masai hunters instruct Trojanow in the art of interpreting footprints and other physical traces of local wildlife.

Trojanow begins his travelogue with a number of reflections on the practice of translation. He suggests that while Burton no doubt played an important role as cultural mediator by presenting then little known works to his English contemporaries, Burton thought little of direct translation, preferring instead to embellish the original works with his own additions and 'corrections'. Accordingly, a direct translation of Burton would be 'nicht nur ein Vergehen an dessen eigener Poetik, es würde ihm nicht gerecht werden' ['not only an affront to his own poetics, it would not do him justice'] (*Nomade* 20). With this disclaimer, Trojanow leaves us to wonder not simply about the accuracy of his own translations, but about larger questions of intercultural encounter, translation, and power.

That the power to interpret and translate is never an innocent one is evidenced in a chapter devoted to Burton's remarkable fluency in approximately twenty-five languages. In an account of his systematic approach to language learning, Burton reveals the extent to which his linguistic pursuits were fuelled not only by intellectual curiosity, but also by a will to mastery and power. The chapter recalls the ambivalent nature of Burton's linguistic abilities which unquestionably allowed him better to understand and even identify with many of the cultures he encountered, but were also crucial to the disguises and alter egos he created to infiltrate various communities in his role as British spy. As Trojanow notes, the acquisition of local languages was enmeshed in colonial relationships of power and exploitation and Burton was fully aware 'daß jede Sprache ein Machtinstrument und die Beherrschung der Sprache ein integraler Bestandteil von Herrschaft ist' ['that every language is an instrument of power and the command of a language an integral component of rule'] (*Nomade* 107).

The translator's authority is however also often undermined in episodes that highlight the transformations texts undergo as they migrate from one linguistic, cultural, and/or temporal realm into another. In Baroda, Trojanow is presented with an excerpt from one of Burton's diaries containing Burton's translation of a Gujarati tale, allegedly told to him by a former teacher. Before presenting his own German translation to the reader, Trojanow warns that: 'dieser Text aus den ursprünglichem Gujurati über das burtoneske Englisch in mein gelegentlich eigenwilliges Deutsch eingewandert ist und daher gewiß einige, von mir nicht kontrollierbare Transportschäden abbekommen hat' ['this text has emigrated from the original Gujurati via Burton's English into my occasionally peculiar German and has thus been damged in transit in ways that I have not been able to check'] (*Nomade* 136). Trojanow's German version represents the final link in a chain of various translations from oral narrative to written tale, from handwritten manuscript to printed text, from Gujurati, to English, to German. Here too, Trojanow undermines notions of authenticity: the source text – itself an oral narrative and therefore not definitive – cannot be verified and attention is instead drawn to the role each interpreter plays in producing and potentially altering the story's meaning.

Elsewhere translation is thwarted altogether. Passages in Burton's manuscripts remain illegible and untranslatable. Unable to read the cultural codes of the dancers in the Mumbai *ladies bar*, Trojanow must admit: 'Vielleicht sandten die Frauen irgendwelche suggestiven Signale aus, die ich nicht wahrnahm' ['Perhaps the women were sending out suggestive signals of one sort or another that I was not picking up'] (*Nomade* 119). The untranslated chapter subtitles provide an instance of what Michael Cronin terms 'translation resistance' and create unequal levels of access to German-speaking readers who may or may not have knowledge of the various languages in question.[26] Most importantly, the prevalence of numerous interpreters – Burton, Trojanow, Carlo da Cunha, Menno Aden and others – suggests that there can be no single interpreter and no direct translation.

---

26   Michael Cronin, *Across the Lines. Travel, Language, Translation* (Cork: Cork University Press, 2000), pp. 94–7.

Attempts to document Burton's significance and the multifaceted nature of the places he inhabited require a polyphonic text that maps no singular truth. Instead, a complex web of interpreters and interpretations confirms the contested and mediated nature of history and visions of place.

However, notwithstanding endeavours to include multiple perspectives, female guides and interpreters are conspicuously absent. Despite repeated reflections on gender, sexuality and travel, women's voices are rarely heard. Considering the lethal consequences of travel, HIV and prostitution in Mlindizi, Trojanow recounts conversations with local truckers, but does not communicate with any of the prostitutes. In an effort to investigate Orientalist fantasies of Indian sexuality, Trojanow consults a male doctor in Mumbai and makes his trip to the *ladies bar* to observe how modern-day successors to the famed *nautch*-girls ply their trade, but he has no occasion to speak to any of the women themselves. Instead, the women in these episodes remain silent objects of the tourist's gaze.

Conclusion: Colonialisms and Cosmopolitanisms Past and Present

As the subtitle of *Nomade auf vier Kontinenten* suggests, Trojanow's journey is ultimately a quest to understand the elusive character of Burton and his era. The travelogue provides a highly ambivalent portrait of Burton, whose intellectual engagement and personal experience with diverse cultures could simultaneously produce a sense of the relativism of religious and cultural practice and the most objectionable racism. While Burton's *The Kasidah* shows how cross-cultural encounters could undermine notions of the superiority of any one belief system, the travelogue's East African episodes recall how Victorian and Wilhelmine travel to Africa fuelled pseudo-scientific racial theories as explorers like Burton were commissioned to bring home human specimens that would fill the ethnographic museums and laboratories of Europe. The section, which also documents

Burton's interest in phrenology, acts as a stark reminder that even someone as culturally sensitive as Burton could ascribe to the specious theories of racial difference that would culminate in the catastrophe of the Holocaust.

Merging his own voice with Burton's, Trojanow subsequently invites us to consider how the contradictory paradigms of difference that characterised Burton's era continue to shape our own. Whether contemplating mass tourism to developing countries, contemporary practices of conservation, or the ongoing war in Afghanistan, Trojanow repeatedly questions the degree to which we have divorced ourselves from nineteenth-century understandings of place and difference, despite our increased ability to traverse and encounter the world, either through physical travel or more virtually through modern media. It is perhaps through the very focus on Burton that Trojanow best escapes the dubious tourist/traveller dichotomy: by presenting us with the ambiguous figure of Richard Francis Burton, he underscores the highly ambivalent nature of travel itself, which even in its most sophisticated forms need not always lead to increased cross-cultural awareness and understanding.

This of course begs the question to what degree Trojanow is willing to submit his own endeavours as traveller and travel writer to the same critical analysis that he performs on Burton. To what extent is he prepared to accept his own implication in the tourist industry he deplores, but that travel writing – at least the more conventional sort in which he also participates – arguably does much to support? Moreover, how can he balance the preservation of his own credibility with a critique of the discursive structures of the genre that paradoxically threatens to undermine the travel writer's authority?

Unlike his more conventional travelogues, *Nomade auf vier Kontinenten* seems above all to be an attempt to come to terms with this dilemma. This perhaps best explains the curious form of his travelogue with its unsuccessful quest for Burton's missing manuscripts. The quest motif is too insistent to be anything but ironic and the failed detective journey leads not to discovery, but absence. That there can be no exhaustive, singular representation of place or past is further underscored in the interweaving of texts, commentary, translations and the conceit of the (incomplete) archive that structures the narrative. In his attempt to collect these documents and present them, however partial, to the reader, Trojanow of course constructs himself as the master archivist, and as such the power of authority, at least for the moment, accrues to him alone. Moreover the failure to include female voices in this travelogue means that *Nomade auf vier Kontinenten* does little to address the historical gender coding of mobility and adventure as inherently masculine. Nevertheless, the insistence on incompleteness, inaccuracy, interpretation and outright untruth nevertheless works to unsettle the author's position of mastery and expertise.

And while the juxtaposition of his own travels with Burton's may on the one hand seem an exercise in self-flattery and romantic longing for a lost age of adventure and exploration, the emphasis Trojanow places on Burton's less admirable qualities makes any comparisons between the two men less favourable. We should furthermore be careful not to see Trojanow's internationalised view as uniquely twenty-first century, and opposed to Burton's; we must consider instead how Burton would also have emphasised his own culturally hybrid identity. As Dane Kennedy writes, the Victorian's self image was

> produced through the encounters that so many of them had with other peoples across the globe as a result of leisure travel, military service, missionary work, merchant enterprise, and more. The Victorian world was in this sense a genuinely transnational and transcultural world, drawing inspiration and insight from wide-ranging, often unexpected sources.[27]

The juxtaposition thus complicates perceptions of the novelty of our current phase of globalisation and recalls Trojanow's assertion that our age resembles Burton's more closely than we may care to acknowledge. In short, Trojanow's travelogue accomplishes something that his more popular novel, *Der Weltensammler*, cannot: while *Weltensammler* skilfully captures the enigmatic and ambiguous figure of Burton, *Nomade auf vier Kontinenten* places equal emphasis on the present moment and historicises our prevailing notions of place and cultural difference. At the same time, the travelogue interrogates the very genre it employs, playing with notions of authenticity and authority and recalling the travelogue's historical implication in Orientalism, exoticism, and imperial expansion.

27   Kennedy, *The Highly Civilized Man*, p. 271.

Together, Trojanow's complex reflections on travel, travel writing, translation, and intercultural encounter point out the potential for travel to disrupt the universalist pretensions of one's own point of view; at the same time they also treat themes such as the resilience of essentialist models of cultural identity and prevailing myths of place, the unequal levels of mobility experienced by citizens of the developed and developing world, and the historical links between travel and imperialism. Trojanow's dual emphasis ensures that his travelogue both challenges the judgments of his colonial predecessor, while at the same time resisting triumphant models of cosmopolitanism that celebrate global interconnectedness while denying its material consequences.

BEN MORGAN

Two Models of Spiritual Life and Narrative Sovereignty: Trojanow and Religion

Introduction

In his sermon on the text 'Blessed are the poor in spirit', Meister Eckhart prays that God might free him from God, for the very idea of God marks a human being's separation from divinity.[1] For the Dominican master, the aim of spiritual life is to work away the habits, attachments and prior commitments that prevent us from doing God's bidding wherever and however it may reach us: 'every moment freely and new, as if [we] had nothing else and neither would nor could do otherwise'.[2] Put in more secular terms, this could be said to mean disencumbering ourselves of routines and fixed ideas to be open to our predicament as it unfolds. This is an aspiration Eckhart shares not just with other Christian but also with Muslim mystics. One of the Sufi teachings recorded by al-Qushayri in eleventh-century Nishapur in North-Eastern Persia is that 'The Sufi is the child of the moment [*as-sufi ibnu waqtihi*][...]. The poor [of heart, *al-faqir*] is not concerned with his past or with his future; he is concerned with the moment in which he is.'[3] In both traditions, therefore, the emphasis is not on particular dogmas or rituals, nor indeed on the cultivation of mystical experiences as an end in

---

1   Eckhart, *Meister Eckhart Werke*, 2 vols, eds Niklaus Largier and Josef Quint (Frankfurt am Main: Deutscher Klassiker Verlag, 1993), i, p. 360.

2   Eckhart, *German Sermons & Treatises*, tr. Maurice O'C. Walshe, 3 vols (Shaftesbury: Element Books, 1979), i, pp. 72–3.

3   Sara Sviri, *The Taste of Hidden Things* (Inverness, CA: The Golden Sufi Center, 1997), p. 16.

themselves. Rather, the goal is to cultivate a certain attitude: an openness to what God brings, however it might relate to our preconceptions, our habits, our hopes, and even our moral code.

A comparable idea of spiritual life can be found in Trojanow's work, which frequently returns to matters religious. There's not space to deal with everything in this brief chapter, so I am taking *Der Weltensammler* as my point of departure. I also draw on four other books by Trojanow: his account of his pilgrimage to Mecca in 2003; *Kampfabsage* [Calling off the Fight], the book-length essay on cultural hybridity that he published with Ranjit Hoskoté in 2007; the account of his own researches into the adventures of the historical figure Richard Francis Burton, who was the inspiration for *Der Weltensammler*; and the collection of excerpts and interviews on spiritual matters published under the title *Sehnsucht* [Yearning] in 2008.[4] Trojanow returns again and again to aspects of spiritual life that do not fit people's preconceptions. Thus in *Der Weltensammler*, Burton's interest in Islam does not fit the expectations of his Hindu servant Naukaram, the Englishman's pilgrimage threatens the conceptual securities of the Muslim authorities in Mecca, while Sidi Mubarak Bombay's rediscovery of his animist heritage does not please his imam, and Burton, at a climactic moment of the hajj remembers the words of his first Hindu guru Upanitsche. Syncretism is at once the ideal to be aspired to and the simple, descriptive truth of how cultures develop in the history reconstructed by Trojanow and Hoskoté in *Kampfabsage* (17–18). In Trojanow's account of the hajj, meanwhile, the community of Islam at its best nurtures cultural differences, as they are evinced by the sartorial variety amongst pilgrims in Mecca; at its worst, it imposes a standardised and alienating model of faith and architecture on the pilgrimage in Saudi Arabia (*Zu den Quellen* 25, 78–9).

---

4   Ilija Trojanow, *Der Weltensammler* (Munich/Vienna: Hanser, 2006). Cited as *DW*;
     Zu den Heiligen Quellen des Islam: Als Pilger nach Mekka und Medina (Munich:
     Piper, 2004); (with Ranjit Hoskoté), *Kampfabsage: Kulturen bekämpfen sich nicht –
     Sie fließen zusammen* (Munich: Blessing, 2007); *Nomade auf vier Kontinenten: Auf
     den Spuren von Richard Francis Burton* (Frankfurt am Main: Eichborn, 2007); and
     Sehnsucht: Mach Dich auf den Weg (Freiburg im Breisgau: Herder, 2008). Further
     references will be given parenthetically in the text.

The way to escape preconceptions, as Trojanow reiterates in a number of his interviews, is to take nothing with you when you travel: no baggage and no guidebook. 'One should strip oneself naked, in order that something can happen' ['Man sollte sich nackt machen, damit was passiert'] (*Sehnsucht* 73).

Trojanow's account of spiritual life thus resembles the views of Eckhart and al-Qushayri because it celebrates openness, and challenges dogmatism. Nevertheless, there's an aspect of his approach that distinguishes it from theirs: the focus on the question of belief. *Der Weltensammler* is structured around something like a twenty-first century *Gretchenfrage*: the puzzle of Burton's faith. At the end of the novel, the Catholic priest who was charged with performing the last rites on the dying Burton by his wife Isabel thinks he has finally answered the question of what Burton believed in. In conversation with the Burtons' Italian maid, Anna, the priest establishes that Burton used to declaim an Islamic *dhikr* or mantra: There is no god but God, *Laa-illaha-ilallah*, a fact which the priest thinks settles the question once and for all: 'Er war Mohammedaner, er war ein verdammter Mohammedaner' ['He was a Mohammedan. He was a damned Mohammedan'] (*DW* 513). The priest is not a character whose views we are asked to endorse. Rather, he is one in a line of figures who look for clear dividing lines in matters of faith where none can be drawn and who cannot imagine, as the figure of Burton puts it at one point in the book, that there is something between friend and foe, black and white, us and them (*DW* 211). Nevertheless, the narrative arc of the novel is structured by the question of Burton's belief, from the death bed rites, through the investigations of the Meccan authorities to the final conversation between the young priest and his bishop. Even if the answer to the question of Burton's faith is that it doesn't finally matter, the question still shapes the novel as a whole.

I want in this chapter to deal with some of the issues raised by this structuring focus, and in particular with two questions. What is the model of inner life underlying the novel's quest to establish what Burton believed? And: what are the consequences of this model of inner life for an understanding of religion? I will start by setting out two contrasting versions of spiritual life, and then go on to look at the way these feature in Trojanow's novel. The frame of reference I will be using is primarily that of the Western tradition: Paul, Augustine, Kierkegaard, Heidegger. This is not the tradition with which Trojanow primarily associates himself, as someone who calls himself a Sufi and has an active interest in the Islamic tradition. At the same time, Trojanow disputes the idea that one culture confronts another, that is to say that Islam confronts the West, and challenges the suggestion, put to him in interview, that he has 'converted' from one to the other, since both cultures are themselves varied and multifaceted as well as being inter-related in many ways.[5] So the juxtaposition of Trojanow's reflections on the Islamic beliefs of a Victorian Orientalist with a tradition of thought stemming from Paul and Augustine is very much in the syncretic spirit of his writing. The argument I want to propose is that the sense of mystery surrounding Burton's religious convictions is one that the novel cultivates in a calculated way and is not an epistemological necessity. This raises the question of the purpose to which the fiction of an inaccessible faith is being constructed. Trojanow's novel does not only fictionalise Burton's biography, it also strategically distances the reader from Burton's inner life. Why would it do that? The issue I want finally to explore is: does this expand our imaginative horizons as readers and facilitate an engagement with unfamiliar habits and responses, or does it create a false sense of mystery: a distracting fiction in place of what in the most general sense could be termed spiritual growth?

Models of Religious Life

Trojanow's preamble to the novel, which introduces the historical figure of Burton, makes the claim that, at some level, we cannot know people and suggests his novel will approach Burton's secret but not try to betray it: 'Jeder Mensch ist ein Geheimnis; dies gilt um so mehr fur einen Menschen, dem man nie begegnet ist. Dieser Roman ist eine persönliche Annäherung

---

5   Wieland Freund, 'Ein Geheimnis drückt mehr aus als eine Erklärung', *Die Welt* (22 March 2006).

an ein Geheimnis, ohne es lüften zu wollen' ['Every person is mystery; this is true all the more for a person one has never met. This novel is a personal engagement with a mystery which I don't want altogether to dispel'] (*DW* 7). In making these assumptions about an inaccessible inner life, Trojanow is situating himself in a tradition that goes back to St Augustine. In his *Confessions*, Augustine assumes that an important part of his life is hidden from others and known only to God. For example, when his mother dies, he is not visibly shaken. His self-control ensures that God alone knows his pain.[6] The privacy of his spiritual life means even those listening to, or reading, Augustine's *Confessions* cannot know whether he is being truthful (*Confessions* 10:3:3). Following the Augustinian model, therefore, we could never answer the question of whether someone believed or did not believe. Indeed, for Kierkegaard, or at least for the character Johannes de silentio, in whose name he wrote *Fear and Trembling*, faith is characterised precisely by its being incommunicable, as he explains using the example of Abraham's sacrifice of Isaac. If there were a rule laying down the circumstances under which it would be acceptable to sacrifice your son, or if there were an intelligible payoff, as there is for Johannes when Agamemnon sacrifices Iphigenia to propitiate Artemis, then the murder of one's child would be intelligible if nevertheless repulsive. For Johannes de silentio, however, Abraham's position as he prepares to murder Isaac is straightforwardly unintelligible. There is no way of bridging the gap between what Abraham sets off to do and moral norms, and this is a situation Johannes suggests is a characteristic of faith generally: 'Faith itself cannot be mediated into the universal, for thereby it is cancelled. Faith is this paradox, and the single individual simply cannot make himself understandable to anyone.'[7] For this model, faith is a private act that remains necessarily beyond the comprehension of our peers.

---

6   Augustine, *Confessions: Text and Commentary*, ed. James J. O'Donnell, 3 vols (Oxford: Clarendon Press, 1992), i, p. 116. Further references will be given parenthetically in the text, giving the standard book, chapter and paragraph number, in this case 9:12:31.

7   Søren Kierkegaard, *Fear and Trembling*, eds Howard V. Hong and Edna H. Hong (Princeton, NJ: Princeton University Press, 1983), p. 71.

If, for Augustine and Kierkegaard, faith is private, inaccessible, and answerable only to God, there is at the same time another facet to their argument, indeed obviously so, since for both thinkers faith is also something to be written about. If Augustine imagines a form of identity with a secret chamber known only to God, he also concedes both that our relation to ourselves involves others at the most fundamental level, and that we can be as mysterious to ourselves as we are to others. Thus in Book III of the *Confessions*, the interpretation of a dream in which Monica, the dreamer, and her son are standing on the same measuring rod is arrived at through the conversation between her and her son, Augustine. She understands what the dream means when presented with Augustine's erroneous and self-interested interpretation of it, namely that she will become a Manichean, when she realises that it means he will join her in the Christian Church (*Confessions* 3:11:20). Monica understands her own inner life by talking to someone else about it, and Augustine has no doubts about the sincerity and truth of her insight, even though the full import will only emerge once he has himself converted to Christianity. If, in *The Confessions*, others help us understand ourselves, they can also affect our behaviour in ways we cannot control, as when Augustine realises that he stole pears as a child because he was ashamed not to join in with the group as it flouted morality for the sake of flouting it (*Confessions* 2:9:17). In both these cases, inner life is not private, but rather something that develops through our interaction with others. Indeed, if this were not the case, Augustine would have no reason to write his book. If he worries that his inner life is finally inaccessible, he also knows that love (or Pauline 'charity') will allow his listeners to hear what he is saying, even if he cannot prove that what he says is true (*Confessions* 10:3:3). Similarly Kierkegaard, speaking in the voice of Johannes de silentio, insists that he may never have found a Knight of Faith but 'meanwhile, [he] may very well imagine him', and goes on to describe the everyday habits of the figure right down to what his wife will cook him for dinner.[8] If faith is inaccessible, it can at the same time be imaginatively engaged with. Furthermore, over and above this play

---

8   *Ibid.*, p. 38.

of masks and imagination, the very fact that Kierkegaard wrote the book suggests that he thinks something of faith can be communicated, if only its incommunicability.

The topos of the inaccessibility of an individual's religious life thus turns out, in Augustine and Kierkegaard, to be part of a larger project to establish contact with the reader and help them to imagine and relate to the spiritual situations described in the books. Augustine and Kierkegaard are both writers who use their rhetorical skills to engage readers, and prompt them to have experiences of their own. For both writers, it is important that the spiritual author does not have experiences in the place of his or her reader, since spiritual experience is not something that can be deputised. This conviction gives their texts their urgency. There is something they cannot say, not so much because it is inaccessible as because it is something that the reader must experience for him- or herself. It is my hunch that, when we turn to Trojanow, we will see that this urgency has been replaced by something more like a cultural or spiritual theme park, where identities can be tried on, and experiences exchanged without the same challenge to take responsibility ourselves for our spiritual growth. That may sound a bit harsh, but behind the suggestion is the question: what is a text being written for? For Augustine and Kierkegaard the texts are being written, amongst other reasons, to offer a space where people take responsibility for their spiritual life. I do not think that is the case with Trojanow, but they may not be his fault so much as an indication of the changing function of the idea of religion in the modern era.

To return to my religious thinkers: if spiritual experience, for writers like Augustine and Kierkegaard, cannot be delegated, it is also something we don't do alone, as Heidegger, who follows in the footsteps of both thinkers, insists. When Heidegger reflects on the communicative situation of a religious text in his lectures on Paul's first epistle to the Thessalonians from 1920–1, he emphasises the degree to which Paul's letter is addressed to a community that shares his experience of having become a Christian, that is to say, which shares the sense of being called to round upon their lives, or, as he puts it, drawing on Paul's frequent use in the epistle of aorist forms of the Greek verb γίγνομαι, their sense of 'having become'. Paul may speak with the authority of an apostle, but Heidegger points out that he simultaneously needs his audience. He depends on the Thessalonians, whom he calls his glory (1 Thess 2,20), and without whom he is orphaned (1 Thess 2,17). Heidegger's lectures specifically draw attention to the shared involvement of Paul and his readers. 'Paulus sieht sie im Schreiben als solche, in deren Leben er getreten ist. Ihr Gewordensein ist mit seinen Eintreten in ihr Leben verknüpft' ['As he writes, Paul sees them as people into whose life he has stepped. Their "Having Become" is bound up with his having entered their life'].[9] Paul's experience of God's call is something that happens with the Thessalonians, something they too knowingly experienced. Facing up to one's spiritual and historical situation for the Heidegger of the early 1920s means uncovering and acknowledging a common predicament.

Drawing on a tradition that spans from Paul to Heidegger, we can thus see two models of religious life, one contained within the other; a mentalist picture (private faith) contained within the wider framework of shared religious practices. The sense of a private experience appears as a topos serving the larger project of being jointly engaged in the unfolding of one's spiritual predicament, or, to put it another way: the idea of an inaccessible life is a means of reaching your reader: appealing to their charity, or challenging them with the paradox of faith to become that 'single individual' who admits that he or she must, to paraphrase Kierkegaard's definition of the self in the opening paragraph of his *Sickness unto Death*, inevitably has a relationship to his or her relationship to God.[10] As we now return to Trojanow's writings, we can follow up two related question. Is the sense of the inaccessibility of Burton's belief part of a wider communicative project, and, if so, what is this project?

9   Martin Heidegger, *Phänomenologie des religiösen Lebens*, eds Matthias Jung, Thomas Regehly and Claudius Strube (Frankfurt am Main: Klostermann, 1995), p. 94.
10   Søren Kierkegaard, *Sickness Unto Death: A Christian Psychological Exposition for Upbuilding and Awakening*, eds Howard V. Hong and Edna H. Hong (Princeton, NJ: Princeton University Press, 1980), pp. 13–14.

Inaccessibility and Narrative Control

When it was first published in 2006, Trojanow's novel was admired for its control of contrasting perspectives: switching between Burton's perspective and that of his servant Naukaram, or of the Ottoman authorities interrogating his companion on the hajj or of Sidi Mubarak Bombay, who acted as the factotum for Burton's journey with Speke in search of the source of the Nile.[11] Günter Grass likened this juxtaposition of the perspective of the master and servant to the contrast between the views of Don Quixote and Sancho Pansa and suggested that the masterful combination of viewpoints put Trojanow's book in the ranks of the great European tradition of the picaresque novel.[12]

The juxtaposition of perspectives is also a central part of the way the novel deals with the question of Burton's religious life. The narrator does not tell us what Burton finally feels about God, but shows us other figures worrying about the issue. The concerns of the priest who conducts the last rites frame the novel; the Hindu servant Naukaram watches Burton's increasing interest in Islam with bafflement and disapproval; the Ottoman authorities collect the views of Burton's fellow pilgrims as to whether or not he was a devout Muslim or an imperialist imposter; Sidi Mubarak Bombay confesses that he will never be able to understand the actions of the Englishmen. This insistence on the inscrutability of Burton's motives is itself given a religious interpretation in one of the conversations between the Ottoman authorities and the pilgrims that assess Burton's attitude to the hajj. Haji Wali suggests that Burton, or 'Sheikh Abdullah' as he called himself on the hajj, was a Shiite and a Sufi hiding this heterodox opinions from his companions, following the practice of *Taqiyya* (*DW* 271), which the historical Burton in the account of his pilgrimage describes as 'A systematic concealment of doctrine, and profession of popular tenets, technically

11   Karl-Markus Gauss, 'Portwein gegen Wortschatz – Wie man Welten sammelt: Ilija Trojanows Abenteuerroman', *Süddeutsche Zeitung* (18 March 2006).

12   'Weltensammler und Blechtrommler: Ein Gespräch mit Günter Grass und Ilija Trojanow' <http://www.ilija-trojanow.de> accessed 28 April 2010.

called by the Shi'ahs "Takíyah": the literal meaning of the word is "fear", or "caution".[13] Following this line of argument, the very inscrutability of the fictional Burton's beliefs is proof that he was following an Islamic mystical path. In the comments of Haji Wali, the protagonist's faith is affirmed and made inaccessible by the same gesture.

This is not the only way in which Burton's inner life is treated. The narrator in the Burton sections can tell us the thoughts of the protagonist. We hear his musings on religion during the hajj as he is simultaneously overwhelmed and sharply analytic in his response to the sight of the Kaaba in Mecca (*DW* 318–19), or when he cannot pray on his own, only as part of the group and thinks to himself: 'Keine andere Tradition hat eine so schöne Sprache für das Unsagbare geschaffen' ['No other tradition has created such a beautiful language for the unsayable'] (*DW* 325). Indeed, the narrator has no difficulty in telling us what Burton thinks in his most private moments. Trojanow has added to Burton's life the story of a temple-dancer-cum-courtesan to whom he gives the allegorical name of Kundalini, which, according to the anatomy of Yoga, is the dormant energy considered to reside at the base of the spine.[14] The first section of the novel is structured around Burton's love for Kundalini and the rivalry between him and Naukaram for her affections. Kundalini asks Burton to marry her and he is unable to say yes because he misjudges the situation. The narrator tells us: 'Er war zu sehr damit beschäftigt, die Situation auszunutzen, um sie richtig einschätzen zu können' ['He was too taken up with exploiting the situation to be able to judge it correctly'] (*DW* 160). Thus, although Trojanow's preamble to the novel insisted that other people remain a secret, he does not have a difficulty in inhabiting the emotions of others where his plot requires it, just as he does not, when writing in the different register of his account of researching Burton's adventures in *Nomade auf vier Kontinenten*, have problems making statements about his subject's motivation and attitudes (*Nomade* 13, 16–17).

---

13   Richard Francis Burton, *Personal Narrative of a Pilgrimage to Al-Medinah & Meccah*, 2 vols (New York: Dover, 1964), i, p. 67. Cited as *Pilgrimage*.

14   Richard W. Maxwell, 'The Physiological Foundation of Yoga Chakra Expression', *Zygon* 44.4 (2009), pp. 807–24.

Trojanow has commented on the similarity that this inhabiting of others, and in particular taking on the voice of Sidi Mubarak Bombay, suggests that there exists between him as the author of a novel with multiple perspectives and Burton as a master of disguise and assimilation.

> Indem ich [Sidi Mubarak Bombay] gegenerzählen ließ, indem ich mich in ihn hineinversetzte, hatte ich ein literarisches Äquivalent für Burtons Verwandlungen, seine Camouflage, sein Eintauchen in die Fremde gefunden. Auf einer anderen Ebene bin ich ein ähnliches Risiko eingegangen.[15]

> By having [Sidi Mubarak Bombay] tell his counter narrative, by placing myself inside him, I had found a literary equivalent for Burton's metamorphoses, his camouflage, his diving into the unfamiliar. At a different level, I took a similar risk.

In both its form and its content, the novel explores the limits of this transformation. In the discussions between the characters, the question is raised whether a transformation can ever be complete, and Naukaram disagrees with his master, suggesting that a change of clothes is not the same as a metamorphosis (*DW* 102). In the form of the novel, the answer remains similarly ambiguous. The narrative perspective is by turns distanced and intimate. We look at Burton from the outside, as he arranges a dinner party for monkeys after the death of his beloved Kundalini, or when he returns from being captured and tortured by the British authorities because they are not aware that he is a spy in disguise. At the same time, we hear his thoughts about Kundalini, or about his responses to the hajj, or his shock when he discovers from Speke's febrile ranting how much his fellow explorer hates him (497).

The framing question, established by the Catholic priest, as to whether or not Burton was a Muslim, runs in parallel to this narrative flexibility, and is in some sense untouched by it. The narrator could tell us the answer without breaking the rules of his narrative world, but he doesn't. Instead he chooses to frame the text with an indirect indication. Trojanow has spoken of the time it took him to find the first sentence of the novel.

---

15   'Recherche als poetologische Kategorie', p. 8. This is Trojanow's Inaugural Lecture as Heiner Müller Visiting Professor at the Free University Berlin <http://www.ilija-trojanow.de> accessed 26 April 2010.

Von irgendwoher tauchte eines Tages der lang erwartete Eröffnungssatz auf: 'Er
starb früh am Morgen, noch bevor man einen schwarzen von einem weißen Faden
hätte unterscheiden können.'[16]

One day the long awaited opening sentence emerged from somewhere: 'He died in the
early morning, before a black thread could have been distinguished from a white one'.

The first sentence draws on an image from the *Qur'an* to be found in the
sura in which the regulations for Ramadan are set out:

You [believers] are permitted to lie with your wives during the night of the fast:
they are [close] as garments to you, as you are to them. God was aware that you were
betraying yourselves, so He turned to you in mercy and pardoned you: now you can
lie with them – seek what God has ordained for you – eat and drink until the white
thread of dawn becomes distinct from the black.[17]

The same image of differentiating between a black and a white thread returns
in the closing section of the novel (*DW* 517). Thus, although the narrator
denies himself the liberty of saying where Burton's true allegiances lay, the
image used to open and close the narrative is Quranic, and it doesn't need
much knowledge of Islam to recognise the allusion (although Trojanow
acknowledges that many readers won't hear it).

To sum up the argument so far: we find narrative ambiguity on two
interrelated levels. On one level, we have a narrator who seems to be able to
choose when to enter the mind of a character and when not do. Characters
are not impenetrable, rather the distance between reader and character can
be manipulated. That then raises the question: to what end? On a second
level, we have the narrator choosing to keep a distance, but suggesting an
answer indirectly through the choice of a textual allusion. The text could
tell us what Burton believed, but chooses to maintain distance and instead
to make the very terms in which the world is introduced to us – what in
a film would be called the *mise-en-scène* – invoke the habits and imaginative world of Islam. We started with Trojanow's statement that people are

16   *Ibid.*, p. 6.
17   *The Qur'an*, tr. M.A.S. Abdel Haleem (Oxford: Oxford University Press, 2004), p. 21
     [2: 187].

enigmas. What we now see is that the enigma of a person is being staged. Trojanow has chosen to construct faith as an enigma.

Before we move on to think about the implications of this choice, it's worth briefly saying how some of Burton's biographers deal with the problem of Burton's relationship to Islam. For Edward Said, Burton's sympathy for, and intelligent grasp of, practices of Islamic culture are not in doubt. However, the very fact that he approaches the everyday life of a culture as a 'collection of rules and practices' means that rather than spontaneously living the culture he is assimilating himself to he is instead 'managing' Oriental life. To manage is to control, so even in Burton's most assiduous attempts to adapt to and understand his surroundings he is introducing an element of mastery that prepares the way for colonial control.[18] Other biographers similarly see a mix of distance and sympathy. Mary S. Lovell concludes that [Burton]

> saw no difficulty in embracing Islam and the creed of Sufism as part of his research; indeed he actively enjoyed the complex rituals which encompassed a sort of brotherhood with fellow worshippers. But he regarded his observance of Islam as the means to an end rather than a statement of faith.[19]

Dane Kennedy concurs:

> It is clear that [Burton] found Islamic faith and culture appealing at a deeply emotional level and he immersed himself in this worldview. At the same time, he maintained his ideological attachment to the British empire, and to the imperatives of power and the opportunities it presented for personal advancement.[20]

Thus whether the mimicry of Islamic practices was for personal advancement, or a genuine engagement with the Orient that was simultaneously distorted by the structure of power it unwittingly reproduced, Burton's faith was, in the view of historians, always also a tool or device.

---

18   Edward Said, *Orientalism: Western Conceptions of the Orient*, 2nd edn (Harmondsworth: Penguin, 1995), pp. 195–7.
19   Mary S. Lovell, *A Rage to Live: A Biography of Richard and Isabel Burton* (London: Abacus, 1999), pp. 84–5.
20   Dane Kennedy, *The Highly Civilized Man: Richard Burton and the Victorian World* (Cambridge, MA: Harvard University Press, 2005), pp. 69–70.

Trojanow chooses to take a different path. He cannot be accused of idealising Burton: the failings of the man who does not support his servant Naukaram in Europe but packs him back to India, or who cannot stop scheming when his mistress declares her love are clear enough.[21] Burton the surveyor and spy is shown as someone helping to catalogue and control the colonies as much as he is portrayed as the collector of new experiences. Nevertheless, licensed by the claim that people are inscrutable – which, as we have seen, his narrative technique does not bear out – Trojanow constructs the image of a mystery.

The process of construction can be seen right down to the smallest details of the text, such as when, in a sort of unexplained and inexplicable synecdoche in the opening paragraph of the novel, we are shown the grotesque image of a hand on the corpse and then on a crucifix before we know it is the hand of Burton's widow (*DW* 13). Trojanow is once more choosing to withhold information, choosing to present us with details, not because the wider context is epistemologically unavailable – Trojanow is not an author who suffers from a sense of language in crisis – but because he wishes to create an effect. Why would he want to do this? The pursuit of mystery is all the more puzzling, since in many places Trojanow uses Burton as a vehicle for his own observations. This might just be small details, such as the fact that, for the historical Burton, the black stone housed in the Kaaba in Mecca is volcanic while Burton in the novel voices the same opinion that Trojanow includes in his personal account of the hajj, namely that the stone might be a meteorite (*Pilgrimage ii*, 169; *DW* 319; *QI* 30).[22] But it also features in relation to more significant issues, as when Trojanow suggests that Burton was overwhelmed by the sight of the Kaaba in Mecca

---

21   Julian Preece notes elements of idealisation, particularly in the presentation of Burton on the hajj, that persist alongside the otherwise critical portrayal. Preece, 'Faking the Hadj? Richard Burton Slips between the Lines in Ilija Trojanow's *Der Weltensammler*', in Preece, Frank Finlay, and Sinéad Crowe (eds), *Religion and Identity in Germany Today: Doubters, Believers, Seekers in Literature and Film* (Oxford: Peter Lang, 2010), pp. 211–25, here p. 224.

22   For review of available evidence by two geologists, see Robert. S. Dietz and John McHone, 'Kaaba Stone: Not a Meteorite, Probably an Agate', *Meteoritics* 9.2 (1974), pp. 173–9.

(*DW* 318–19), when Burton's own account suggests only a pride in his own daring: '[The pilgrims'] was the high feeling of religious enthusiasm, mine was the ecstasy of gratified pride' (*Pilgrimage* ii, 161). The novel thus claims to put Burton at a distance while at the same time ignoring passages where the historical figure explicitly narrates – albeit in a manner that doesn't fit Trojanow's undertaking – what he felt or did.

This revision could be seen to be an indirect tribute to Burton's own style, which, as Trojanow points out, entailed altering, improving and copiously annotating the texts he purported to be merely translating (*Nomade* 20–1). But I think that would be too easy a way out. I think it's more interesting to point up the tension in Trojanow's approach: on the one hand, laying claim to Burton's voice even to the point of replacing his words; on the other hand, manufacturing the sense of Burton's inaccessibility. Why would Trojanow do this? The stated aim of his cultural project, in the essay he wrote with Ranjit Hoskoté, is to find a position beyond the false opposition between relativism and universalism – that is to say, beyond the complete inaccessibility of other cultures on the one hand and, on the other, their total uniformity – and to opt instead for confrontation, engagement and interaction: *Auseinandersetzung* and *Interaktion* (*Kampfabsage* 194–6). However, having looked at what Trojanow does, as opposed to what he says he does, I think the picture is a little different. The dominant aspect of Trojanow's writing practice is not so much an engagement with cultural difference as the sovereign management of disorientation. I want to end the chapter by thinking through some of the consequences of this literary technique, in particular what it suggests about the relationship between religion and the novel.

Religion and Autonomy: Two Related Fictions

When we looked at religious texts from the tradition stretching from Paul to Heidegger we saw how the idea of an inaccessible private experience needed to be qualified. To use the topos of a private faith was to engage with a reader: an invitation to charity, in Augustine's case, or a dialectical provocation in that of Kierkegaard. In the cases of a Pauline epistle, Augustine's confession, Kierkegaard's 'dialectical lyric' and even Heidegger's lectures, the *address to readers*, and the concomitant appeal to spiritual life they share, or could share, with the writer, is clear. Is Trojanow inviting the reader on such a journey? I'm not sure that he is, because the problem that he creates around the figure of Burton doesn't seem to be necessary in the same way that the obstacles to a genuine communication are for Kierkegaard or Augustine. The difficulties of Augustine as he forms the genre of the written confession, or Kierkegaard as he uses pseudonyms to prompt people to engage in their spiritual life are palpable and inevitable, since spiritual experience, for both writers, cannot be delegated. Instead, Augustine and Kierkegaard draw on and provocatively adapt shared habits of reading and reflection that encourage readers to become active participants in the traditions to which they are committed. What is Trojanow's equivalent? The figure of Burton and Trojanow as writer can alike be seen as examples of a form of sovereign flexibility. The fictional Burton is presented as a mystery, and kept as a mystery by narrative control. Nevertheless, as Michaela Haberkorn points out, we see him choosing to be a mimic: inscrutable as he may be, he lives the choice of his flexibility.[23] The air of mystery is only the superficial form of an individual opting for a self-made fluidity, a form of self-creation which fits the lines from Burton's *The Kasidah* that Trojanow quotes as an epigraph for his novel: 'He noblest lives and noblest dies/Who makes and keeps his self-made laws' (*DW* 7). Trojanow, as the creator of Burton's character, exhibits a parallel sovereignty as he stage manages the reader's relationship with Burton and chooses when we hear what. Is this sovereign individual connected in any way to religion? The anthropologist Talal Asad, who has studied the development of the modern idea of religion as it informs anthropological engagements with non-Western cultures would say: through and through. From an anthropologist's view,

---

23   Michaela Haberkorn, 'Treibeis und Weltensammler: Konzepte nomadischer Identität in den Romanen von Libuše Moníková und Ilija Trojanow', in Helmut Schmitz (ed.), *Von der nationalen zur internationalen Literatur: Transkulturelle deutschsprachige Literatur und Kultur im Zeitalter globaler Migration* (Amsterdam: Rodopi, 2009), pp. 243–61, here pp. 258–9.

what we call religion appears as a collection of shared practices, legitimised and regulated by a discursive tradition.[24] Nevertheless, it has in Christian thought since the seventeenth century increasingly been identified with private conviction, with the mere fact of faith, separated from the particular ways this faith is lived, regulated and related to a shared social existence.[25] Associated with this private faith is the ideal of an individual subject whose actions, like his faith, are not entangled with or constrained by traditions and shared practices.[26] The autonomous individual and the idea of private faith are two sides of the same coin.

The figure of Burton as he is constructed in Trojanow's novel, and Trojanow himself, as the interventionist narrator choosing when and how to manage his readers and their understanding of Burton's faith, both exhibit the same cultural habits: privatised religion and the pursuit of an isolated and isolating sovereignty. These habits take attention away from the shared practices of which Burton and Trojanow are both in fact a part to emphasise instead the fictions of faith and individual autonomy. One aspect of Islam that particularly appeals to Trojanow is the living community it embodies (*IQ* 31, 92–3). Nevertheless, the literary project of *Der Weltensammler* is not shaped by a commitment to community but by the interrelated and questionable tropes of private faith and individual action. These are not terms it is easy to escape as citizens of the modern world. Nevertheless, a self-questioning attention to what we actually do, as opposed to what we think or hope we do, might allow us to be surprised beyond our preconceptions about religion and individual identity, and so, for instance, to give up the reassuring stereotype of the heroic, if flawed, individual of the type represented by Trojanow's Burton. The account of the hajj by the anthropologist Abdellah Hamoudi records just such a journey of disrupted certainty when he concludes:

24 Talal Asad, 'The Idea of an Anthropology of Islam', *Poznań Studies in the Philosophy of the Sciences and the Humanities* 48 (1996), pp. 381–403, esp. pp. 397–402.
25 Talal Asad, *Genealogies of Religion: Disciplines and Reasons of Power in Christianity and Islam* (Baltimore, MD: Johns Hopkins University Press, 1993), pp. 40–3.
26 Talal Asad, 'Reading a Modern Classic: W.C. Smith's *The Meaning and End of Religion*', *History of Religions* 40.3 (2001), pp. 205–22, here p. 215.

I thus had no other choice but to abandon a certain language: 'arbitrary choices', 'construction', 'fabrication', 'invention' of the self, of tradition, of institutions, of humanity. Put simply: the emergent being, human being, being human, does not choose, build, create. If one wants to keep those words, one must use them to mean 'working at' something, as a painter works at colors, an inexhaustible memory.[27]

If spiritual life for Eckhart or al-Qushayri entails endeavouring to leave behind unhelpful habits, then it seems a set of habits to leave behind might be a model of religion associated with individuality and a private faith, and a model of the novel, associated with a hero, however flawed, following his 'self-made laws'.

27   Abdellah Hammoudi, *A Season in Mecca: Narrative of a Pilgrimage*, tr. Pascale Ghazaleh (Cambridge: Polity, 2006), pp. 261–2.

JULIAN PREECE

From Kisch to Kapuściński: Trojanow and the European Tradition of Reportage

At the centre of my attention in this chapter is a term which Ilija Trojanow himself has employed in the titles or first lines of three of his own travelogues and of two anthologies that he has edited or introduced: the term is 'reportage', plural 'reportagen'. It may be used quite loosely today to denote journalism written (usually) from abroad but reportage has a literary lineage which is distinct both from travel writing and reports by foreign correspondents, not to mention literary fiction which is set in other countries. Writers of reportage tend to have a point to get across and a commitment to uncovering the truth that justifies their bringing what they have experienced to life through literary means. This may include imaginative invention which leads in turn to charges that they have embellished the truth. They often show solidarity with the subjects of their writing, however, by living side by side with them and reporting from their point of view. Classical travel writing, in contrast, has often been associated with the privileged, as a domain of the gentleman of leisure. Goethe taking off in his carriage to spend three years exploring Italy, with a stipend arranged retrospectively with his royal employer, is the classic German example.

The two anthologies of reportage that Trojanow has edited are by the Prague-born journalist Egon Erwin Kisch (1885–1948) and the Polish author Ryszard Kapuściński (1932–2007).[1] Both Kisch and Kapuściński

---

1   Egon Erwin Kisch, *Die schönsten Geschichten und Reportagen* [The Most Beautiful Stories and Dispatches], ed. and intro. by Ilija Trojanow (Berlin: Aufbau, 2008) and *Die Welt des Ryszard Kapuściński. Ausgewählte Geschichten und Reportagen* [The World of Ryszard Kapuściński. Selected Stories and Dispatches], intro. by Ilija Trojanow (Frankfurt am Main: Eichborn, 2007).

wrote for mass readerships, upset the powerful with their mixture of investigative critique and imaginative reconstruction of events. They also extended our understanding of the literal truth. In two brief essays which accompany the two volumes, Trojanow offers his thoughts on how these classic practitioners approach this particular mode of writing which allows them to cross generic boundaries rather as they crossed national borders on their travels. He quotes with approval the Somali novelist Nurrudin Farah's comment on Kapuściński's portrayal of the last days of Haile Salassie in *The Emperor: Downfall of an Autocrat*, that this supposedly eye-witness account of the self-styled Ethiopian Emperor was in fact 'a novel', though one based of course on first-hand reporting.[2] In Kisch's vignettes written from visits to five continents much more is 'literature' too than a reader is at first likely to suspect. Kapuściński begins with metaphors rather than statistics, although he does uses figures too and, to my knowledge, in the recent controversy over the literal truthfulness of his reporting, nobody has suggested that these are wrong. He opens his account of the last days of the Emperor of Ethiopia with a comment about dogs on the streets of Addis Ababa and chronicles the corruption at his court. Trojanow begins with the same motif in his narration of the fall of Tidor Zivkov, who ruled Bulgaria with similar brutality and for nearly as long, in *Dog Times*.[3] In *Shah of Shahs*, on the Iranian Revolution in 1979, Kapuściński turns events into stories by imposing narrative patterns, in particular the pattern of repetition, to produce an idea of history as process.[4] He fills in gaps by imagining and inventing characters, or at least that is what he appears to do because

2   'Die Wahrheit der verwischten Fakten', in *Die Welt des Ryszard Kapuściński*, pp. 7–14, here p. 12. Ryszard Kapuściński, *The Emperor. Downfall of an Autocrat*, trs William R. Brand and Katarzyna Mroczkowska-Brand (London: Quartet, 1983). First published in Polish in 1978.

3   Ilija Trojanow, *Die fingierte Revolution. Bulgarien, eine exemplarische Geschichte* [The Simulated Revolution: Bulgaria. An Exemplary History] (Munich: Deutscher Taschenbuch Verlag, 2006), previously published as *Hundezeiten. Heimkehr in ein fremdes Land* [Dog Times. Coming Home to a Foreign Country] (Munich/Vienna: Hanser, 1999).

4   Ryszard Kapuściński, *Shah of Shahs*, trs William R. Brand and Katarzyna Mroczkowska-Brand (London: Quartet, 1985). First published in Polish in 1983.

he blurs the lines between facts, which can be checked, and fiction, which cannot. Facts become fiction when, for example, statistics help to generate metaphors which illuminate an epoch or explain a country.

Reportage, while it may have something to do with the news, is not staple fare in newspapers. It is contemporary history which depends on observations of daily life, conversations and interviews with real people, as well as background research. In a 1982 German critical study, it is characterised as 'a subversive form', which uncovers facts that the ruling class want to remain covered up, reporting on the truncheon-wielding policemen and denouncing the generals who wanted to be celebrated as heroes of freedom while they planned the next coup.[5] Reportage was revived in Germany by the 'documentarists', in particular Günter Wallraff in the 1960s and 1970s. Wallraff knows the truth and distinguishes between right and wrong, good and bad. He went undercover to reveal what went on at the *Bild* newspaper and most famously of all he posed as a Turkish guestworker, which caused a furore in Germany but was not an original ploy.[6]

In Germany reportage is associated above all with the interwar period when it was epitomised by writer reporters such as Kisch himself or the intrepid interwar campaigner Maria Leitner (1892–1942). As a genre it belongs to the left, as it deals with poverty and injustice. Leitner also wrote fiction on the subjects of her journalism, such as working conditions in the USA or everyday life in Nazi Germany, where she returned as an undercover reporter after going into exile on account of her Jewish heritage and communist sympathies. In English the tradition is arguably older. Trojanow mentions Charles Dickens' *Sketches by Boz* (1837–1839), Jack London's *The People of the Abyss* (1903), as well as George Orwell's *Down and Out in Paris and London* (1933) as forbears for Kapuściński.[7] While Charles Dickens wrote his individual sketches, which became increasingly literary in nature, for publication first in magazines, Jack London and George Orwell

---

5   Michael Glaser, *Die literarische Reportage in Deutschland. Möglichkeiten und Grenzen eines operativen Genres* (Königstein: Skriptor, 1982), p. 7.
6   Günter Wallraff, *Ganz unten* (Cologne: Kiepenheuer & Witsch, 1985) and *Der Aufmacher: Der Mann der bei Bild Hans Esser war* (Cologne: Kiepenheuer & Witsch, 1982).
7   'Die Wahrheit der verwischten Fakten', p. 9.

sent their work to literary publishers rather than journals or newspapers. It was meant to appear between the covers of a book and was not to be confused with ephemeral journalism. They all nonetheless wrote during a hundred-year period when the printed word ruled supreme in the media. Other forms of mass communication, such as radio or cinema newsreel, were still in their infancy in the 1930s. Kisch and Leitner use humour for German readers. They place themselves too at the centre of his narrative reports and fashion what purport to be their own experiences into acerbic vignettes, which are designed to amuse and inform their readers and often to make them think.

Trojanow's own journalistic writing is occasional in nature. Since November 2007, for instance, he has written a column entitled 'Schlagloch' (pothole) for the leftwing *tageszeitung*. The column appears infrequently: there were only 16 in total in the four years to the end of 2011. In 2011 his subjects ranged from the financial crisis, to famine in Somalia and the 'Arab Spring'. He also reviews books and writes essays on subjects such as the American revolutionary Emma Goldman or the British novelist Salman Rushdie. Little of this cultural and political journalism (what in German would generally be called *Feuilleton*) is 'reportage'; none of it has so far been made into a book. It serves other purposes in Trojanow's thinking; 'reportage' is clearly something else. Trojanow earns his keep from his pen, though once on the road he does not pay his way by taking casual jobs like Orwell or Leitner. Goethe, in contrast, certainly did not take a job and did not even publish his *Italienische Reise/Italian Journey* for some twenty-five years after his return. As Trojanow writes under the constraints of the market, if he wants to campaign against injustice or give a voice to the disenfranchised, then he has to entertain and as well as to inform. *Gebrauchsanweisung für Indien/*India: A User's Manual is a commissioned work designed to appeal to travellers to the subcontinent, but it incorporates a vision of the country, in particular its rich mix of languages and religions. Yet while a writer like Kisch is not shy to recommend solutions and point fingers, Trojanow is more circumspect. He points out inequality and suggests how specific instances be put right, challenging western attitudes and ignorance, but unlike the classic 'muck-rakers' he does not have a set of solutions. He is immunised by his family experience of communist Bulgaria against any creed or movement which calls itself 'socialist'. Even if he were inclined to do so, there are no longer any local liberation struggles or anti-colonial movements in Africa or elsewhere that he could support. He also does not directly blame the West, the legacy of colonialism, or multinational companies in the context of globalised capitalism for the plight of the poor in the countries that he visits.

In the essays accompanying the Kisch and Kapuściński volumes he explains what attracts him to the two writers. It is the ways that they use reality as a springboard for their imaginations and challenge prejudiced thinking. He recognises a kindred spirit in Kapuściński who sets out 'die Stereotypen über Afrika zu überwinden' ['to overcome the stereotypes about Africa']. The problem for Trojanow with 'Nackte-Fakten-Journalismus' ['journalism of naked facts'] is that 'in solchen Zeiten gewaltiger Umbrüche [... er ...] eine Übersicht simuliert, die der Unordnung der vorbeirauschenden Ereignisse nicht gerecht wird' ['in such times of violent upheaval [it] simulates an overview which does not to justice to the chaos of the events as they whoosh by']. It is the joy in Kapuściński's reporting on Angola that impresses him too. Life resembles literature before the writer has put pen to paper:

> Es wirkt so frisch, weil man dem Text anmerkt, mit welch sinnlicher Lust der Autor die neugefundene Freiheit genießt, Menschen zu beschreiben, als seien sie Figuren in einem Roman, Szenen zu komponieren, als seien sie Kurzgeschichten und Dialoge festzuhalten, die für ein Theaterstück geschaffen sein könnten.[8]

> It seems so fresh because you can tell from the writing that the author is getting immense sensual pleasure from the new found freedom to describe people as if they were characters in a novel, to compose scenes as if they were short stories and to note down dialogues which could come straight out of a play.

As Trojanow cites this principle with approval, we should assume that in his own reportage the individuals whom he cites do not always exist in quite the way he pretends or that their opinions and experiences may be

---

8   *Ibid.*, pp. 8–9. Ryszard Kapuściński, *Another Day of Life*, tr. William Brand (Harmondsworth: Penguin, 2001).

those of a number of different individuals, or even perhaps that he imagines
what someone might say or might have said. For the section on the street
children of Bombay Central Station in *Der Sadhu an der Teufelswand/The
Sadhu on the Devil's Wall*, Trojanow spent a few days with the boys, talking to them and to the social workers at the Hamara Club. The boys take
drugs, they come to Bombay from the poorest regions of India, they have
lost touch with their families, they are bullied and exploited by the police
who steal the money they earn from buying tickets or 'reserving' seats on
trains for travellers with more money than time. In 'reportage' it does not
matter whether the boys that he introduces to his readers really were called
'Soni' and 'Sanjay'.[9] While a journalist is not, on the whole, permitted to
proceed like this, a literary writer of reportage is.

Trojanow also makes some other comments which, after the furore
caused by a Polish biography of Kapuściński published in March 2010,
sound prophetic.[10] They contain too a key to his own method, as he states:
'Erst das Verwischen der faktischen Vorlage bewirkt eine empathische
Annäherung und einen existentiellen Erkenntiswert' ['Empathy and existential insight can only come when the factual basis is blurred'].[11] The
posthumous arguments over Kapuściński centred on two things: his coop-
eration with the secret services, which Trojanow already took as a given,
and his imaginative reconstructions of events. The key word in Trojanow's
sentence is 'empathy', which is the quality unites the writer with the people
he is writing about. In the Afterword to the Kisch volume he imagines
a conversation with Kisch and quotes him to the same effect, as Kisch
invokes what he calls 'logische Phantasie' ['logical fantasy'] through which
'das grauenhafte Modell' ['the terrible model'], or reality itself, is endowed

9   'Im Takt des Fahrplans: Die Kinder vom Bahnhof Bombay Central' [In the Rhythm
      of the Time Table: the Children of Bombay Central Station], in *Der Sadhu an der
      Teufelswand. Reportagen aus einem anderen Indien* [The Sadhu on the Devil's Wall.
      Dispatches from a Different India] (Munich: Frederking & Thaler, 2002), pp. 177–85.
10   The title of the recent Polish biography translates as 'Kapuściński Non-Fiction'. See
      Timothy Garton Ash, 'Bearing Witness is a Sacred Trust', Guardian 10 March 2010.
      Artur Domosławski, *Ryszard Kapuściński: The Biography*, tr. Antonia Lloyd-Jones
      (London: Verso, 2012).
11   'Die Wahrheit der verwischten Fakten', p. 9.

with colour and viewed in perspective, setting the present into a context with the past and future.[12] Trojanow is writing about his own method and metier when he writes about two former masters of the genre.

The self-styled 'rasende Reporter' ['raging reporter'], who first made his name by exposing the spy scandal surrounding the Austrian Colonel Redl in 1913 (Kisch), and the doyen of Soviet-bloc travel-writers (Kapuściński) may have, however, more in common with each other than either does with Trojanow himself. While they operated in two very different sets of circumstances and periods of twentieth-century history, both battled against repression and censorship. In contrast, their twenty-first century admirer is allowed to say more or less what he likes within the limits usually imposed in a western democracy. His output is more varied too. Just as the lines of demarcation between his fiction and travel writing are not clear cut, so his works which contain reportage have elements of contemporary history, political harangue, as well as didacticism, and travelogue. Kapuściński was always also writing about Poland and never needed to spell that out because parallels were self-evident to his first readers. His section in *Shah of Shahs* on why the Iranians came to adopt the minority Shiite form of Islam because it fitted their inferiority complex as hard-done by losers of history is about Polish identity through the nineteenth and twentieth centuries. Similarly, when Kisch goes to America he writes about modernity which for German readers was synonymous with the United States. Trojanow is different in this respect. When he says India or Africa, he means India or Africa, not Europe; when he says Bulgaria, he does not mean Germany or Austria.

What both Kapuściński and Kisch shared was a rootedness in the culture of their mother tongue and a relationship with readers which was based on common experience. They could both regard that culture, however, as partial outsiders. When Kapuściński, who was born in an impoverished, underdeveloped region of eastern interwar Poland, was asked about his interaction with 'the third world' he replied that he grew up there.

---

12   'Hommage an einen Rastlosen' [Homage to a Restless Spirit], in *Die schönsten Geschichten und Reportagen*, p. 305.

> Because Pińsk, even though borrowing so much from Europe, was not part of Europe
> [...] I have always rediscovered my home, rediscovered Pińsk in Africa, in Asia, in
> Latin America [...] The society of Polesia was, really, a feudal one, a tribal society:
> it prepared me for Africa.[13]

We travel through time as well as space; the recent past can be the strangest
country of all. Can it be a coincidence that Kapuściński, who spent his professional life writing home from Africa, Central America, and the Middle
East, should come from a multi-ethnic, multi-lingual border region? Or
that Kisch should be a German-speaking Jew who grew up among Czech-
speaking gentiles, like his close contemporary and compatriot Franz Kafka?
Home can be the first experience of abroad.

Trojanow spends years rather than weeks in the originally alien culture and he writes his account for a readership whose cultural references
he does not necessarily share, since German is not his mother tongue.
When he arrives at the medieval Indian city of Jaisalmer, for example, the
'fortress with the ninety-nine towers', and he wonders whether he should
compare it with Quedlinburg or Rothenburg ob der Tauber.[14] He does not
answer his own rhetorical question which sticks in the memory because
he so rarely mentions Germany or Germans. The overwhelming majority
of his literary references are to Anglophone writers or the African and
Indian traditions rather than the German. Apart from Kisch I have only
found references to Hermann Hesse (but not his writings on India) and
Günter Grass (he is positive on *Die Blechtrommel/The Tin Drum*, negative
on *Zunge zeigen/Show Your Tongue*), and a mention of the birthplace of
Elias Canetti in *Dog Times*. (In the lecture printed in this volume he dis-
cusses Lessing's *Nathan der Weise*). In contrast to Grass in *Zunge zeigen*,
which is on the subject of a six-month visit to Calcutta, Trojanow tries
to explain what he experiences in its own terms. He tries to find out why
the Bengalis behave in the ways that they do, how they understand their

---

13   Quoted by Carl Tighe, *The Politics of Literature: Poland 1945–1989* (Cardiff:
      University of Wales Press, 1999), p. 204.
14   *Gebrauchsanweisung für Indien* [India: A User's Manual] (Munich: Piper, 2006),
      p. 93.

environment, and how their self-understanding is embedded in their history. Grass is shocked by dirt, noise, and poverty and he stays in his own little Germanic bubble, 'ein Menhir auf Reisen, der sich nie selbst in der Verunsicherung durch eine andere Perspektive verliert' ['a menhir on a journey, who never upsets his self-composure by disconcerting himself through a different perspective'].[15] Cultures, like the individuals who are formed by them, cannot behave as if they are ancient stones which could only get damaged were they to clash together. Trojanow prefers the image of flowing water because when two rivers meet they blend together to form a new one. He does not even allow language to be a barrier between him and the people that he comes across. After all in multilingual Africa and India, or cosmopolitan Mecca, he may be at no less of a disadvantage than most of the other supposedly native people.

The three books in which he uses the term 'reportage' are *Hundezeiten (Die fingierte Revolution)*, *Der Sadhu an der Teufelswand. Reportagen aus einem anderen Indien*, and the volume of occasional pieces written over more than two decades, *Der entfesselte Globus. Reportagen.* There are also examples of reportage in his other travel books, in particular his writings on India: *An den inneren Ufern Indiens. Eine Reise entlang des Ganges* (translated as *Along the Ganges*) and *Gebrauchsanweisung für Indien.*[16] Trojanow uses the term as more than a casual label but his writing fits uneasily in the German and international tradition for a number of reasons. *Along the Ganges* and its counterpart about Islam *Zu den heiligen Quellen des Islam. Als Pilger nach Mekka und Medina* (translated as *From Mumbia to Mecca*) are accounts of religious journeys, which explain mythology, history, and current devotional practice, as well as reporting on more everyday

---

15   'Auf den Spuren von Günter Grass: Zunge zeigen in Kalkutta' [On the Trail of Günter Grass. Show your Tongue in Calcutta], in *Der Sadhu an der Teufelswand*, pp. 152–60, here p. 160. See also 'Oscar in Afrika. Nairobi 1982', in *Der entfesselte Globus. Reportagen* [The Unchained Globe. Dispatches] (Munich/Vienna: Hanser, 2008), pp. 18–22.

16   *An den inneren Ufern Indiens. Eine Reise entlang des Ganges* (Munich: Hanser, 2003), translated as *Along the Ganges* by the author with Ranjit Hoskoté (London: Haus, 2005).

traveller experiences. These books are interventions of a sort, as they seek to counter inaccurate preconceptions in the German-speaking lands and the West generally of Hinduism and Islam and the cultures in which the two religions are practised. The books dismantle prejudices about little known places and peoples, explaining how they see and experience their own worlds. In the wake of 9/11, the Muslim case is more urgent. Neither of these books, however, is classic 'reportage': current affairs, contemporary politics, economics, controversies are also present in small doses only.

In his best reportage Trojanow runs with his metaphor, as in his account of the efforts made by the Indian authorities to shield American President Bill Clinton from any glimpse of the true aspect of their country by erecting walls along the route of his cavalcade. Trojanow has published this essay twice, but as it was already more or less perfectly formed the first time and undergoes negligible changes when it is reprinted.[17] Reality would appear to need little elaboration in this case. The charade was first enacted in eighteenth-century Russia, from where the term 'Potemkin villages' is derived after the Russian first minister. Another essay in *Der entfesselte Globus* also takes up material which first appeared in *Der Sadhu an der Teufelswand*, for which co-author Rainer Hörig is also credited. In the intervening seven years it seems unlikely that Trojanow has carried out new research or discovered new facts.[18] The basic ideas in both versions are the same: that poverty is abolished by being banished out of sight. Golf clubs or even golf villages are islands of privileged serenity in the midst of what the privileged themselves regard as chaos and disorder. Slums, on the other hand, can appear over night and extend like a weed over an empty area of ground. They can tame ground previously thought uninhabitable, thus doing the developers' hard work for them. As they do

---

17 'Willkommen in Clintonnagar! Oder Kommt ein Präsident geflogen' [Welcome to Clintonnagar or When a President Flies in], in *Der Sadhu an der Teufelswand*, pp. 210–13 and *Der entfesselte Globus*, pp. 85–7.

18 See 'Die Abschaffung der Armut' [The Abolition of Poverty], sub-titled 'Bombay. 1998–2003', in *Der entfesselte Globus*, pp. 65–74, and 'Für die Reichen, für die Armen: Die Wahl zwischen Golfplatz und Slum' [For the Rich, for the Poor: The Choice between a Golf Course and a Slum], in *Der Sadhu an der Teufelswand*, pp. 197–210.

not own the land, the slum dwellers are at the mercy of crooks and officials who demand extortionate sums as a kind of rent. They can be evicted at any time. In this case there are distinct differences between the two versions of the report. The second version, which appears in a volume of 'reportagen', is more literary than the first. It has more similies and metaphorical language. It introduces the notion of the South African 'laager' to account for the behaviour of Bombay's elites which opens up an historical perspective: 'Sie führte schließlich zur Apartheid und verkrüppelte ein ganzes Volk' ['It lead to apartheid and crippled a whole people'].[19] The second version also has fewer numbers and dates, it is shorter and more compact, with no quotations from politicians and no debate between two sides. It is punchier, ending with a damning quotation from a best-selling work of investigative sociology (and reportage) about grotesque inequalities in income distribution in the USA.[20] In the second version, instead of a report we have something more like a parable.

Trojanow admits on occasion to a desire to intervene. Taking a camel ride in North-West India, he discovers in that the men who own the camels receive only a fifth of the 10-euro fee he has paid for the entire day, the rest of which goes to the lords ('die Herren') of Jaisalmer. 'Worauf sich eine mustergültige Diskussion anbahnt: "Wieso verlangt ihr nicht mehr?"' ['Which provoked an archetypal discussion: "Why do you not ask for more?"'] To the European visitor it is obvious that the camel owners simply need to organise themselves in order to take control of the market and cut out the exploitative middle men, but the discussion gets nowhere. What seems straightforward to the visitor is riven with danger for the local. 'Worauf der Besucher seufzt und in der letzten Zitadelle des ohnmächtigen Touristen Zuflucht sucht: dem Trinkgeld. Mit einem großzügigen Bakschisch wird für einen Moment für ausgleichende Gerechtigkeit gesorgt' ['Which makes the visitor sigh and take refuge in the last bastion of the powerless tourist: a tip. A generous bakshish brings about a moment of compensatory justice'].[21]

19   *Der entfesselte Globus*, p. 66.
20   See Barbara Ehrenreich, *Nickel and Dimed: On (not) Getting by in America* (New York: Metropolitan Books, 2001).
21   *Der Sadhu an der Teufelswand*, p. 96.

On the whole, what class injustice was to politically motivated writers of reportage like Leitner and Wallraff, identity is to Trojanow. Identity
politics has replaced the class war; he knows in this regard what is right and
what needs to be done. If there is a force for bad in the writings on India, it
is Bal Thackeray and his chauvinist Hindu movement, the Sangh Parivar.[22]
Thackeray stands for everything that Trojanow's writings do not because
he opposes variety and cosmopolitanism. He is the villain of the chapter
on cricket for attempting to stop the Indian and Pakistani teams playing
each other. According to him, being Indian means being Hindu; reports
of Hindu massacres of Muslims cannot be reproduced because he cannot
acknowledge that anything can happen which disrupts his understanding
of how the world is put together. The India which Trojanow loves is syncretic, accepting of different faiths as expressions of a common religious
impulse. If there is a point at which he idealises India, it is his dating of its
contemporary inter-communal strife to independence. The original wound
is partition which took place as the British Empire crumbled and the former
colony lurched into independence as two separate states, Pakistan (for the
Muslims and India for the Hindus). The antithesis of Trojanow's writing
on India was written by James Mill, father of the liberal philosopher, in
1817. Whereas earlier British writing on India reflected a pre-Imperialist
interest in the foreign cultures which showed respect for their difference,
Mill never visited India, did not know any of its languages and even rejected
on principle earlier writings in English on India. He asserts his opinions
as *a priori* correct. Because its purpose was ideological, his three-volume
History of British India was an instant classic.[23] Other misinformation has
a less insidious purpose but when it develops into myth it shows a related
disrespect born of objectification.

Trojanow's writing on Bulgaria is by some distance his bitterest.
Hundezeiten recounts his visits to his native country twenty years after
he left as a young child. While he calls it a 'literarische Reportage', he
employs the mode sparingly, wanting instead to show how the ruling elite

22   *Gebrauchsanweisung für Indien*, pp. 69–72.
23   *Ibid.*, pp. 74–5.

in Bulgaria prepared for the collapse of communism and survived the sup-posed cataclysm unscathed, remaining in positions of power. The section entitled 'Bulgariens Kohlhaas' ['Bulgaria's Kohlhaas'] is an account of an elderly dissident's attempts to read the secret police files on his case which accrued over half a century. In theory he now enjoys the right to read them, in practice former state security officials still control his access. What makes Georgi Konstantinow a latter-day, Bulgarian version of Michael Kohlhaas, an historical figure from the time of the Reformation made by famous by Heinrich von Kleist's novella, is that Konstantinow patiently exhausts each legal or pseudo-legal avenue which is open to him and still cannot get justice. This book is more factual and less lyrical than any of Kapuściński's reports of political upheaval in faraway lands. Perhaps in homage to Kapuściński, Trojanow starts off with a richly evocative tale about the plague of wild dogs which ran wild in parts of Bulgaria after the communist regime was toppled. They were purchased initially by citizens concerned for their security after the partial breakdown of law and order with the end of communism, but were then turned loose when the price of food made keeping a dog too expensive. *Hundezeiten* is a book which needed to be written but it is a polemic and his tone in some of the shorter pieces is acerbic. He is returning home rather than visiting somewhere new.

If there is one objective which *all* these travel books share it is to bring the cultures that he has visited closer to the cultures of the language in which Trojanow writes. So far, so conventional, one may think, but that has not always been the point of travelogues and Trojanow achieves his objective in a distinctive way. Each time he writes over and corrects what we think we already know. This makes each book into a particular sort of palimpsest. Western ignorance of Islam is so profound that a fairly matter-of-fact account of a hajj such as that in *Zu den heiligen Quellen des Islam* can be radically enlightening. *Hundezeiten* argues against our understanding that a revolution of any sort took place there in 1989 with the collapse of communism in Eastern Europe: '1989' is a myth, not just in Bulgaria but across the former Soviet bloc. *Gebrauchsanweisung für Indien* contrasts uninformed clichés with facts and often shows too where those clichés originated: in nineteenth-century imperialist British discourse, the purpose of which was to demonstrate the inferiority of all things Indian.

What differs slightly from book to book is how Trojanow positions himself, his writing or narrating 'ich', relative both to the people and the situations that he encounters and to his readers. His first person pronoun does not take pride of place. The idea of the individual is after all a Western construct of fairly recent origin. In a short piece in *Der entfesselte Globus* he gives an account of the African practice of friendship and conviviality, as it exists among, but not between, the sexes. The friendship group or network is what counts, not an individual person within it.[24] Trojanow is a presence in his non-fiction books and he projects if not a persona, then an identity which he positions between the fixed identities which are adopted by or imposed on non-travellers. Most of his books are prefaced by a comment on his origins, which make them into an indirect form of autobiography or an expression of that primal experience of border-crossing and resulting exposure to lived cultural difference. He begins his first book with a memoir of the move to an entirely new place in his early childhood.[25] *Gebrauchsanweisung für Indien* begins: 'Nach Indien kam ich über Kenia. Nach Kenia kam ich über Zirndorf. Nach Zirndorf kam ich über Triest. Und nach Triest kam ich über den Fluchtweg. Bei soviel Umwegerei erschien mir Indien gar nicht so fremd' ['I came to India via Kenya. I came to Kenya via Zirndorf. I came to Zirndorf via Trieste. And I came to Trieste via an escape route. All this travelling via places made India appear far from foreign to me'].[26] In the first item in *Der entfesselte Globus*, he frequently uses the first-person plural ('wir' and 'uns') but writes 'ich' only once in some six pages. For a memoir this takes some beating. *Der entfesselte Globus* has a deliberate structure and this first autobiographical piece has a methodological purpose, rooting what is to follow in his own experience and personality. He reflects on what his unusual childhood and schooling brought him and his schoolmates in Nairobi's 'Deutsche Schule':

---

24 'Nichts Schlimmeres als Alleinsein' [Nothing Worse than Being Alone], in *Der entfesselte Globus*, pp. 29–32.

25 'Wie ich die Fremde kennenlernte ...' [How I Got to Know Foreign Parts], in *In Afrika: Mythen und Alltag* [In Africa: Myths and Everyday Life] (Munich: Frederking & Thaler, 2001), pp. 9–12.

26 *Gebrauchsanweisung für Indien*, p. 9.

Das Aufwachsen in mehreren Sprachen. Die selbstverständliche Existenz des Anderen. Der umgekehrte Blick auf vermeintliche Wahrheiten. Die Erfahrung, daß man mehrere Heimate ('Plural selten', sagt Brockhaus Wahrig) und eine dynamische Identität besitzen kann.[27]

Growing up in several languages. Accepting the existence of difference. The reversed view of what are supposed to be truths. The experience than one can have several homelands (the German word Heimat rarely exists in the plural according the the dictionaries) and a dynamic identity.

Bulgaria, the land of his birth, can be read through Africa, its deposed communist dictator Zivkov compared with his African 'dictator colleagues', such as Zaire's Mobutu and Ivory Coast's Houphouët-Boigny. All three were originally peasants who bestowed their native villages with wide streets and impressive buildings.[28] How can this be if their respective fiefdoms belonged to the 'third world', which is defined in opposition to the 'first world' (the west), which all Europeans inhabit today, and the 'second world' which supposedly ended in 1989 when the Soviet empire crumbled? One answer is that Eastern Europe was never a part of the West.

In travel writing we are used to viewing the relationship between the traveller and the place visited as that between subject and object. Whether Alfred Döblin in Poland in the mid-1920s or Elias Canetti in Marrakesh in the mid-1950s, the destination is alien and the languages spoken incomprehensible.[29] The traveller traditionally makes sense of what he sees and hears, the fragments that he can understand, and he does this from the outside, implicitly using his own culture, which he assumes that he shares with his readers, as a point of reference and comparator. Yet Döblin (a Prussian-Polish Jewish-Catholic) and Canetti (a German-speaking Bulgarian Jewish Englishman) both had multiple identities and questioned some of the

---

27 'Szenen aus der Savanne der Jugend. Nairobi 1981–1984' [Scenes from the Savannah of Youth. Nairobi 1981–1984], in *Der entfesselte Globus*, pp. 11–17, here p. 16.

28 *Ibid.*, p. 29.

29 Alfred Döblin, *Reise in Polen* (Frankfurt am Main: Fischer, 1925); Elias Canetti, *Die Stimmen von Marrakesch. Aufzeichnungen nach einer Reise* (Munich/Vienna: Hanser, 1967).

cultural assumptions in classical travel writing. What attracted Trojanow to Richard Burton's brief account of his visit to the Passion Plays in Oberammergau is the apparently provocative narrative perspective that he adopts: 'Er beschreibt die Oberbayern so, als wären sie ein unbekanntes, primitives Völkchen, das tief im Gebirge im Schatten eines dunklen Berges, am Ufer eines wilden Flusses haust und erst jüngst "entdeckt" wurde' ['He describes the Upper Bavarians as if they were an unknown minor tribe of primitives that lived deep in the mountains in a dark valley on the bank of a wild river and had only recently been "discovered"'].[30] Trojanow takes a different approach and strives to write as if from within. In *An den inneren Ufern Indiens* he reports that according to a centuries old doctrine of non-violence, which has influenced mainstream Hinduism, violence is practised when another person is defined as 'other'. 'Wenn man seinen Mitmenschen begrenzt, begrenzt man sich selbst [...] In der Konsequenz bewahrt Ahimsa den Menschen vor der Manipulation durch fiktive Identitäten, seien sie nationaler, ethnischer oder kultureller Prägung' ['If one limits one's fellow human being, one limits oneself [...] As a result Ahimsa protects human beings from being manipulated through fictitious identities, be they of a national, ethnic or cultural nature'].[31] This is an extreme view but in *Der Weltensammler* it is elevated at times into a narrative principle; it is also the most extreme form of empathy that Trojanow demands of the writer of reportage.

30 (with Susann Urban) *Oberammergau. Richard F. Burton zu Besuch bei den Passionsspielen/Oberammergau. Richard F. Burton. A Glance at the Passion-Play.* Zweisprachige Ausgabe/bilingual edition (Zurich: Arche, 2010), pp. 9–10.

31 *An den inneren Ufern Indiens*, p. 153.

Bibliography

This bibliography contains only items which have been cited in this volume. For a list of Trojanow's major book publications, see also 'Biographical/ Bibliographical Chronology: Ilija Trojanow'. For details of editions cited by the contributors, see the notes in their chapters. For a comprehensive list of items of journalism both by and about Trojanow, I recommend the Innsbrucker Zeitungsarchiv (<http://www.uibk.ac.at/iza>).

Ilija Trojanow

An den Inneren Ufern Indiens. Eine Reise entlang des Ganges (Munich: Hanser, 2003). Translated by the author with Ranjit Hoskoté as *Along the Ganges* (London: Haus, 2005)

(with Juli Zeh) *Angriff auf die Freiheit. Sicherheitswahn, Überwachungstaat und der Abbau bürgerlicher Rechte* [Attack on Freedom. Security Mania, the Surveillance State and the Demolition of Civil Rights] (Munich/Vienna: Hanser, 2009)

'Antarktis. Die letzte Leere' [Antarctica. The Last Emptiness], *Die Zeit* (12 December 2008)

Der entfesselte Globus. Reportagen [The Unchained Globe. Dispatches] (Munich/ Vienna: Hanser, 2008)

(with Rudolf Spindler) *Autopol* (Munich: dtv, 1997)

Der Sadhu an der Teufelswand. Reportagen aus einem anderen Indien [The Sadhu on the Devil's Wall. Dispatches from a Different India] (Munich: Frederking & Thaler, 2002)

Der Weltensammler (Munich/Vienna: Hanser, 2007). Translated by William Hobson as *The Collector of Worlds* (London: Faber and Faber, 2008)

'Die Wahrheit der verwischten Fakten' [The Truth in the Blurring of the Facts], in *Die Welt des Ryszard Kapuściński. Ausgewählte Geschichten und Reportagen* [The World of Ryszard Kapuściński. Selected Stories and Dispatches] (Frankfurt am Main: Eichborn, 2007), pp. 7–14

Die fingierte Revolution. Bulgarien, eine exemplarische Geschichte [The Simulated
  Revolution: Bulgaria, an Exemplary History] (Munich: Deutscher Taschen-
  buch Verlag, 2006)
Die Welt ist groß und Rettung lauert überall [The World Is Large and Salvation Lurks
  Around Every Corner] (Munich/Vienna: Hanser, 1996)
EisTau [Melting Ice] (Munich/Vienna: Hanser, 2011)
Gebrauchsanweisung für Indien [India: A User's Manual] (Munich: Piper, 2006)
'Hommage an einen Rastlosen' [Homage to a Restless Spirit], in Egon Erwin Kisch,
  Die schönsten Geschichten und Reportagen, ed. and intro. by Ilija Trojanow [The
  Most Beautiful Stories and Dispatches] (Berlin: Aufbau, 2008)
Hundezeiten. Heimkehr in ein fremdes Land [Dog Times. Coming Home to a Foreign
  Country] (Munich/Vienna: Hanser, 1999)
(with Chenjerai Hove) *Hüter der Sonne. Begegnungen mit Zimbabwes Ältesten: Wur-
  zeln und Visionen afrikanischer Weisheit*, ed. Monika Thaler, tr. Ilija Trojanow
  [Guardians of the Sun. Encounter with Zimbabwe's Elders] (Munich: Frederking & Thaler, 2007)
(with Ranjit Hoskoté) *Kampfabsage: Kulturen bekämpfen sich nicht - Sie fließen
  zusammen* [Calling off the Fight: Cultures do not Fight each other - They Flow
  Together] (Munich: Blessing, 2007)
'Komplot(t) – Wie plant der Autor den perfekten Plot' [How Does an Author Plan
  the Perfect Plot], *Wespennest 149*, November 2007, 6–10
Nomade auf vier Kontinenten. Auf den Spuren von Sir Richard Francis Burton [Nomad
  on Four Continents. On the Trail of Sir Richard Francis Burton] (Munich:
  Deutscher Taschenbuch Verlag, 2008)
(with Susann Urban) *Oberammergau. Richard F. Burton zu Besuch bei den Passions-
  spielen/Oberammergau. Richard F. Burton. A Glance at the Passion-Play*. Zweisprachige Ausgabe/bilingual edition (Zurich: Arche, 2010)
'Recherche als poetologische Kategorie' [Research as a Poetological Category], Inaugural Lecture as Heiner Müller Visiting Professor at the Free University Berlin
  <http://www.ilija-trojanow.de/downloads.cfm> accessed 30 August 2012
'Requiem for the Future. Writing a Novel about Catastrophic Climate Change'
  <http://www.vanderleeuwlezing.nl/sites/default/files/LectureTrojanow.pdf>
  accessed 30 August 2012
'Requiem auf die Zukunft' [Requiem for the Future], *Der Standard (Album)* (26
  November 2010)
(with Fatma Sagir) *Sehnsucht: Mach dich auf den Weg* [Yearning: Hit the Road]
  (Freiburg im Breisgau: Herder, 2008)
'Vor der Katastrophe' [Before the Catastrophe], in conversation with Stefan Gmünder,
  Der Standard (Album) (27 August 2011)

'Weltensammler und Blechtrommler: Ein Gespräch mit Günter Grass und Ilija Tro-janow' [Collector of Worlds and Beater of the Tin Drum. A Conversation between Günter Grass and Ilija Trojanow] <http://www.ilija-trojanow.de/downloads.cfm> accessed 30 August 2012

Zu den heiligen Quellen des Islam. Als Pilger nach Mekka und Medina (Munich: Malik, 2004). Translated by Rebecca Morrison as *From Mumbai to Mecca* (London: Haus, 2007)

Other Primary Material

Alfred Andersch, *Wanderungen im Norden. Mit 32 Farbtafeln nach Aufnahmen von Gisela Andersch* (Zurich: Diogenes, 1970)

Margaret Atwood, *The Handmaid's Tale* (Toronto: McClelland and Stewart, 1985)

Augustine, *Confessions: Text and Commentary*, ed. James J. O'Donnell, 3 vols (Oxford: Clarendon Press, 1992)

Ray Bradbury, *Fahrenheit 451* (London: Transworld, 1957)

Richard Francis Burton, *Personal Narrative of a Pilgrimage to Al-Medinah & Meccah*, 2 vols, ed. Isabel Burton (New York: Dover, 1964)

Elias Canetti, *Die Stimmen von Marrakesch. Aufzeichnungen nach einer Reise* (Munich/Vienna: Hanser, 1967)

Thomas Carlyle, *On Heroes, Hero-Worship, and the Heroic in History.* (Berkeley: University of California Press, 1993)

Alfred Döblin, *Reise in Polen* (Frankfurt am Main: Fischer, 1925)

Eckhart, *German Sermons & Treatises*, tr. Maurice O'C. Walshe, 3 vols (Shaftesbury: Element Books, 1979)

——, *Meister Eckhart Werke*, 2 vols, eds Niklaus Largier and Josef Quint (Frankfurt am Main: Deutscher Klassiker Verlag, 1993)

Barbara Ehrenreich, *Nickel and Dimed: On (not) Getting by in America* (New York: Metropolitan Books, 2001)

Penelope Fitzgerald, *The Blue Flower* (London: Flamingo, 1995)

The Great White Silence (dir. Herbert Ponting, 1924)

Abdellah Hammoudi, *A Season in Mecca: Narrative of a Pilgrimage*, tr. Pascale Ghaz-aleh (Cambridge: Polity, 2006)

Martin Heidegger, *Phänomenologie des religiösen Lebens*, eds Matthias Jung, Thomas
Regehly, and Claudius Strube, *Gesamtausgabe*, vol. 60 (Frankfurt am Main:
Klostermann, 1995)
Thomas Hettche and Jana Hensel (eds), *Null* (Cologne: DuMont, 2000)
Aldous Huxley, *Brave New World* (London: Chatto & Windus, 1932)
An Inconvenient Truth (dir. David Guggenheim, 2006, USA)
Ryszard Kapuściński, *Another Day of Life*, tr. William Brand (Harmondsworth:
Penguin, 2001)
——, *The Emperor. Downfall of an Autocrat*, trs William R. Brand and Katarzyna
Mroczkowska-Brand (London: Quartet, 1983)
——, *Shah of Shahs*, trs William R. Brand and Katarzyna Mroczkowska-Brand
(London: Quartet, 1985)
Daniel Kehlmann, *Die Vermessung der Welt* (Reinbek: Rowohlt, 2005)
Søren Kierkegaard, *Fear and Trembling*, eds Howard V. Hong and Edna H. Hong,
Kierkegaard's Writings, vol. 6 (Princeton, NJ: Princeton University Press, 1983)
——, *Sickness Unto Death: A Christian Psychological Exposition for Upbuilding and
Awakening*, eds Howard V. Hong and Edna H. Hong, *Kierkegaard's Writings*,
vol. 19 (Princeton: Princeton University Press, 1980)
Jack London, *People of the Abyss* (London: Pluto, 2001)
Herman Melville, *Moby-Dick* (New York: Harper & Brothers, 1851)
Norman Ohler, *Die Quotenmaschine* (Hamburg: Hoffmann & Campe, 1996)
Christopher Ondaatje, *Journey to the Source of the Nile* (Toronto: HarperCollins, 1998)
——, *Sindh Revisited: A Journey in the Footsteps of Captain Sir Richard Francis Burton:
1842–1849, the India Years* (Toronto: HarperCollins, 1996)
George Orwell, *Down and Out in Paris and London* (London: Gollancz, 1933)
——, *Nineteen Eighty-Four* (London: Secker & Warburg, 1949)
Fernando Pessoa, *Lisboa: o que turista deve ver/What the Tourist Must See* bilingual
edition (Lisbon: Livros Horizonte, 1992)
Matthias Politycki, *Marietta – die Idee, der Datensatz und der Strohhut. Schreiben
und Schreiben-Lassen im Internet* (Mainz/Stuttgart: Steiner, 2000)
The Qur'an, tr. M.A.S. Abdel Haleem (Oxford: Oxford University Press, 2004)
Rainer Maria Rilke, *Neue Gedichte* (Frankfurt am Main: Suhrkamp, 1976)
Lawrence Sterne, *The Life and Opinions of Tristram Shandy, Gentleman* (1759–1767),
London: Dodsley
Italo Svevo, *Zeno's Conscience*, tr. William Feaver (London: Penguin, 2002) [also
known as *The Confessions of Zeno*, tr. Beryl de Zoete (London: Putnam, 1948)]
Colm Tóibín, *The Master* (London: Picador, 2004)
Günter Wallraff, *Der Aufmacher: Der Mann der bei Bild Hans Esser war* (Cologne:
Kiepenheuer & Witsch, 1982)

——, *Ganz unten* (Cologne: Kiepenheuer & Witsch, 1985)

Martin Walser, *Muttersohn* (Frankfurt am Main: Suhrkamp, 2011)

Joseph von Westphalen, *Lametta lasziv. Ein kleiner scharfer Roman* (Zurich: Kein & Aber, 2001)

Christa Wolf, *Kein Ort. Nirgends* (Berlin: Aufbau, 1979)

Malcolm X, *The Autobiography of Malcolm X* (New York: Grove Press, 1966)

Criticism on Trojanow

Florian Breitsameter, 'Autopol.' (21 February 1998) <http://www.sf-fan.de/rezensionen/ilija-trojanow--autopol.html> accessed 30 August 2012

Stephanie Catani, '(Re-)Thinking History: Ilija Trojanows *Der Weltensammler*', *Angermion* 2 (2009), pp. 91–108

Wieland Freund, 'Ein Geheimnis drückt mehr aus als eine Erklärung', *Die Welt* (22 March 2006) [review of *Der Weltensammler*]

Karl-Markus Gauss, 'Portwein gegen Wortschatz – Wie man Welten sammelt: Ilija Trojanows Abenteuerroman', *Süddeutsche Zeitung* (18 March 2006) [review of *Der Weltensammler*]

Michaela Haberkorn, 'Treibeis und Weltensammler: Konzepte nomadischer Identität in den Romanen von Libuse Monikova und Ilija Trojanow', in Helmut Schmitz (ed.), *Von der Transnationalen zur Internationalen Literatur* (Amsterdam/New York: Rodopi, 2009), pp. 256–7

Gert Hofmann, 'Literarische Kosmographie, oder Was kostet die Vermehrung der Welt. Ilija Trojanows Roman *Der Weltensammler*', *Literatur für Leser* 35.4 (2011), pp. 247–62

Michael Hofmann, 'Postkoloniale Begegnungen in der globalisierten Welt. Indien und Afrika in der deutschsprachigen Gegenwartsliteratur: Ilija Trojanow: *Der Weltensammler* und Christof Hamann: *Usambara*' (February 2010) <http://www.germanistik.ch> accessed 30 August 2012

Sigrid Löffler, 'Verschmelzungsgeschäfte auf vier Kontinenten', *Literaturen* (July/August 2007), p. 54 [Review of *Nomade auf vier Kontinenten*]

Gabriele Lotz, 'Historische Reiseromane: Erzählprosa von Christoph Ransmayr und Ilija Trojanow', in Christoph Parry and Liisa Voßschmidt (eds), *'Kennst Du das Land …?': Fernweh in der Literatur* (Munich: Iudicium, 2009), pp. 75–84

Beat Mazenauer, 'Aufstand in der Sonderzone', *Freitag* (20 March 1998) [review of *Autopol*]

Stefan Neuhaus, 'Kein ewiges Eis. Ilija Trojanows neuer Roman: Eine Anklageschrift gegen die Zerstörung der Welt', *Die Furche* (1 September 2011)

Andreas Mittermayr, *Kosmopolitische und kosmopolitisch-engagierte Literatur am Beispiel Ilija Trojanows*, PhD thesis, University of Vienna, 2011

Julian Preece, 'Faking the Hadj? Richard Burton Slips between the Lines in Ilija Trojanow's *Der Weltensammler*', in Preece, Frank Finlay, and Sinéad Crowe (eds), *Religion and Identity in Germany Today: Doubters, Believers, Seekers in Literature and Film* (Oxford: Peter Lang, 2010), pp. 211–25

——, 'Ilija Trojanow, *Der Weltensammler*: Separate Bodies, or: An Account of Intercultural Failure?', in Lyn Marven and Stuart Taberner (eds), *Emerging German-Language Novelists of the Twenty-First Century* (Rochester, NY: Camden House, 2011), pp. 119–32

Janna Rakowski, *Der Weltensammler – ein postkolonialer Roman?* (Hamburg: Igel, 2012)

Ulrich Rüdenauer, 'Der Weltbesserwisser', *Süddeutsche Zeitung* (21 September 2011) [review of *EisTau*]

Other History and Criticism

William H. Adams and Jon Hutton, 'People, Parks and Poverty. Political Ecology and Biodiversity Conservation', *Conservation and Society* 5.2 (2007), pp. 147–83

Talal Asad, 'The Idea of an Anthropology of Islam', *Poznań Studies in the Philosophy of the Sciences and the Humanities* 48 (1996), pp. 381–403

——, *Genealogies of Religion: Disciplines and Reasons of Power in Christianity and Islam* (Baltimore, MD: Johns Hopkins University Press, 1993)

——, 'Reading a Modern Classic: W.C. Smith's *The Meaning and End of Religion*', *History of Religions* 40.3 (2001), pp. 205–22.

Bill Ashcroft, Gareth Griffiths, and Helen Tiffin, *Post-Colonial Studies. The Key Concepts* (New York/London: Routledge, 2000)

Raffaela Baccolini and Tom Moylan, 'Introduction: Dystopia and Histories', in Raffaela Baccolini and Tom Moylan (eds), *Dark Horizons: Science Fiction and the Dystopian Imagination* (London: Routledge, 2003), pp. 1–12

Jens Balzer, 'In antiliberaler Mission', *Berliner Zeitung* (6 December 1997)

Felix Baron, *The Persian Girl* (London: Nexus, 2008)

Roland Barthes, *Empire of Signs*, tr. Richard Howard (New York: Hill and Wang, 1982)

Henri Bergson, *Das Lachen. Ein Essay über die Bedeutung des Komischen*, tr. Roswitha Plancherei-Walter (Darmstadt: Luchterhand, 1998). First published in French in 1900.

Peter Best, 'Die amerikanische Strafkultur und die Privatisierung: Kein Vorbild für die europäische Kriminalpolitik', in Thomas Feltes, Christian Pfeiffer and Gernot Steinhilper (eds), *Kriminalpolitik und ihre wissenschaftlichen Grundlagen. Festschrift für Professor Dr Hans-Dieter Schwind zum 70. Geburtstag* (Heidelberg: C.F. Müller, 2006)

Kimberly M. Blaeser, 'Trickster: A Compendium', in Mark Lindquist and Martin Zanger (eds), *Buried Roots and Indestructible Seeds: The Survival of American Indian Life in Story, History and Spirit* (Madison: University of Wisconsin Press, 1995)

Keith M. Booker, *The Dystopian Impulse in Modern Literature. Fiction as Social Criticism* (Westport, CT: Greenwood Press, 1994)

Pierre Bourdieu, *Acts of Resistance. Against the Tyranny of the Market*, tr. Richard Nice (New York: The New Press, 1998)

Jobst-Ulrich Brand, 'Gerüstet für das neue Lesen', *Focus* 42 (18 October 1999)

Stephen Brockmann, 'Juli Zeh, *Spieltrieb*: Contemporary Nihilism', in Lyn Marven and Stuart Taberner (eds), *Emerging German-Language Novelists of the Twenty-First Century* (Rochester NY: Camden House, 2011), pp. 62–74

Fawn Brodie, *The Devil Drives: A Life of Sir Richard Burton* (London: Eland, 2002)

W.B. Carnochan, *The Sad Story of Burton, Speke, and the Nile: Or, Was John Hanning Speke a Cad* (Stanford: Stanford General Books, 2006)

Nils Christie, *Crime Control as Industry: Towards GULAGS, Western style*, 2nd edn (London: Routledge, 1994)

Contemporary Travel Writing in French: Tradition, Innovation, Boundaries, Special Issue of *Studies in Travel Writing* 13.4 (2009)

Michael Cronin, *Across the Lines. Travel, Language, Translation* (Cork: Cork University Press, 2000)

Colin Davis, 'David Rousset (1912–1997)', in S. Lillian Kremer (ed.), *Holocaust Literature: An Encyclopedia of Writers and their Work*, vol. 2 (New York: Routledge, 2003), pp. 1048–52

Matthew Davis, 'On Travel and Travel Writing', *World Hum* (30 November 2006), <http://www.worldhum.com/features/travel-interviews/pico_iyer_travel_writing_20061104/> accessed 24 August 2012

Robert. S. Dietz and John McHone, 'Kaaba Stone: Not a Meteorite, Probably an Agate', *Meteoritics* 9.2 (1974), pp. 173–9

Artur Domosławski, *Ryszard Kapuściński: The Biography*, tr. Antonia Lloyd-Jones (London: Verso, 2012)

Jane Donawerth, 'Genre Blending and the Critical Dystopia', in Raffaela Baccolini and Tom Moylan (eds), *Dark Horizons*, pp. 29–46

David Downes, 'The Macho Prison Economy. Mass Incarceration in the United States – A European Perspective', *Punishment & Society* 3.1 (2001), pp. 61–80

Joel Dyer, *The Perpetual Prisoner Machine. How America Profits from Crime* (Boulder, CO: Westview Press, 2000)

James F. English, *Comic Transactions. Literature, Humor, and the Politics of Community in Twentieth-Century Britain* (Ithaca, NY/London: Cornell University Press, 1994)

Malcolm M. Feeley, 'Entrepreneurs of Punishment. The Legacy of Privatization', *Punishment & Society* 4.3 (2002), pp. 321–44

Bernhard Fetz and Hannes Schweiger (eds), *Die Biographie: Zur Grundlegung ihrer Theorie* (Berlin: de Gruyter, 2009)

Charles Forsdick, Feroza Basu and Siobhán Shilton, *New Approaches to Twentieth-Century Travel Literature in French: Genre, History, Theory* (New York: Peter Lang, 2006)

Michel Foucault, *Discipline and Punish. The Birth of the Prison*, tr. Alan Sheridan (New York: Vintage Books, 1995)

Timothy Garton Ash, 'Bearing Witness is a Sacred Trust', *The Guardian* (10 March 2010)

Daniel Gilpin, *Burton and Speke's Source of the Nile Quest* (Oxford: Heinemann, 2008)

Alessandro de Giorgi, *Re-thinking the Political Economy of Punishment. Perspectives on Post-Fordism and Penal Politics* (Aldershot: Ashgate, 2006)

Michael Glaser, *Die literarische Reportage in Deutschland. Möglichkeiten und Grenzen eines operativen Genres* (Königstein: Skriptor, 1982)

Jon R. Godsall, *The Tangled Web: A Life of Sir Richard Burton* (Abingdon: Matador, 2008)

Erika Gottlieb, *Dystopian Fiction East and West. Universe of Terror and Trial* (Montreal: McGill-Queen's University Press, 2001)

Ben Grant, *Postcolonialism, Psychoanalysis and Burton: Power Play of Empire* (London: Routledge, 2009)

Michael Hallett, 'Imagining the Global Corporate Gulag: Lessons from History and Criminological Theory', *Contemporary Justice Review* 12.2 (2009), pp. 113–27

Simon Hallsworth, 'Rethinking the Punitive Turn: Economies of Excess and the Criminology of the Other', *Punishment & Society* 2.2 (2000), pp. 45–60

J.B. Harley, 'Maps, Knowledge and Power', in Denis Cosgrove and Stephen Daniels (eds), *The Iconography of Landscape* (Cambridge: Cambridge University Press, 1988), pp. 277–312

Wilhelm Hemecker, 'Anton Weberns Tod. Eine Metabiographie von Gert Jonke', in Bernhard Fetz and Hannes Schweiger (eds), *Spiegel und Maske. Konstruktionen biographischer Wahrheit* (Vienna: Zsolnay, 2006), pp. 160–74

Christoph Hickmann, 'Hinter Gittern ist ein Traum geplatzt', *Süddeutsche Zeitung* (31 March 2008)

Eric Hobsbawm, 'Interview – World Distempers', *New Left Review* 61 (2010), pp. 133–50

Patrick Holland and Graham Huggan, *Tourists with Typewriters. Critical Reflections on Contemporary Travel Writing* (Ann Arbor: University of Michigan Press, 1998)

Richard Holmes, *Footsteps. Adventures of a Romantic Biographer* (London: Hodder and Stoughton, 1985)

Michael Holroyd, *Lytton Strachey: The New Biography* (London: Chatto & Windus, 1994)

Stefan Horlacher, 'A Short Introduction to Theories of Humour, the Comic and Laughter', in Gaby Pailer, Andreas Böhn, Stefan Horlacher and Ulrich Scheck (eds), *Gender and Laughter. Comic Affirmation and Subversion in Traditional and Modern Media* (Amsterdam/New York: Rodopi, 2009), pp. 18–42

Peter Hulme, 'Travelling to Write (1940–2000)', in Peter Hulme and Tim Youngs (eds), *The Cambridge Companion to Travel Writing* (Cambridge: Cambridge University Press, 2002), pp. 87–101

Maya Jasanoff, 'Let in the Djinns', *London Review of Books* (9 March 2006), pp. 34–5

Christa Karpenstein-Eßbach, 'Mediale Wirkungsästhetik: Formierungen von Reiz und Gefühl', in Brigitte Häring and Knut Hickethier (eds), *Buchstaben, Bilder, Bytes* (Norderstedt: Books on Demand, 2004), pp. 27–46

Dane Kennedy, *The Highly Civilized Man. Richard Burton and the Victorian World* (Cambridge, MA: Harvard University Press, 2005)

Dragan Klaic, *The Plot of the Future. Utopia and Dystopia in Modern Drama* (Ann Arbor: University of Michigan Press, 1991)

Barbara Korte, *English Travel Writing. From Pilgrimages to Postcolonial Explorations*, tr. Catherine Matthias (New York: Palgrave Macmillan, 2000)

Nicola Lacey, *The Prisoners' Dilemma: Political Economy and Punishment in Contemporary Democracies* (Cambridge: Cambridge University Press, 2008)

Beate Lakotta and Dorothee Stöbener, 'Liebe zum Klammeraffen. Spezial-Gespräch mit Autor Matthias Politycki über das Schreiben im Netz', *Spiegel Spezial* 10 (October 1999), p. 44

Paul Lewis, *Comic Effects: Interdisciplinary Approaches to Humour in Literature* (New York: State University of New York Press, 1989)

J. Robert Lilly and Paul Knepper, 'The Corrections-Commercial Complex', *Crime & Delinquency* 39.2 (1993), pp. 150–66

Eunice Lipton, *Alias Olympia: A Woman's Search for Manet's Notorious Model and Her Own Desire* (New York: Scribner's, 1992)

Debbie Lisle, *The Global Politics of Contemporary Travel Writing* (Cambridge: Cambridge University Press, 2006)

Ian Loader, 'Ice Cream and Incarceration: On Appetites for Security and Punishment', *Punishment & Society* 11.2 (2009), pp. 241–57

Bjørn Lomborg, *Cool It: The Skeptical Environmentalist's Guide to Global Warming* (New York: Knopf, 2007)

Mary S. Lovell, *A Rage to Live: A Biography of Richard and Isabel Burton* (London: Abacus, 1999)

Dean MacCannell, *The Tourist: A New Theory of the Leisure Class* (London: Macmillan, 1976)

Richard W. Maxwell, 'The Physiological Foundation of Yoga Chakra Expression', *Zygon* 44.4 (2009), pp. 807–24

Claudius Messner and Vincenzo Ruggiero, 'Germany: The Penal System between Past and Future', in Vincenzo Ruggiero, Mick Ryan, and Joe Sim (eds), *Western European Penal Systems: A Critical Anatomy* (London: Sage, 1995), pp. 128–48

Barbara D. Metcalf, 'The Pilgrimage Remembered: South Asian Accounts of the Hajj', in Dale F. Eickelman and James Piscatori (eds), *Muslim Travellers: Pilgrimage, Migration and the Religious Imagination* (London/New York: Routledge, 1990), pp. 85–107

Robert Michael and Karin Doerr, *Nazi-Deutsch/Nazi-German: An English Lexicon of the Language of the Third Reich* (Westport, CT: Greenwood Press, 2002)

Ira Bruce Nadel, *Biography: Fiction, Fact and Form* (London: Macmillan, 1984)

James L. Newman, *Paths without Glory: Richard Francis Burton in Africa* (Washington, DC: Potomac Books, 2010)

Caitríona Ní Dhúill, 'Lebensbilder: Biographie und die Sprache der bildenden Künste', in Bernhard Fetz (ed.), *Die Biographie – Zur Grundlegung ihrer Theorie* (Berlin: de Gruyter, 2009), pp. 473–500

——, 'Widerstand gegen die Biographie: Sigrid Weigels Bachmann-Studie', in Wilhelm Hemecker (ed.), *Die Biographie – Beiträge zu ihrer Geschichte* (Berlin: de Gruyter, 2009), pp. 43–70

David E. Nye, *The Invented Self. An Anti-Biography, from Documents of Thomas A. Edison* (Odense: Odense University Press, 1983)

James Parakilas, 'The Soldier and the Exotic. Operatic Variations on a Theme of Racial Encounter', *The Opera Quarterly* 10.2 (1993), pp. 32–56

Gregory Paschalidis, 'Modernity as a Project and as Self-Criticism: The Historical Dialogue between Science Fiction and Utopia', in Karen Sayer and John Moore (eds), *Science Fiction, Critical Frontiers* (New York: St Martin's Press, 2000), pp. 35–47

Anne Petersen and Johannes Saltzwedel, 'Absturz der Netz-Poeten', *Der Spiegel* 51 (16 December 2002), p. 178

Manfred Pfister, 'Introduction: A History of English Laughter?' in Pfister (ed.), *A History of English Laughter. Laughter from Beowulf to Beckett and Beyond* (Amsterdam/NewYork: Rodopi, 2002)

Loredana Polezzi, *Translating Travel: Contemporary Italian Travel Writing in English Translation* (Aldershot/Brookfield: Ashgate, 2001)

John Pratt, *Penal Populism* (New York: Routledge, 2007)

Mary Louise Pratt, *Imperial Eyes. Travel Writing and Transculturation* (London/New York: Routledge, 1992)

Susan Purdie, *Comedy. The Mastery of Discourse* (Hemel Hempstead: Harvester Wheatsheaf, 1993)

David Rousset, *A World Apart*, trs. Yvonne Motse and Roger Senhouse (London: Secker and Warburg, 1951)

Nicolaas A. Rupke, *Alexander von Humboldt: A Metabiography* (Chicago: University of Chicago Press, 2008)

Mick Ryan, *Privatization and the Penal System: The American Experience and the Debate in Britain* (New York: St Martin's Press, 1989)

Edward Said, *Orientalism: Western Conceptions of the Orient* (New York: Vintage, 1979)

Viktor Schlawenz, 'Novel in Progress. Matthias Polityckis Roman *Ein Mann von vierzig Jahren* entstand im Internet', *literaturkritik.de* 2.4 (April 2000) <http://www.literaturkritik.de> accessed 30 August 2012

Ulrich von Schwerin, 'Kann Privatisierung im Strafvollzug Kosten sparen?' *Stuttgarter Zeitung* (18 April 2008)

Joe Sim, 'Militarism, Criminal Justice, and the Hybrid Prison in England and Wales', *Social Justice* 31.1–2 (2004), pp. 39–50

Roberto Simanowski, *Interfictions. Vom Schreiben im Netz* (Frankfurt am Main: Suhrkamp, 2002)

Jonathan Simon, 'Fear and Loathing in Late Modernity. Reflections on the Cultural Sources of Mass Imprisonment in the United States', in David Garland (ed.), *Mass Imprisonment. The Social Causes and Consequences* (London: Sage, 2001), pp. 15–27

Jeanne Rosier Smith, *Writing Tricksters: Mythic Gambols in American Ethnic Literature* (Berkeley: University of California Press, 1997)

Rolf Spinnler, 'Namenloser Thriller im Netz', *Stuttgarter Zeitung* (26 March 1998).

Gayatri Spivak, 'Can the Subaltern Speak?', in Cary Nelson and Lawrence Grossberg (eds), *Marxism and the Interpretation of Culture* (Basingstoke: Macmillan, 1988), pp. 271–313

Vivien Stern, 'Mass Incarceration: "A Sin Against the Future"?', *European Journal on Criminal Policy and Research* 4.3 (September 1996), pp. 7–25

Rolf Stober (ed.), *Privatisierung im Strafvollzug?* (Cologne: Heymann, 2001)

Dorothee Stöbener, 'Dicht am Dichter. Deutsche Autoren schaffen die Literatur ins Internet', *Spiegel Spezial* 10 (1 October 1999), p. 36

Lytton Strachey, *Eminent Victorians: Cardinal Manning – Florence Nightingale – Dr Arnold – General Gordon* (London: Chatto & Windus, 1918)

Sara Sviri, *The Taste of Hidden Things* (Inverness, CA: The Golden Sufi Center, 1997)

A.J.A. Symons, *The Quest for Corvo: An Experiment in Biography* (London: Cassell, 1934)

Carl Tighe, *The Politics of Literature: Poland 1945–1989* (Cardiff: University of Wales Press, 1999)

'Trojanows Pferd' (Anon.), *Der Spiegel* 12 (17 March 1997)

Victor Turner, *The Ritual Process: Structure and Anti-Structure* (Hawthorne, NY: de Gruyter, 1995)

John Urry, *The Tourist Gaze: Leisure and Travel in Contemporary Societies* (London/ Thousand Oaks, CA: Sage, 1990)

Jon Vagg, *Prison Systems. A Comparative Study of Accountability in England, France, Germany, and the Netherlands* (Oxford: Clarendon, 1994)

Chris R. Vanden Bossche, *Carlyle and the Search for Authority* (Columbus: Ohio State University Press, 1991)

Barry Vaughan, 'The Punitive Consequences of Consumer Culture', *Punishment & Society* 4.2 (2002), pp. 195–211

Fritz Vorhols, 'Der Castor-Skandal zeigt: Selbstkontrolle der Atomindustrie ist nicht genug', *Die Zeit* (28 May 1998)

Immanuel Wallerstein, *After Liberalism* (New York: The New Press, 1995)

Thomas Wegmann, 'Verschaltbar statt haltbar? Eine unvollständige Bestandsaufnahme zur Literatur im Internet', in Matthias Harder (ed.), *Bestandsaufnahmen. Deutschsprachige Literatur der neunziger Jahre aus interkultureller Sicht* (Würzburg: Königshausen & Neumann, 2001), pp. 43–62

Sigrid Weigel, *Ingeborg Bachmann. Hinterlassenschaften unter Wahrung des Briefgeheimnisses* (Vienna: Zsolnay, 1999)

L. Zedner, 'In Pursuit of the Vernacular: Comparing Law and Order Discourse in Britain and Germany', *Social Legal Studies* 4 (1995), pp. 517–34

John Zilcosky, *Kafka's Travels: Exoticism, Colonialism, and the Traffic of Writing* (New York/Basingstoke: Palgrave Macmillan, 2003)

Notes on Contributors

SEIRIOL DAFYDD is currently working on his doctoral dissertation at Swansea University, on the subject of intercultural and intertextual encounters in Michael Roes' travel fiction. He has previously published a Welsh translation of a selection of stories from Bertolt Brecht's *Geschichten vom Herrn Keuner* and an English translation of Michael Roes' story 'As-Samt/ Das Schweigen'.

EVA M. KNOPP holds a first degree in English, German and Music from the University of Cologne. Between 2006 and 2010 she taught German as DAAD-Lektor at the Universities of Edinburgh and St Andrews in Scotland and in London at King's College London and University College London. She is currently a doctoral candidate and research assistant in the English Department at the University of Cologne.

CHRISTINA KRAENZLE (PhD, University of Toronto, 2004) is Associate Professor and Director of the Canadian Centre for German and European Studies at York University, Toronto. Her research focuses on modern German literature, film, and culture, with an emphasis on transnational cultural production, migration, travel and globalisation. Her recent publications include the co-edited volume *Mapping Channels Between Ganges and Rhein: German-Indian Cross-Cultural Relations* (with Jörg Esleben and Sukanya Kulkarni) as well as articles in *The German Quarterly*, *German Life and Letters*, *Transit: A Journal of Travel, Migration and Multiculturalism in the German-Speaking World* and the volume *Searching for Sebald: Photography after W.G. Sebald*.

BEN MORGAN is Fellow and Tutor in German at Worcester College Oxford. He is author of *On Becoming God: Late Medieval Mysticism and the Modern Western Self* (2012), and (with Carolin Duttlinger and Antony Phelan) editor of *Walter Benjamins anthropologisches Denken* (2012). He has also published on the Frankfurt School, German film (Lang, Riefenstahl, the 'Heimat' film) and contemporary writing (Jelinek).

CAITRÍONA NÍ DHÚILL lectures in German at Durham University. Her first book, *Sex in Imagined Spaces: Gender and Utopia from More to Bloch* (Legenda, 2010), offers a critical account of the imaginary sex-gender systems of utopian thought and fiction. Her research aims to bring the collective fantasy of utopia into dialogue with the singular reality of biography, and to show that these two categories are not as far apart from each other as it might seem. She held a research position at the Ludwig Boltzmann Institute for the History and Theory of Biography, Vienna, from 2005 to 2009, and has published widely in English and German on the theory of biography and on the relationship between biography and literature. Among her recent and forthcoming articles and essays are contributions on Hugo von Hofmannsthal, Ingeborg Bachmann, Frank Wedekind and Ernst Bloch.

CORNELIUS PARTSCH received his PhD in German Studies from Brown University and is Professor of German in the Department of Modern & Classical Languages at Western Washington University in Bellingham, Washington. He is the author of *Schräge Töne. Jazz und Unterhaltungsmusik in der Kultur der Weimarer Republik* (Metzler, 2000) and has published on various aspects of twentieth- and twenty-first-century German popular culture, including jazz literature, post-World War II spy fiction, film and early German science fiction in an article titled 'Paul Scheerbart and the Art of Science Fiction' (2002).

JULIAN PREECE graduated from Oxford, where he also wrote a DPhil on Günter Grass. He was made Professor of German Studies at Swansea University in 2007, after teaching posts at Huddersfield and Kent. He has written, edited or translated more than a dozen books, including most recently the monograph *Baader-Meinhof and the Novel: Narratives of the Nation/Fantasies of the Revolution, 1970–2010* (2012). With Frank Finlay he is a founding co-editor of Peter Lang's new series *Contemporary German Writers and Filmmakers*.

ERNEST SCHONFIELD is a Teaching Fellow in German at University College London. His main research interests are German narrative fiction from around 1800 to the present day and German visual culture since 1900. He is author of *Art and its Uses in Thomas Mann's Felix Krull* (2008), and has published essays on Thomas Mann, Johann Peter Hebel, Raabe, Brecht, Döblin, Max Ernst and Hubert Fichte. He is the editor of a website on German literature: <http://www.germanlit.org>.

Index

CONTEMPORARY GERMAN WRITERS AND FILMMAKERS

Edited by

Julian Preece (Swansea University)
Frank Finlay (University of Leeds)

Editorial Board

Professor Stephen Brockmann (Carnegie Mellon University)
Professor Friederike Eigler (Georgetown University)
Dr Michael Minden (University of Cambridge)
Professor Moritz Baßler (Westfälische Wilhelms-Universität Münster)
Professor Sabine Hake (University of Texas at Austin)

Contemporary German Writers and Filmmakers aims to reflect the continuing and dynamic developments in German culture since the reunification of Germany in 1990. The fall of communism, the forging of the new Berlin Republic and increasing ethnic diversity have coincided with growing international acclaim for writers of German (such as Nobel Laureates Günter Grass, Elfriede Jelinek and Herta Müller) and renewed interest in German cinema (such as award-winning film *Das Leben der Anderen / The Lives of Others*).

Each volume is devoted to the work of a contemporary German-speaking novelist, poet, playwright or filmmaker, containing an interview with its subject and, in the case of writers, an original piece of previously unpublished writing presented in parallel English translation. The other chapters on key aspects of the emerging oeuvre and its international significance are by scholars in the field. As the volumes are intended for readers with little or no knowledge of German, all quotations are translated into English. The volumes are designed as a resource for specialists and students alike and to stimulate debate within and beyond the academy.

Proposals for new volumes on significant contemporary practitioners in the literary and cinematic fields are welcomed. The language of the series is English.